teach yourself... Delphi

By Devra Hall

MIS:
PRESS

A Subsidiary of
Henry Holt and Co., Inc.

First Edition—1995

Printed in the United States of America.

Library of Congress Cataloging-in-Publication Data

Hall, Devra.
    Teach yourself-- Delphi / Devra Hall.
        p. cm.
    Includes index.
    ISBN 1-55828-390-0
    1. Windows (Computer programs)   2. Delphi (Computer file)
I. Title.
QA76.76.W56H36 1995
005.265--dc20   95-7106
                                             CIP

10 9 8 7 6 5 4 3 2 1

MIS:Press books are available at special discounts for bulk purchases for sales promotions, premiums, fund-raising, or educational use. Special editions or book excerpts can also be created to specification.

For details contact: Special Sales Director
                        MIS:Press
                        a subsidiary of Henry Holt and Company, Inc.
                        115 West 18th Street
                        New York, New York 10011

Editor-in-Chief: Paul Farrell   Copy Editor: Suzanne Ingrao
Managing Editor: Cary Sullivan   Technical Editor: Bruneau Babet
Development Editor: Mike Sprague   Production Editor: Erika Putre

ACKNOWLEDGMENTS

I would like to thank the following people for their invaluable assistance with this book:

- ◆ Paul Farrell, Editor-In-Chief
- ◆ Michael Sprague, Development Editor
- ◆ Bruneau Babet, Technical Editor
- ◆ Suzanne Ingrao, Copy Editor
- ◆ Erika Putre, Production Editor

Table of Contents

CHAPTER 1

Getting Acquainted with Delphi

- ◆ Examining Delphi icons on the Windows desktop
- ◆ Launching the Delphi program
- ◆ Introducing the Delphi interface
    - –Forms
    - –Code window
    - –Component palette
    - –Object Inspector
- ◆ Examining a few form and button properties
- ◆ Customizing the Component palette
- ◆ Exiting the Delphi program

1

The best way to learn how to create applications in a visual programming environment is to jump right in. Using this book, you'll create two applications: a presentation program and an order placement program that interacts with a database. As you progress through each chapter, you'll learn everything you need to learn in order to build these applications step-by-step. So let's get started.

In this chapter you'll become acquainted with the basic parts of the Delphi interface. After a brief examination of the different desktop icons, you'll launch the program and begin exploring the interface. Using the Component palette, you'll create two components: a label and a button and place them on a form. Then you'll inspect their properties and events using the Object Inspector. Finally, you'll create your own custom component page for use with this book, and then exit the Delphi program.

Launching Delphi

First, take a look at the Delphi icons on your desktop. If you did a complete installation, you should have a Windows group that looks something like the one shown in Figure 1.1. You should also create a TEACH subdirectory on your system and install the files from the diskette accompanying this book. You won't actually need any of the files in this chapter, but you will need the files in Chapter 2, and it's often easier to do your setup first and get it out of the way. (If you haven't installed Delphi yet, you should do so now. If you need assistance installing the files from the Teach Yourself diskette, see Appendix A.)

Delphi is the main icon (it's the one that looks like a Greek temple). This icon launches the whole application, and it's the only one you'll need for this book. Some of the other icons launch programs that you can access from inside Delphi, such as Help. The rest of the icons launch more advanced programming tools for debugging, configurations, and remote access. The Delphi Icons on Your Windows Desktop sidebar contains a brief description of each icon. To launch Delphi, double-click on the main Delphi icon.

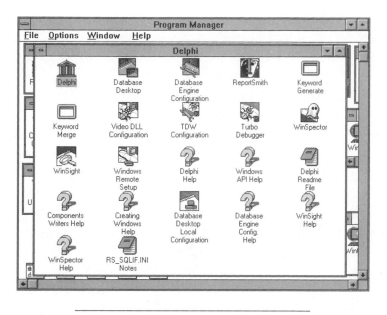

Figure 1.1 *Delphi Group window on desktop*

Delphi Icons on Your Windows Desktop

Delphi: Launches the Delphi programming environment.

Database Engine Configuration: Launches the IDAPI Configuration Utility. IDAPI stands for Independent Database Application Programming Interface. The configuration utility is used to set standards such as the formatting for time, date, and numeric fields. Other settings relate to how applications are started, the creation or modification of driver aliases, and how tables are created, sorted, and handled. It is these settings that allow for proper interaction with the specified database.

Database Desktop: Launches an application that allows you to open existing tables and create new ones. You can also add, modify, or delete aliases, set up working and/or private directories, customize.

the database view, edit table data, and perform queries. (See Chapter 7 for more information.) You can also launch this from the Tools menu when running Delphi.

Database Desktop Local Configuration: This feature allows you to specify the names of your working and private directories, and your IDAPI configuration file.

ReportSmith: Launches the Report Smith program. You can also launch this from the Tools menu when running Delphi. (See Chapter 10 for more information.)

Video DLL Configuration: Launches the Turbo Debugger Video DLL Configuration Utility, allowing you to change current video DLL settings without having to edit the TDW.INI file.

Turbo Debugger: Launches the main debugging tool. You can also launch this from the Tools menu when Delphi is running.

TDW Configuration: Launches a program that allows you to configure your Turbo Debugger window. Configuration settings include such things as the colors used, display options such as lines per screen and integer format, the type of source file, and how you want to save your configuration settings.

WinSight: Launches an advanced programmers tool that allows you to monitor the Windows system as it sends and receives messages. Used for debugging.

WinSpector: Launches an advanced programmers tool that creates a report log of Unrecoverable Application Errors and General Protection Errors. Used for debugging.

Windows Remote Setup: Launches the utility for controlling remote driver settings, including communication port and baud rate.

Keyword Generate: Launches a dialog box that allows you to generate the keywords for the Help Builder. Keywords are like index entries; they're the words you use when searching for help.

Keyword Merge: Launches a utility that merges the keyword files for use in a Help Project (HPR files).

Help Files: Delphi provides individual icons for launching the separate Help files. This is useful if you wish to look up information without running the program. Delphi Help can also be launched from the Help menu inside Delphi. Windows API Help can also be launched from inside Delphi. Component Writers Help and Creating Windows Help must be launched independently. WinSight Help, WinSpector Help, and Database Engine Configuration Help can be launched independently, or from within their respective programs.

Introducing the Main Interface Elements

When you launch Delphi, you'll see that the program contains several elements. Because each element is actually a separate window, the application does not take over your entire screen. This can result in quite a clutter unless you minimize your Program Manager and any other applications that you might have running. With your Program Manager minimized, your screen should look something like the one shown in Figure 1.2.

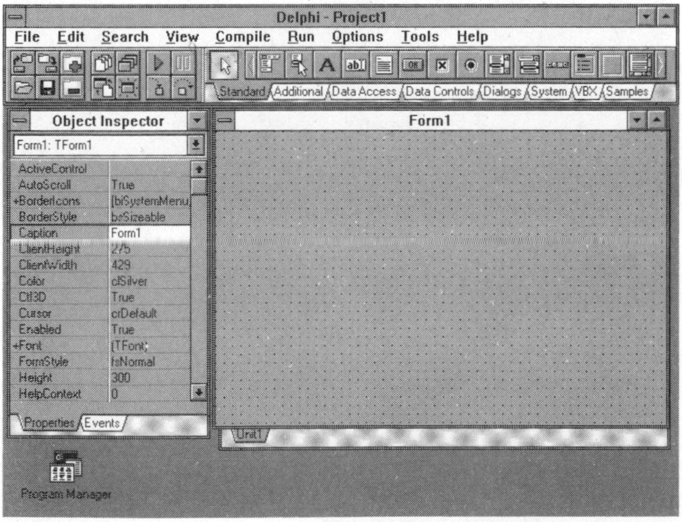

Figure 1.2 *The Delphi screen when first launched*

Across the top of your screen you'll see the Delphi title and menu bar. Immediately below the menu is the toolbar—actually it's two toolbars, the Speedbar and the Component palette. Take a look at the View menu. The last two items on the menu are Speedbar amd Component Palette, and the check mark indicates that both are displayed. Click on the **Speedbar** item and the check mark disappears along with the Speedbar. To display the Speedbar again, reselect the **Speedbar menu item**. The Speedbar holds 14 glyphs representing shortcuts for tasks such as Open, Save, View Form, View Unit, and more, as shown in Figure 1.3.

Figure 1.3 *The Speedbar contains 14 glyphs*

As for the Component palette, the first question is "what's a *component?*" Components, sometimes called *controls* or *objects*, are the building blocks for your applications. Text boxes, picture boxes, buttons, labels, even menus, are all components, and they are just a few of the many components that are available for your use.

Delphi is an object-oriented Pascal-based *visual* programming environment. The visual part of this description means that you can see what you're building as you go along. If you're designing a presentation, for example, and you know that on your first screen you want to have a picture (perhaps a company logo) and some text (probably the title of your presentation), you can choose a label component and place it right on the screen so that you can see how it looks. Then you can select and position the image component. You can drag the boxes around on the screen and resize them, until you are satisfied with how they look. This is part of the visual aspect of building your application.

In Delphi, your application windows are called *forms*. When you launch Delphi, one of the elements that appears is Form1, which is the smaller window in the middle of your screen, the one that says Form1 in its own title bar.

Forms

A *form* is like the canvas of a painting. In Chapter 6 you'll learn how to draw and paint lines and shapes directly on the canvas. For now, however, just think of a form as the surface on which you place all of your components. As a window, forms have all of the standard window features including a control menu, minimize/maximize buttons, title bar, and resizable borders, as shown in Figure 1.4. These standard window features are *properties* of the form, and as such, you can determine the settings for these and other form properties. In a moment I'll talk about form properties in more detail, but first let's take a look at the Code Editor and Component palette elements of the interface.

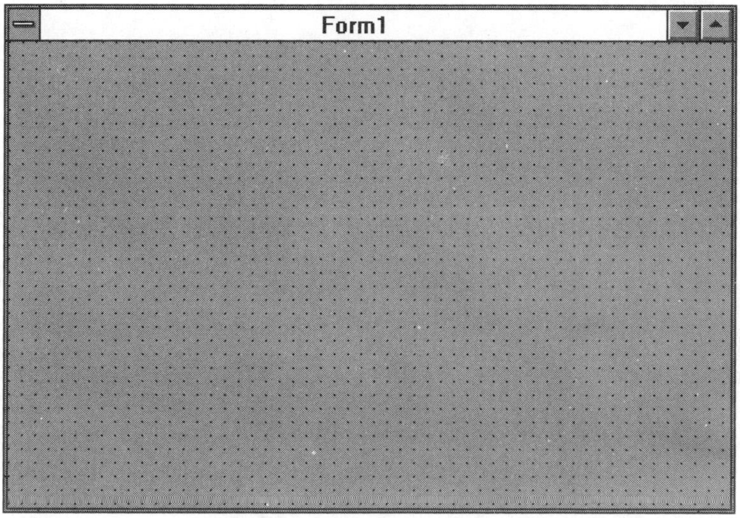

Figure 1.4 *A Form window*

Code Editor

Did you notice the little Unit1 tab sticking out from the bottom of the Form1 window? Actually that tab is part of the Code Editor window that just happens to be hiding underneath. Drag the form away, or better yet, minimize it by clicking on the **down arrow** in the top-right corner of the Form window. Voila, the Code Editor window.

As you can see, the Code Editor already contains some code, but I'll get to that in Chapter 3. For now, I just wanted you to see the window. You can restore the Form1 window by double-clicking on the **Form1** icon at the bottom of your screen. If you don't like a cluttered screen, or you find the Code Editor window distracting, you can always minimize it.

You can also display a form by pressing **Shift+F12** to bring up the View Form dialog box. This is useful when you are working with several forms, because you can simply select the form you wish to see from the list and click on **OK**.

Component Palette

Back in Figure 1.2, you saw that the Component palette was located on the right portion of the bar directly under the menus. Components are categorized into eight basic groups: Standard, Additional, Data Access, Data Controls, Dialogs, System, VBX, and Samples. Each group has its own page in the Component palette, and you can move from page to page by clicking on the **corresponding tab**.

As you might imagine, basic components such as text boxes and buttons are located on the Standard page. If you hold your mouse over a component and pause for a moment without clicking, a pop-up label will appear to tell you the name of the component. Working with so many different icon images can become confusing, but with these tool tips, working with components becomes much easier.

Take a moment to explore the Component palette. Use the tabs to move from page to page, and browse the icons using your mouse to activate the tool tips. Figures 1.5, 1.6, 1.7, 1.8, 1.9, 1.10, 1.11, and 1.12 represent the Component palette pages with annotations to identify each component.

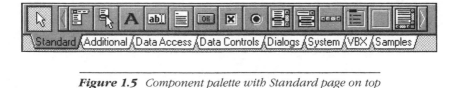

Figure 1.5 *Component palette with Standard page on top*

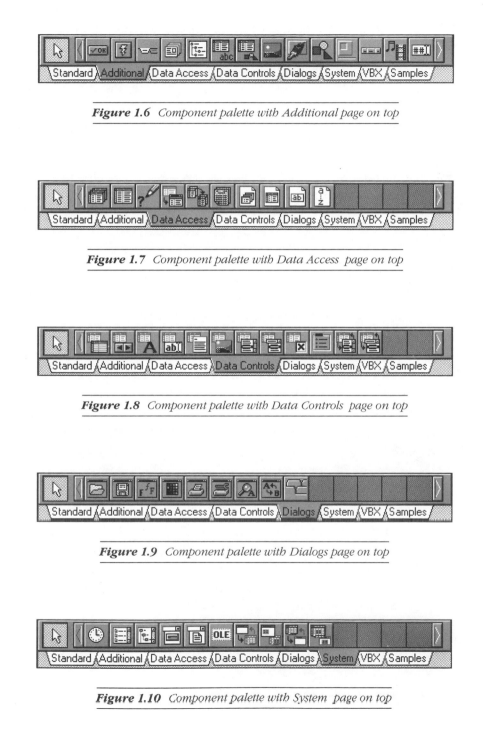

Figure 1.6 *Component palette with Additional page on top*

Figure 1.7 *Component palette with Data Access page on top*

Figure 1.8 *Component palette with Data Controls page on top*

Figure 1.9 *Component palette with Dialogs page on top*

Figure 1.10 *Component palette with System page on top*

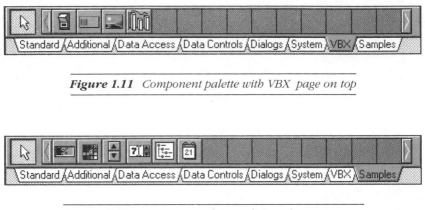

Figure 1.11 *Component palette with VBX page on top*

Figure 1.12 *Component palette with Samples page on top*

To place a component on your form, click on the component and then drag out an area on the form where you want the component to appear. Try placing a button in the bottom right-hand corner of Form1. Click on the button component (it's on the Standard page; see Figure 1.5)and then drag out a small area on Form1. Then add a label component (also on the Standard page) and place it a little below center on your Form1. When you're done, your Form1 should look something like the one shown in Figure 1.13

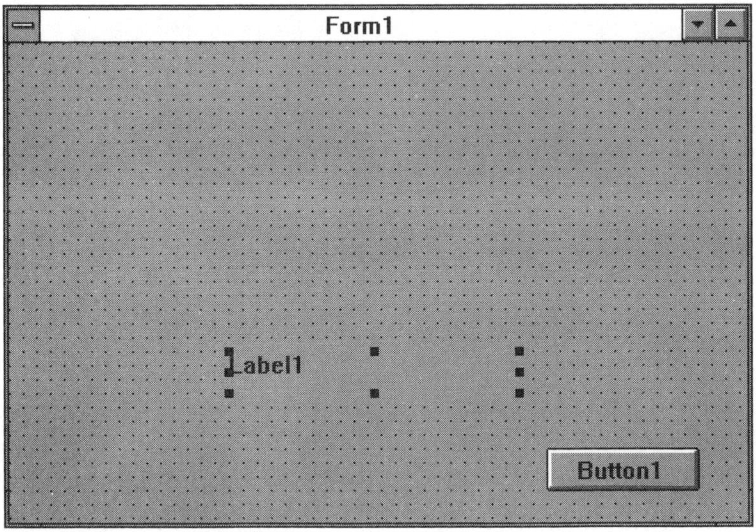

Figure 1.13 *A Form1 window with a label component and a button component*

You won't get to use every available component while building the sample applications presented in this book, but Delphi's Online Help contains a complete listing of all the available components. To see this list, select Contents from the Help menu and click on Component Library reference. From there you can access descriptions of every component in Delphi, and instructions for working with each one. At the end of this chapter, you're going to create your own customized page containing the components that you'll need for the first few sample applications. But first, let's take a look at some of the other elements in the Delphi interface.

Object Inspector

The Object Inspector is the smaller window to the left of your Form1 window. You can't miss it because the title bar says `Object Inspector`. The Object Inspector keeps track of the properties and events for each object (same thing as a component) in your application. If you look at your Object Inspector right now, it might say `Form1:TForm1`, `Button1:TButton`, or `Label1:TLabel` at the top, depending on which of your objects is currently active. Single-click on your button object. See the black handles that appear around the edges of the button? That means it is active. You can now use your mouse to drag on the handles to make the button smaller or larger, and the Object Inspector should say `Button1:TButton` at the top in the display box. The same is true for your label component. Click on it. Notice that the handles around the button are now gone, and instead the label now has handles. The Object Inspector also changes to show that Label1 is now the active object.

Most of the time you will only want to select one object or component at a time. It is possible, however, to select more than one component at a time by holding down **Shift** as you select each component. This saves time when you want multiple components to share one or more of the same property values.

There is one object that must exist in every visual application, so that's the one we'll look at first. Can you guess which one it is? If you guessed Form1, you're right. To select **Form1**, click your mouse on any empty part of Form1 (that means anywhere except where a component exists). You won't see any handles appear, but if you take a look at the Object

Inspector it should say `Form1:TForm1` in the display box, and it should look like the one shown in Figure 1.14.

Object Inspector	
Form1: TForm1	
ActiveControl	Button1
AutoScroll	True
+BorderIcons	[biSystemMenu
BorderStyle	bsSizeable
Caption	Form1
ClientHeight	275
ClientWidth	429
Color	clSilver
Ctl3D	True
Cursor	crDefault
Enabled	True
+Font	[TFont]
FormStyle	fsNormal
Height	300
HelpContext	0
\Properties /Events/	

Figure 1.14 *The Object Inspector showing the default Form1 properties*

The Properties Page

You already saw how the Properties page of the Object Inspector automatically changes to reflect the properties of whatever component is currently active, displaying the name of that component just below the Object Inspector's title bar. You may also have noticed that at the right of that space is a downward arrow. If you click on that arrow you'll find that it displays a drop-down list of all of the objects that currently exist in your application. And yes, selecting an object from that list has the same effect as selecting a component on the form. Try it and watch the handles appear around the chosen component on your form.

Delphi supports 62 different properties for a form. Some of these are subproperties, and I'll explain those in a moment. Earlier in this chapter I referred to some standard window properties such as system menu, minimize and maximize buttons, and resizable borders. Take a look at the third property on the list—BorderIcons. The default value for a form's BorderIcons is [biSystemMenu,biMinimize,biMaximize].

Sometimes the value or setting of a property is too long to be completely visible in the right column. If you click on the property name in the left column, the corresponding value in the right column becomes active. You can use your left and right arrow keys to move through the characters, and as you near the end of the visible portion, the text will move automatically, sort of like a de facto scroll bar. Your other option is to resize the Object Inspector window, but it tends to take up too much space.

Did you notice the plus sign in front of the property name? And did you notice that the setting was embraced by square brackets? Actually, I should have said that contains subproperties.

Double-click on **BorderIcons** to display the subproperties as shown in Figure 1.15. Each of these three subproperties can have a setting of True or False. The biMinimize and biMaximize properties represent the buttons that are found in the top-right corner of most windows. Minimize reduces the window to an icon at the bottom of your screen, and Maximize enlarges a window to full screen. The biSystemMenu property represents the button in the top-left corner of most windows, the one that drops down a menu with choices such as Restore, Move, Minimize, Maximize, and Close. Simply double-clicking on a **SystemMenu** will close the form.

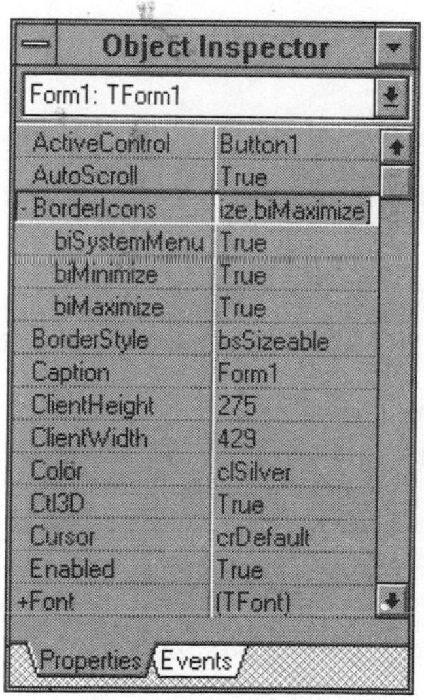

Figure 1.15 The Object Inspector displaying the BorderIcons subproperties

You can change a property setting in the Object Inspector in three different ways:

◆ Double-click on the value (this cycles through the available settings)

◆ Use the down arrow to the right of the value field to display a drop-down list of available settings and select from there

◆ Type in the value

When you're finished examining the BorderIcon subproperties, double-click on **BorderIcons** again to hide the subproperties. If you changed one or more of the subproperty settings you'll notice that only properties set to **True** appear in the composite property value.

N O T E   If you changed one of the BorderIcon settings to **False**, the Minimize property for example, you may be wondering why the Minimize button is still visible on your Form1. These form property settings will only take effect when you run your application.

All properties are listed in alphabetical order, and the next form property on the list is BorderStyle. The default value for a form's border style is resizable, but if you click on the **down arrow** to the right of the value column (where it says bsSizeable), the drop-down list reveals your property value choices—in this case, bsDialog, bsNone, bsSingle, and bsSizeable.

Scroll through the list just to get a feel for some of the other form properties. The Height, Left, Top, and Width properties indicate the size and placement of the form on your screen. You can manually drag the edges of a form to the size and placement you desire, or you can enter the position by indicating the pixel position. The Top and Left settings together indicate the top-left corner of your form, where top is the *Y*-axis and left is the *X*-axis. The top-left corner of your screen is 0,0. So if Top = 50 and Left = 25, the top-left corner of your form would be 50 pixels down from the top, and 25 pixels in from the left. The Width and Height settings then specify the form's width and height in pixels, starting from the Top and Left positions.

NOTE

You could actually set the Top and Left properties to 0,0 and Height and Width properties to 480 and 640, respectively, but this would force your window to go full screen even while designing.

The last form property on the alphabetical property list is WindowState, with three available settings: Normal, Minimized, and Maximized. If you select **Normal**, then the form will adhere to the Height, Left, Top, and Width settings when your program runs. If you select **Maximized**, the form will appear full screen when it runs, ignoring the size settings. Similarly, selecting **Minimized** will show your form as an icon, also ignoring the Height, Width, Left, and Top settings.

The Events Page

Now look at the bottom of the Object Inspector and notice the two tabs: One tab says Properties (it's the page you've been examining), and the other says Events. Click on the **Events** tab to display that page. Just like the Properties page, the Events page corresponds to the object that is currently selected. If you've been following along, your form should still be active and your Events page should look something like the one shown in Figure 1.16.

Object Inspector

Form1: TForm1

OnActivate	
OnClick	
OnClose	
OnCloseQuery	
OnCreate	
OnDblClick	
OnDeactivate	
OnDestroy	
OnDragDrop	
OnDragOver	
OnEnter	
OnExit	
OnKeyDown	
OnKeyPress	
OnKeyUp	

Properties / Events

Figure 1.16 *The Object Inspector Events page for a form object*

Delphi automatically supports specific *events* for each object or component. An event is some action relating to an object that is caused by either the user or the program itself. Before you look at the events associated with a form object, think about which events would be logical. What actions do you think might be taken with a form? Perhaps you thought about closing or resizing a window. Close and Resize are both good examples, representing two of the 20 different form events.

Now select your button component, either by choosing it from the Object Inspector's drop-down list or by clicking on it in the form. What types of actions might relate to a button object? If the user clicks on a button, that button experiences an OnClick event caused by the user. In some applications, buttons can be controlled by pressing a single key, or a combination of keys, instead of a mouse click. For this purpose, Delphi also provides the OnKeyPress and OnKeyDown events. Delphi supports lots of different events, and they vary by object type.

Every time an event occurs, Delphi executes any programming code that is associated with the event. If you don't think of yourself as a programmer, don't worry! You can create many applications with little or no Pascal code. That's because some Delphi components have preexisting code built in. One very powerful example of this is the DBNavigator component that allows you to navigate through the records of a database without having to write one line of code.

In Chapter 2 you'll begin the programming process by setting component properties, and by Chapter 3 you'll start writing simple Pascal code. But before I end this chapter, you're going to create that customized page for your Component palette that I mentioned earlier.

Customizing the Component Palette

After you've been using Delphi for a while, you may find that you use certain components over and over, and that they are inconveniently located on different pages. Delphi lets you customize the Component palette to suit your own needs. When you select **Environment** from the Options menu, you'll see the Environment dialog box containing seven pages. Click on the **Palette** tab to view the Palette page as shown in Figure 1.17.

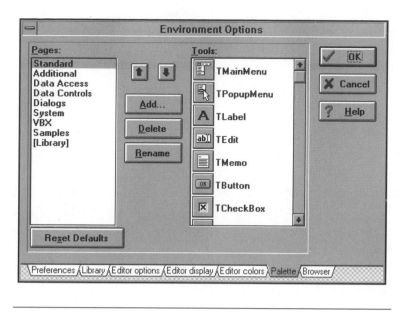

Figure 1.17 *The Environment dialog box with the Palette page displayed*

When you click on the name of a component page in the left box, the corresponding tool icons appear on the right. You can drag icons from the right side over to a page name on the left. But before you try it, let's create a page for you to use when working with the early samples in this book.

Click on the **Add** button to create a new page. When the little Add Page dialog box appears, type in **Teach** for the page name, and click on the **OK** button. The Teach page name should now be on the list. Later on, when you're done with the examples in this book, you can go back to the Palette Page dialog box and reset the defaults. Or, if you prefer, you can delete this page, rename it, or recustomize it for some other use.

You're going to need a few components from the Standard page, so click on the Standard page name to display the components. Moving a component to a page is a simple click-drag-and-drop maneuver. Click on the **TLabel** component and while holding your mouse button down, drag it over to the Teach page name, then drop it there by releasing your mouse button. Follow this same procedure to add the TEdit, TMemo, TButton, TComboBox, and TGroupBox components to your Teach page.

When you move a component from one page to another, it will no longer be available in its original location. In other words, you are not copying the component tool, but taking it away from one position and placing it into another. When you click on **OK** in the Environment - Palette page, you will save these changes, and they will remain this way even when you open another project or exit from the Delphi program. Of course, you always have the option of changing them again or resetting them to the default settings.

You're also going to need some components from the Additional page. Click on the page name to display the corresponding components, and drag **TImage** and **TBitBtn** from the Additional page over to the Teach page. Finally, highlight the Teach page name and click on the **up arrow** inside the dialog box. Notice that the Teach page name moves up a position each time you click the **up arrow**. Keep clicking until Teach is at the top of the list. Now click **OK** to close the Environment dialog box, and notice that not only do you have a new page in the component palette, but Teach is the first page.

Depending on your video monitor settings, you may find that the Samples page is no longer visible on your Component palette. (It was the one on the far right, and when you added the Teach up front, Samples may have been pushed off the screen. If so, you'll also see a small right and left arrow next to the last visible page tab. Click on the **right arrow** to slide the palette pages over—sort of like scrolling. Then use the left arrow to move back until you can see the Teach page.

Exiting the Delphi Program

Exiting from Delphi is pretty much the same as exiting most Windows programs. Just select **Exit** from the File menu. Because you've been working on a project, one that has not yet been named, Delphi will ask you if you want to save the project. You might be tempted to answer "no" because you haven't officially begun work on the sample presentation program, but you can use the work you've done so far, so I'd like you to save it. When you select **Yes**, the Save Unit dialog box appears. A project can contain one or more forms and units in addition to the project file.

To save Unit1, select your **TEACH** subdirectory and type in **PRES-U01.PAS** and click on **OK**. (The filename extension, PAS, stands for Pascal, and it's the required extension for Delphi source files.) Delphi will automatically create the corresponding form file, naming it PRES-U01.DFM and placing it in the same directory. (The filename extension, DFM, stands for Delphi form, and it's the required extension for Delphi form files.) It's always good to have a file-naming convention, so we'll use PRES as the prefix for all your Presentation files. As you probably guessed, U in your unit file name stands for unit, and 01 represents the first unit. When the Save Project dialog box appears, type in **PRESENT.DPR** and select **OK**. (The filename extension, DPR, stands for Delphi Project, and it's the required extension for Delphi project files.)

Summary

- A complete installation of Delphi creates a Windows program group called Delphi, which contains 22 icons. The Delphi icon is the main icon for launching the programming environment.

- Delphi has several interface elements. *Forms* are the windows in which you place your components.

- *Components*, which include objects such as buttons, labels, text, and image boxes, are the main building blocks of your applications.

- The component tools are held in another interface element called the *Component palette*. Components on the palette are grouped by pages: Standard, Additional, Data Access, Data Controls, Dialogs, System, VBX, and Samples.

- The *Object Inspector*'s Properties page keeps track of all the properties associated with each object, and allows you to set the value for these properties. The Events page lists all of the events that may be associated with each object.

- BorderIcons is a composite form property that includes three sub-properties: biSystemMenu, biMinimize, and biMaximize. True/False settings determine which of these elements is available on the form.

◆ The form's BorderStyle property determines if a form is resizable or fixed. It can also be used to remove the border completely or to identify the form as a dialog box.

◆ The Top, Left, Width, and Height properties specify the size and placement of the form on your screen. However, if the Window State property is set to **Maximized** or **Minimized**, the Top, Left, Width, and Height settings are ignored.

◆ OnClose and OnResize are two events associated with forms. OnClick, OnKeyPress, and OnKeyDown are three events associated with buttons. (It turns out that these three events are also associated with forms.)

◆ The Component palette may be customized to meet your needs. Components can be placed on specified palette pages, and the pages can be added, renamed, and deleted. To access this feature, select **Environment** from the Options menu and click on the **Palette page** in the Environment Options dialog box.

◆ To exit the Delphi program, select **Exit** from the File menu. If you haven't saved your project, Delphi will prompt you to do so. Unit and project files must be saved individually.

In the Next Chapter

In the next chapter you'll learn about a phased approach (my ABCD plan) to creating applications, and you'll begin creating a sample presentation application. You'll create the first form in the presentation, using a button, a label, and an image box; examine the properties of those components in more detail; and learn a few terms relevant to event-driven programming.

CHAPTER 2

Beginning Your Application

◆ Presenting the ABCD approach to project design

◆ Setting some property values

–The difference between, and importance of, Name and Caption properties

–Individual Font and Color properties versus parent values

–Cursors shapes and keystroke alternatives

–The image component versus a form's Picture property

◆ Introducing events, methods, procedures, and other action-related terms

In this chapter you will learn about a four-phase approach to creating applications and begin creating the sample presentation application. You'll create the opening form for the application using a button, a label, and an image box; examine the properties of those components in more detail; and learn some event-driven programming terminology.

ABCD: An Overview

You can approach the task of creating an application as a four-phase process. You'll soon find that the process is not strictly sequential because the phases will overlap and even repeat. Nevertheless, the phased approach is a good way to look at the overall process when you're first beginning.

The first step in any project is *advance planning*. This part of the process begins with the conceptualization of your application and may include the creation of text and/or graphic specifications.

Phase 2 is the *building* phase, beginning with the selection and visual placement of the components on your forms and ending with the definition of properties for each object. Every object has a set of properties (this includes component and form objects). In Chapter 1 you got your first look at some of the properties associated with forms, buttons, and labels. Other examples of component properties include the font size and style of the text displayed in a particular label, edit, or memo box.

Once the components are in place and their properties are set, you can begin *coding*; this is phase 3. The code you write might be as simple as `Form2.Show`, or it could be a complex Pascal routine. In some cases Delphi will create code for you. The beauty of event-driven programming is the ability to create blocks of code that are invoked by the appropriate events as needed. This means that code blocks are reusable.

Debugging is the fourth phase. No matter how experienced the programmer, a new application is bound to have some bugs in it. Sometimes those errors are simple typos in the program code, and Delphi will prompt you with error messages whenever it identifies a problem such as a misspelled command or missing punctuation. Logic errors are a little harder to find. Thorough testing will usually uncover most of them, and Delphi comes with some special debugging aids. The subject of debugging and error handling is covered in Chapters 11.

A Little Planning Goes a Long Way

Before you launch Delphi, you should ask yourself several questions. First, what is the purpose of the application you want to create? Don't laugh. That is not always a simple question. In choosing the first sample application for this book, I started with the idea of a presentation of some sort. If you're in the business of selling goods or services, for example, you might want to create a presentation of your product line. Okay, that sounds simple enough. But then I ran into the next problem. Because I wanted to include some data files that you could use for building a sample application, I had to use materials to which I owned the copyrights. This is an important issue, because you cannot legally use data in your applications unless you have the rights (either through ownership or license). My solution for this book is to have you create a photo presentation using some of my own photos. I own the rights to these pictures, and you may use them for the purposes of creating the sample application. You may not use them in your own programs (not that you would want to anyway).

So now we know that the first sample application will be a photo presentation. But that is too broad a statement. When you are planning an application, you need to consider the potential audience, decide what type of information should be included, and decide how it should be accessed. First I decided to limit the scope of the presentation to nature photos, and more specifically landscape photos. This eliminates all my animal photos, as well as the usual people and event photos we all tend to accumulate.

I also decided that information about the photos should be grouped by subject, as you'll see when we get to Chapter 4. The purpose is straightforward presentation or display of some photos with corresponding information about each. If you are in sales, for example, you might want to create a similar type of presentation for your product line.

When you feel that you have clearly defined the scope of your project, you need to consider the functions required to fulfill your needs. For example, in a sales presentation you want to find ways to present the strongest selling points as dynamically as possible. This could mean adding animation or special graphics or changing colors to highlight your "best sellers." You'll also want to have enough information available to answer questions about your products, so you'll need to give some thought to what questions might be asked. If you are creating a sales presentation at work, you might want to provide product information such as item name, description, part number, single unit price, and volume price. For the sample photo presentation project I decided to provide a simple label containing the location and date of each photo and a brief comment.

Equipment must also be considered. If your sales force is working with monochrome laptops, then you can't use color to get your point across. Also, visual displays and resolution make a difference. You're most likely working on a VGA monitor; SVGA will look different, and EGA will be more different. While my photos were originally scanned at 16 million colors, I reduced them to 256-color bitmaps for your use.

If you're working with a development team, then much of your planning should be documented so that everyone is working with the same set of information. The level of detail, however, can vary. Some people create very detailed specifications, listing each data item and function. Sometimes a general description is sufficient. In some cases, designers create complete storyboards, diagramming the placement of all data, and adding narration to describe the functionality. For many, however, the beauty of a visual programming environment is the ability to design your screens dynamically as you create your application. How you choose to go about your planning will be a function of your own work habits—or those required by your employer. Each of you will find your own comfort zone.

The written specification for the sample presentation project was not extensive, including only some rough sketches of what each window would display. We will see these notes as we go along. And we might as well start now, with the sketch for the opening presentation screen (see Figure 2.1).

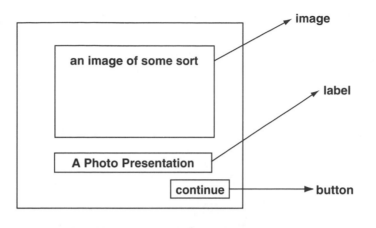

Figure 2.1 *Rough sketch of opening presentation window*

Visual Construction for Look and Feel

In Chapter 1 you placed a button and a label on a form and then saved the project. Now you're going to open that project and use that form to create your opening presentation screen. Launch Delphi from your desktop. (Don't forget to minimize your Program Manager and any other programs you might be running.) Select **Open** from the File menu, and when the Open dialog box appears, select **PRESENT.PRJ** from the list of available projects.

When Delphi has retrieved your project, Form1 should be visible. If it is not, select **Forms...** from the View menu, press **Shift-F12**, or click on the **Select Form From List** glyph on the Speedbar (top row, third from right), to bring up the View Form dialog box. From there you can choose to view any form listed.

When you're designing with Delphi, you can drag a form around on your screen and resize the borders until you like the way it looks. The same is true for positioning and sizing components. This is part of what I described as a visual part of the building phase. You can also control the positioning and sizing of forms and components by setting certain property values with the Object Inspector.

Let's begin with the form properties. In Chapter 1 you explored the Object Inspector and some of the form properties. You also saw how some properties could be nested (composite properties), and you saw the three different ways to set property values: double-clicking on the value, selecting from a drop-down list, and typing.

Table 2.1 contains a list of only those form properties and values that you'll need to set for the sample application. In the following sections I will discuss these properties, specifying settings as we go along. Toward the end of this chapter I'll suggest that you review your settings by checking them against the tables. Some of the form properties are not applicable to the first form in the sample application and others have default values that are acceptable, so any properties not shown in the table can be left as is.

Table 2.1 *Property Settings for Opening Screen of Present Program*

Property	Value
+BorderIcons	[biSystemMenu]
biSystemMenu	True
biMinimize	False
biMaximize	False
BorderStyle	bsSingle
Caption	Teach Yourself Delphi - Sample Presentation Program
Color	clBlack
Name	OpeningScreen
Visible	True
WindowState	wsMaximized

Let's start with the composite property +BorderIcons. You may need to change this property setting, depending on what alterations you made when you explored this property in Chapter 1. Because the first sample program is a presentation, the user does not need to be able to alter the size of the opening screen, so the form doesn't need to have minimize and maximize buttons. To remove these buttons, display the subproperties by double-clicking on **+BorderIcons**. Then change the biMinimize and biMaximize values from True to **False**.

You'll also need to change the setting for BorderStyle. The default value is bsSizeable (see Figure 2.2), but because I decided that the user need not be able to resize the first screen, you should change the property value to **bsSingle**. All three of the other value choices will prevent the form from being resizable; however, the bsDialog value is only used with dialog boxes, so it doesn't apply here (see Figure 2.3). The BsSingle value will create a single-line border around the form (as shown in Figure 2.4). The bsNone value removes the border and all the BorderIcons completely (as shown in Figure 2.5). If you used this setting, you would not need to set the BorderIcons property at all. I chose **bsFixed** for our presentation because I like the look of a single-line border, and I want to retain the SystemMenu icon as well.

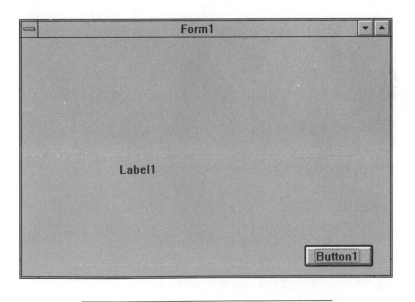

Figure 2.2 *A form where BorderStyle is Sizeable*

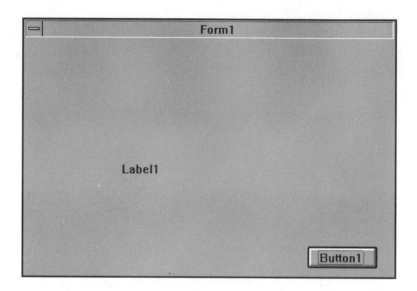

Figure 2.3 *A form where BorderStyle is Dialog*

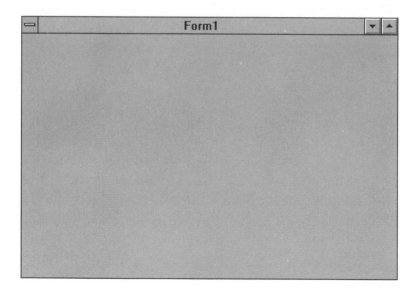

Figure 2.4 *A form where BorderStyle is Single*

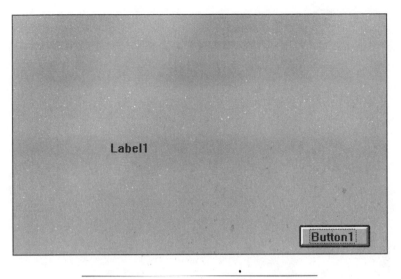

Figure 2.5 *A form where BorderStyle is None*

Another related property is WindowState. The default value is wsNormal, but I want our first presentation window to take up the whole screen. In other words, I want Delphi to automatically maximize the window, so you'll need to change the property setting to **wsMaximized**. The WindowState property has three possible values:

◆ **wsMaximized** automatically maximizes the window, ignoring the Height, Left, Top, and Width property settings that normally control the window size

◆ **wsMinimized** automatically minimizes the window, displaying it as an icon and therefore ignoring the four window-size properties just mentioned

◆ **wsNormal** initially displays the window according to the four size settings and allows resizing if the BorderStyle is set to **bsSizeable**.

At this point you should have your BorderIcons property set to **[biSystem Menu]**, BorderStyle to **bsFixed**, and WindowState to **wsMaximized**. Before I move on to the components, let's look at two more properties: Name and Caption.

What's in a Name? Form Names and Captions

The value of a form's Caption property is what appears in the form's title bar; it is for the benefit of persons viewing the application. The value can contain any characters you want, including spaces. This is not true for the value of a form's Name property. The Name is critical to the functioning of Delphi because it is the name by which Delphi identifies each form within a project.

The Name of a form must be unique. In other words you cannot have two forms within the same project that have the same Name. Whenever you create a new form, Delphi automatically assigns unique sequentially numbered default names: Form1, Form2, Form3, and so on. From a programmer's point of view, the default names are not terribly useful because they are not descriptive. It is good programming practice to give descriptive names to your forms and components.

The Name value is used by Delphi to identify each object. Because the Delphi program uses this value, the setting must conform to certain rules. First, it must be only one word, which means you can't use any spaces. You may, however, use up to 63 letter, number, and underscore characters, and the Name value is not case-sensitive. The following are some examples of valid form Name settings:

Form1

Form_1

FirstPresentationScreen

First_PresentationScreen

First_Presentation_Screen

You may use the underscore as the first character, but you may not use a number as the first character, as follows:

`_1Form`	Valid.
`1Form`	Not valid.
`1_Form`	Not valid.
`_FirstForm`	Valid.

Go ahead and change the form's Name property from Form1 to OpeningScreen and press **Enter**. Did you notice what happened? The Object Inspector window now shows OpeningScreen:TForm1, reflecting the object's new name. But something else also happened when you changed the Name property—the form's Caption changed with it. You should now see `OpeningScreen` in the form's title bar. This sometimes leads people to confuse the Name and Caption properties with one another. Here's the rule: *If you have not yet set the Caption property, Delphi will automatically set it to match the Name property.* However, once you set the Caption property, Delphi will not override it, even if you change the Name property again later. Assuming you haven't already done so, change the Caption value to `Teach Yourself Delphi - Sample Presentation Program`.

Another important thing to remember is that when you use the Object Inspector to change the Name property value, Delphi automatically changes all references to that name throughout your program—in each place it is mentioned in all of the existing code units. If, however, you change the name directly in a code window, the change will only appear where you type it.

Some Button and Label Properties

Now we'll look at some of the properties for the button and label components. In the previous section I mentioned that the value for a form's Caption property could contain freeform text and that it appears in the form's title bar. I also discussed the fact that Name property values had to be unique, as they are used as identifiers by the program code, and that making them descriptive is useful to the programmer. The same rules apply to button and label components.

The Name property values for buttons and labels must also be unique, and their Caption property values can be freeform text. With buttons, the caption appears on the face of the button. Label captions appear inside the label area. You can also control the font size and style and text alignment of captions using the font subproperties.

T I P

If you want the text inside a label to appear as if superimposed over the form so that you can't tell where the label area begins and ends, you can set the label's Transparent property to **True**. This will eliminate the label's background completely.

Table 2.2 contains the property settings for the button and label components on your first form. I will continue to discuss these properties, specifying settings as I go along. And you will still have an opportunity to double-check the settings against the tables.

Table 2.2 *Property Settings for the Button and Label Components*

Component	Property	Value
Button	Caption	Continue
	Cursor	crDefault
	Default	True
	Font	[Tfont]
	Color	clYellow
	Name	Roman
	Size	12
	Style	[fsBold]
	fsBold	True
	Height	40
	Left	500
	Name	btnContinue
	ParentFont	False
	Top	410
	Visible	True
	Width	100

Label	Alignment	taCenter
	Caption	A Photo Presentation
	Cursor	crDefault
	Font	[Tfont]
	Color	clRed
	Name	Roman
	Size	48
	Style	[fsBold]
	fsBold	True
	Height	75
	Left	20
	Name	lblTitle
	ParentFont	False
	Top	340
	Transparent	True
	Width	600

N O T E

You may think that your label component is gone, but it's still there. The black background just makes it impossible to see. Just use the Object Inspector's drop-down list to select the label whenever you want to set its properties or events.

Notice that I used the abbreviation btn as a prefix to the button Name, and lbl as a prefix to the label Name. This is a naming convention that you will use throughout this book. Using prefixes such as these is very helpful. Not only can you can tell at a glance what type of component you're working with, but you can also use a prefix to make a name unique.

Fonts, Colors, and Parents

Both the button and label components have a font property consisting of six subproperties: color, height, name, pitch, size, and style. The Style property itself has four subproperties: fsBold, fsItalic, fsUnderline, and fsStrikeout. All of these are fairly self-explanatory, except perhaps height and pitch. You can use the Height property of a font to ignore screen resolution when specifying a font's point size. This is a more advanced property, so for our sample application we'll let Delphi control the height automatically. Just in case you're curious, however, the height calculation requires the use of the form's PixelsPerInch property. Delphi divides the PixelsPerInch by 72 and multiplies the result by the Size setting to calculate the value of height, as follows:

```
Height = Size * PixelsPerInch / 72
```

SHORTCUT Using a standard Windows Font dialog box for setting font properties is much easier than revealing the font subproperties and setting each individually with the Object Inspector. You can access the Font dialog box by selecting the **Font** property and then double-clicking on the ellipsis (**...**) that appears to the right of the Font property value box.

Button and label components also have a ParentFont property. When this property is set to **True** (the default value), then the component's font will be the same as the font settings of the parent. Great! But what is a parent? Some of you may be familiar with the use of the words *parent* and *child* with reference to windows. For example, when you're working with a program and a dialog box appears, that dialog box is usually a child window, and the window in which the application is running is the parent.

When you're working in an object-oriented environment, this logic is extended to include *parent* as an object or component that contains another component. For example, if you place a button on a form, the form is the parent to that button. However, if you have radio buttons inside a group box on a form, the form is parent to the group box, and the group box is parent to the radio buttons. And of course the reciprocal relationship applies. The radio buttons are children of the group box, which is in turn a child of the form. It's just like life, where a mother can have many children, but the children have only one mother. This may not seem like a big deal at the moment, but in the next chapter, when you create a group box with radio buttons, you'll get to see the benefit first-hand. For now, the important point is that using ParentFont and ParentColors is an easy way of maintaining consistency.

In the sample presentation program your button and label font settings will be different than those of the parent (i.e., the form), so be sure to set ParentFont to **False**.

Labels also have a ParentColor property that works the same way. When set to True, the label color (i.e., the background color of the label) will be the same as that of the parent. This holds true even if you set the Label's Color property to a different value. The only way to make Delphi pay attention to a component's Color and Font property settings is to set the ParentColor and ParentFont values to **False**.

Cursors and Keystrokes

The Cursor property, which can be used with forms as well as buttons and labels, determines the shape of the cursor when it passes over the component. The default setting for the Cursor property, crDefault, is the safest choice because when it is used, Delphi automatically uses the standard Windows cursor shapes as appropriate for each circumstance. For example, using crDefault, the arrow you see when moving your mouse around the form right now is used for pointing at objects, clicking on buttons, and selecting check boxes. However, the cursor changes into a double-ended arrow shape when you move it over the border of a resizable form, and upon entering an edit box the cursor changes into an I-beam shape to indicate the cursor location in text. There are certainly times, however, when you want to select a specific cursor shape for a component. For a change of pace, you'll use the cross-hairs cursor for selecting radio buttons when you work on the second form for the sample application.

While we're talking about the crDefault value for the Cursor property, it would be a good time to point out that this is something altogether different from the Default property of a button. Every button component has a property called Default, and it has only two possible value settings: True and False. When Default is set to **True**, pressing **Enter** will have the same effect as a mouse click when a button is selected or active. Providing keyboard capability in addition to the mouse is a standard practice that is useful to both power users and novices, so for our sample application, set the button's Default property to **True**.

Another opportunity exists to provide keyboard control, and it relates back to the Caption property. When you use an ampersand character (&) within a caption, Delphi underlines the letter following the ampersand. The user may then press that character (usually a letter) along with the **Alt** key instead of using the mouse. This technique is most often used with menu items, and you'll have a chance to try it in Chapter 9.

Adding a Picture

Before we finalize the opening screen, let's add a picture. For the sample application, you'll use the image component and select the **IMAGE1.BMP** file for the Picture property. (The file is on the diskette that accompanies this book. If you did not create a TEACH subdirectory and install the Teach Yourself diskette, you should do so now. If you need assistance, see Appendix A.) Also, before you create the image component, use the Object Inspector to switch back to **OpeningScreen** and change the form's color setting to **clBackground**. You'll see why in a moment.

Okay, now click on the image component in the palette, then drag out an area on the OpeningScreen form. Set the Height property to **320**, Left to **50**, Top to **10**, and Width to **550**. Then double-click on the **Picture** property to bring up the Load dialog box. Click on the **Load** button, and using the Find File dialog box, select **IMAGE1.BMP** from the TEACH directory. When it appears in the dialog box window, click **OK**.

The image should now be visible in the upper-left section of the OpeningScreen form, as shown in Figure 2.6. You can see that the image does not fill up the whole image component space and you might be wondering if the settings I gave you are incorrect. What is that small image doing in the upper-left section of the window? Why isn't it centered? And why is the size of the image space so big? I wanted to illustrate a point (one you wouldn't have been able to see if you had left the form's color setting as black). When you place an image, Delphi aligns the top-left corner of the image itself with the top-left corner of the image component space created. If the image itself is smaller than the allotted componenet area, then there will be leftover space visible. If the image is larger than the component space, not all of the image will be seen.

Figure 2.6 *The OpeningScreen after setting the Picture property for the image component*

If you don't know exactly how much space an image will need, you can always adjust the component borders after you bring in the picture. Another alternative might be to use the Stretch property. This is one of the most interesting properties of an image component. If you set the Stretch property to **True**, then the image will stretch to fit the component space. Try that now: set Stretch to **True**. Hmmm. Distorted my picture, didn't it? Your screen should look something like Figure 2.7. The lesson here is that you have to be knowledgable about graphics. If the image had been created with greater color depth, then Stretch might have worked without distortion. However, I kind of like the abstract effect, so if you don't mind, let's leave Stretch set to True, and move on with the sample presentation.

Figure 2.7 *The OpeningScreen after setting the Stretch property for the image component to True*

Table 2.3 contains the property settings you need for the image component. Use the table to set the properties, then go back and double-check all your component properties against the values shown in Tables 2.1, 2.2, and 2.3, just in case you missed any. Don't forget to reset the form's Color property to **clBlack**. When you're done, you can run the program to see how it looks in action.

Table 2.3 *Property Settings for the Image Component*

Property	Value
Height	320
Left	50
Name	OpeningImage
Picture	(Tbitmap) *
Stretch	True
Top	10
Width	550

*The Value setting for Picture reads (**Tbitmap**) after you use Load to place the IMAGE1.BMP.

Run the Program

Now that the three components are in place with their properties set, you can run the program. Before you do, however, I suggest you save the project. That way, if you should run into any fatal errors, you won't lose all the work you've done. Because you saved the project once before (in the last chapter), and you haven't added any new forms or units, you will not need to specify any file names. Have you saved it? Okay, now let's run it.

To run your project, select **Run** from the Run menu, or press **F9**. What happens? Not much, that's true. But you should be able to see the opening screen (as shown in Figure 2.8), and when you click the button you should be able to see it depress. You might expect something to happen when you press a button, as well you should, but you haven't yet told the program what to do when the button is pressed. This leads us directly to a discussion of event-driven programming.

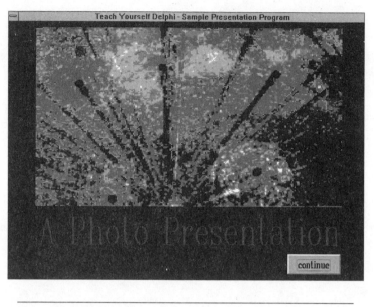

Figure 2.8 *OpeningScreen of Present program, up and running*

In a moment I'll define some terms that should smooth the way a bit, but before I do, I want to show you one more thing. While your program is running, the Delphi title bar reads `Delphi - Present[Running]`. You can't see it at the moment because OpeningScreen is running in the maximized position and hiding the entire Delphi program. In order to see it, you'll have to drag the OpeningScreen window down a little on your screen. We did set the form's BorderStyle to **Fixed**, so you can't resize the window, but you can drag it around on the screen.

To stop running your presentation program, double-click on the **SystemMenu** icon in the top-left corner of the form. Now take a look at the Delphi title bar again; it simply reads `Delphi - Present`.

The Great Event

What is event-driven programming? An event-driven program is one that bases its activity on the occurrence of events. In Chapter 1, while examining the Object Inspector, I touched briefly on the concept of events. I defined an *event* as some action relating to an object or component that is caused by either the user or the program itself. Examples included clicking on a button and resizing a form. When you write code that is to be executed on the occurrence of a specific event, you're creating an event handler. *Event handlers* are special procedures that tell the program what to do when a specific event occurs. So what's a procedure?

Procedures, and *functions*, are blocks of code that tell the program what to do. A procedure is a subroutine, nested within the main program, that can be called from anywhere in the program. A function is a special type of subroutine that computes and/or returns a value. As mentioned a moment ago, event handlers are also special procedures.

This may still seem a bit confusing, and you don't really need to have a crystal-clear understanding of which is which in order to use Delphi. When you get into advanced programming, it may become necessary to know the difference because some programming rules will apply to one and not the other. But by then, you'll know what's what from your own experience. Let's tackle one more term, just to complete the overall picture.

A *method* is a procedure, function, or command that is related directly to a specified object or component. In fact, when you use a method (as you will in the next chapter), the object is named first, followed by a period, followed by the method. In some cases methods are commands, and in other cases a method can be the name of an event handler. Don't let that confuse you. In the next chapter you'll see examples of both.

Add a Form

In the next chapter you're going to write some code so that when you click on that button you can move from your OpeningScreen form to a second form. But you don't have a second form yet, so before I close out this chapter, I'd like to show you how to add another form to your project.

Select **New Form** from the File menu, or you can use the New Form glyph on the Speedbar (bottom row, third from left). Either option brings up the Browse Gallery (see Figure 2.9) from which you can select the type of new form that you want. Right now what you need is a blank form, so make sure that it's selected and click **OK**. That's it, you have a new form. Set the form's Name property to **SelectScreen**. Then exit the Delphi program. Of course, because you have added a new form, you'll be prompted to save the new file. To maintain our file-naming conventions, name this new one **PRES_U02.PAS**. Don't be thrown by the fact that Delphi thinks this is Unit1 when you know it's the second unit. Delphi's automatic naming with numbers doesn't take into account any forms or units that you have already named.

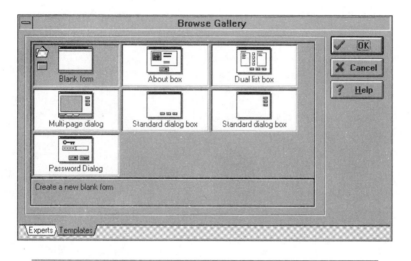

Figure 2.9 *The Browse Gallery appears when you select New Form*

Summary

◆ ABCD, a four-phase approach to creating an application, stands for *a*dvance planning, *b*uilding, *c*oding, and *d*ebugging.

◆ Advance planning should include: definition of your purpose, goals, and required functionality; consideration of your target audience and their equipment; and, optionally, written specifications and drawings. The latter is particularly desirable when working with a team.

◆ The BorderIcons property of a form determines whether a form has SystemMenu, Minimize, and/or Maximize buttons. The BorderStyle property controls whether a form is resizable, is to be treated as a dialog box, or has any borders at all. The WindowState property allows you to ignore the Top, Left, Width, and Height settings in favor of displaying the form full-screen (i.e., maximized) or as an icon (i.e., minimized).

◆ The Name property of any component must be unique among the same-type components. Descriptive names are useful to the programmer. A Name may consist of up to 63 letter, number, and underscore characters, and it is not case-sensitive. However, a name may not contain any spaces or begin with a number. Delphi uses the Name to identify each object in a project.

◆ The Caption property may contain freeform text, including spaces. A form's caption is displayed in the form's title bar. The caption for a button appears on the face of the button. Label captions appear inside the label area. You can control the font size and style used for the caption by setting the component's font subproperties or by accessing the Font dialog box.

◆ A parent is an object or component that contains another component. If you want to set the font or color of a button to match that of the form on which the button sits, you can set the button component's ParentFont and/or ParentColor properties to **True**. This is an easy way to maintain visual consistency.

◆ A component's Cursor property determines the shape of the cursor as it passes over the component. Shapes include the pointer arrow, I-beam, and cross-hairs.

◆ A button has a property called Default. When Default is set to **True**, pressing **Enter** when the button is selected or active will have the same effect as a mouse click.

◆ You can place a picture on a form using an image component. By default, a picture will appear in its original size, so if it is larger than the component space, not all of the image will be visible. If it is smaller, there will be unused component space. However, when the image component's Stretch property is set to **True**, the image will resize to fit the component.

◆ To run your program, select **Run** from the <u>R</u>un menu or press **F9**. While the program is running, the word Running appears in brackets in the Delphi title bar. To stop running, double-click on the **SystemMenu** in the top-left corner of your form.

◆ Some terminology for event-driven programming: *Event handlers* are special procedures that tell the program what to do when a specific event occurs. A *procedure* is a subroutine, i.e., a block of code nested within the main program, that can be called from anywhere in the program. A *function* is a special type of subroutine that computes and/or returns a value. A *method* is a procedure, function, or command that is directly related to a specified object or component.

◆ To add a new form to your project, select **New <u>F</u>orm** from the File menu.

In the Next Chapter

In the next chapter you're going to begin with some simple Pascal programming. You'll learn about expressions, punctuating code, statement types, and syntax. I'll also describe the parts of a Delphi project.

CHAPTER 3

Pascal Is the Language

- ◆ Using the Show and Hide methods
- ◆ Finding and displaying forms using View Form
- ◆ Creating an OnClick event
- ◆ Examining a procedure
- ◆ Exploring units
  - –Unit structure
  - –Communication between units
  - –The project unit
- ◆ Idenitfying statements
  - –Assigning values
  - –Evaluating expressions

45

As of the end of the last chapter, you completed the design and layout for the first form in the sample application. The form, named OpeningScreen, now contains a label with the title of the presentation, an image component to display a bitmap graphic, and a button. You also added a second form to the project and named it SelectScreen. The design intention is that after viewing the opening screen, the user will click on the button to move on to the next screen. At this point, however, when you click on the button, nothing happens. This brings us to the Pascal, the underlying programming language that drives applications created with Delphi.

Using a Method

All programming languages use certain words and characters for special purposes. In Delphi these are known as reserved words and special symbols. For example, as you'll see shortly in Figure 3.1, `begin` and `end` are reserved words used to mark the beginning and ending of blocks of code. You'll also see characters used as special symbols, such as the semicolon indicating the end of a statement, and curly bracket characters used to surround words that are intended as comments and not program code.

Every programming language also needs some action words or commands. Getting back to our sample application, when you click on the button, you want to invoke an action that will display the SelectScreen form. In Pascal, display is not a recognized word. What you need is the Show method, as follows:

```
SelectScreen.Show
```

At the end of the last chapter, I defined a method as a procedure, function, or command that is related directly to a specified object or component. As you can see, the method follows the name of the object or component to which it applies and is attached to that object or component by a period. (This means that the period character is also a special symbol.)

Great! That seems simple enough. But where do you put it? In Chapter 2 I introduced the concept of event handlers. Now you'll get to put that concept into action.

Where Did It Go?

Assuming that you saved your project and exited Delphi as instructed at the end of the last chapter, you'll need to get Delphi running and open your PRESENT project before you can code your event. When you open your project, you'll find your OpeningScreen form on top of the Code Editor window displaying only the PRES_U01 code page and tab. What happened to the SelectScreen form and its PRES_U02 code page and tab?

Don't worry, they're still part of the project, but once again you've got to use the **Forms...** item on the <u>V</u>iew menu, press **Shift-F12**, or click on the **Select Form From List** glyph on the Speedbar, to bring up the dialog box where you can select a specific form. Alternatively, you can bring back the SelectScreen form by selecting **Project Manager** from the <u>V</u>iew menu. From the Project Manager window you can highlight the **SelectScreen** form and use the **View Form** glyph, or simply double-click on **SelectScreen**, listed on the right side of the window under the form heading.

N O T E

You use similar procedures when you want to display the a code page. For example, to display the PRES_U01 code page, you can double-click on **Pres_u01**, listed on the left side of the Project Manager window under the Unit heading. If a form is displayed, you can always access its corresponding code page by simply double-clicking on the form. You can also access code windows by selecting <u>U</u>nit... from the View menu, pressing **Ctrl-F11**, or using the **Select Unit From List** glyph from the Speedbar to bring up the View Unit dialog box.

When you choose to display another form, the form window appears in addition to the other windows on your screen. So if you choose to display SelectScreen now (and it's completely up to you), both forms will be on your screen. As you can imagine, building a project with many forms could create a cluttered screen, like so many papers strewn across a desk. Of course you can always minimize an open window. The View tools provide an alternative—making it easy to find what you want when you need it—but each of you will find your own working preferences.

Okay, now we'll continue with our discussion about event handlers.

The First Event

As you probably remember, an event corresponds to an object or component. The component in question here is the button named btnContinue on the OpeningScreen form, and the event is a Click event. Select your button component either by clicking on it or by choosing it from the drop-down list at the top of the Object Inspector. Now choose the Events page from the Object Inspector, select the **OnClick** event from the top of the list, and double-click in the empty value area to the right.

When you do this, your Code Editor window should appear, displaying the Pres_u01 code page. The following code should be visible at the top of the window:

```
procedure
TOpeningScreen.btnContinueClick(Sender:
TObject);
begin

end;
```

and you'll notice that the position of the scroll bar on the right side of the Code Editor window indicates that what you're seeing is not at the beginning of the code page.

When you double-clicked on the event in the Object Inspector, Delphi generated this piece of code for you and placed it at a specific location in your code unit. And guess what? It's not only a procedure (as you can tell, because it says so), but it's also an event handler. Let's examine this code.

The first line is called the *procedure heading*. It begins with the reserved word, **procedure**, displayed in bold. Also on this line is a two-part text string. The first part, *TOpeningScreen*, is the name of the form containing the component with which the event is associated. The second part, *btnContinueClick*, names the specific component and event, and it is separated from the first part by a period. Looks like a method, doesn't it?

At the end of Chapter 2, I said that a method can be the name of an event handler, and that's just what this is.

The procedure heading line ends with (*Sender: TObject*). The parentheses contain the procedure's list of formal *parameters*, if there are any, and the type of each parameter. A parameter is something that allows the program to pass and/or receive data to and from a procedure or function. In this case the Sender parameter and its TObject type are system generated. Sender carries the name of the object in which the event occurred, and TObject is the Sender's system-assigned object type.

The only other Delphi-generated lines for this event handler are the **begin** and **end;** lines. Begin marks the beginning of the code that you want executed whenever this particular event occurs. End, followed by a semicolon, indicates the end of this event-handler. (The other **end.** line denotes the end of the procedure, as you'll see shortly.)

Earlier I discussed using the SelectScreen.Show method as the statement to be executed when the Click event occurs, so let's try it. Type in the code so that your event handler looks like this:

```
procedure
TOpeningScreen.btnContinueClick(Sender:
TObject);
begin
SelectScreen.Show
end;
```

Now press F9 to run your program. Oops. At the bottom of your code window you got a colorful error message that says `Error 3: Unknown identifier.`, and the code line you added is now highlighted and displayed in another color too (see Figure 3.1). Delphi highlights the line that caused the error, so that you know where to look for the problem. The problem is that Pres_u01 has never heard of SelectScreen because SelectScreen is part of Pres_u02, and Pres_u01 doesn't automatically know about Pres_u02. This leads us to a discussion about the overall structure of a program created with Delphi.

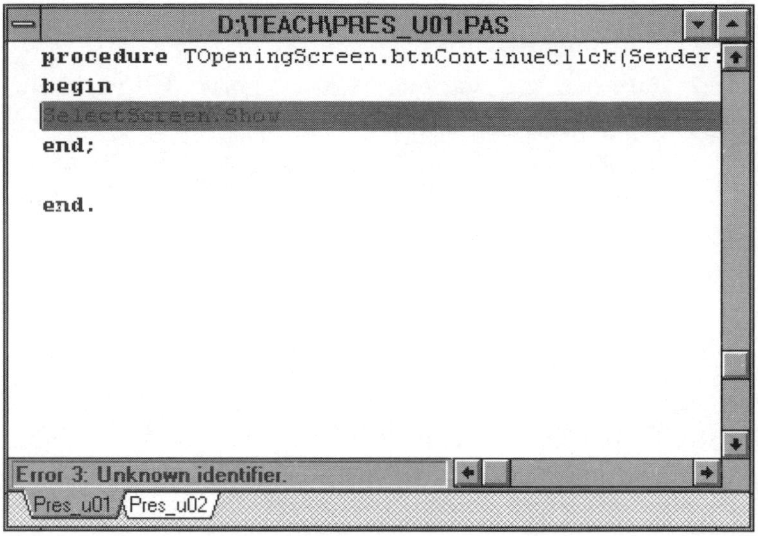

```
┌─────────────────────────────────────────────────────┐
│ ─          D:\TEACH\PRES_U01.PAS          ▼  ▲        │
├─────────────────────────────────────────────────────┤
│ procedure TOpeningScreen.btnContinueClick(Sender ▲   │
│ begin                                                │
│ SelectScreen.Show                                    │
│ end;                                                 │
│                                                      │
│ end.                                                 │
│                                                      │
│                                                  ▼   │
├─────────────────────────────────────────────────────┤
│ Error 3: Unknown identifier.        ◄      ►         │
│  \ Pres_u01 / Pres_u02 /                             │
└─────────────────────────────────────────────────────┘
```

Figure 3.1 *The Pres_u01 code window after encountering an unknown identifier*

What's in a Unit? The Big Picture

You may have heard people refer to *blocks of code*. A code block contains declarations and statements. A *unit* is a large code block that also contains smaller code blocks, each of which is either a procedure, function, or method. When you begin a new project, Delphi automatically generates a unit to go along with Form1. Every form has a corresponding code unit to contain the event handlers, procedures, and functions relevant to that form. And unless otherwise specified, what is in a particular unit is local to that unit, meaning that the statements and objects can only be recognized from inside that unit.

When you first began creating the sample application, Delphi started you off with FORM1 and a corresponding unit for code called UNIT1.PAS. You then renamed the form by setting its Name property to **OpeningScreen**, and when you first saved the project, you renamed the code unit **Pres_u01**. Let's go line-by-line through the code currently in

Pres_u01, as shown in Figure 3.2. Scroll to the top of the code window, and I'll start from the beginning.

```
Unit Pres_u01;

interface

uses SysUtils, WinTypes, WinProcs, Messages,
Classes, uGraphics, Controls, Forms, Dialogs,
StdCtrls;

type
  TOpeningScreen = class(TForm)
     btnContinue: TButton;
     lblTitle: TLabel;
     OpeningImage: TImage;
     procedure btnContinueClick(Sender: TObject);
  private
     { Private declarations }
  public
     { Public declarations }
  end;

var

  OpeningScreen: TOpeningScreen;

implementation
```

```
{$R *.DFM}
procedure
TOpeningScreen.btnContinueClick(Sender:
TObject);
begin
SelectScreen.Show
end;

end.
```

Figure 3.2 *The code in Pres_u01 after adding the SelectScreen.Show method*

Units begin with a *unit heading* consisting of *unit* (a reserved word), the unit name (Pres_u01 in this case), and a semicolon. After the heading, the first section of a unit is the *interface section*, which begins with the word *interface* (again a reserved word) on a line by itself. This section is used to specify procedures, functions, and other elements that are public, meaning they may be accessed from outside the unit in which they are contained.

The *uses* clause, which is part of the interface section, is a list of the names of other units that are used directly by this unit. In Pres_u01 the uses clause lists SysUtils, WinTypes, WinProcs, and several other units that Delphi has determined are needed by this unit. That code was genera- ted automatically for you. You can, however, add to that list, and as you'll see shortly, that is exactly how you're going to solve your current code error.

The *type* section comes next, listing the forms, components, and pro- cedures available in this code unit. First comes the form itself, and Delphi has used the class reserved word to note that it may be referred to as an object of TForm type. The three components on that form are each named and their type identified. These lines should remind you of the parameter statement I discussed earlier—Sender: TObject;—because they serve similar purposes and use the same syntax:

```
name: type;
```

Following the list of components comes the list of procedures. For each procedure, Delphi automatically inserts a copy of the procedure heading line in this section. So far in Pres_u01 you only have one procedure, your event handler.

The last part of the type section is the area for *private* and *public* declarations. Private means local, so private declarations are only available within the unit. Conversely, anything declared as public means it is available to other units. The section officially concludes with the **end;** line.

The *var* section is used to declare variables, and we'll talk more about variables in Chapter 5. For now, notice that the declaration includes the name of the variable and its type—just like the type and parameter declarations I discussed a moment ago. In the type section, TOpeningScreen was identified as a TForm type, and here Delphi as associating TOpeningScreen with OpeningScreen (no T), the Name property value you assigned to the form.

The last section in the unit begins with the reserved word *implementation* and concludes with a period (.) at the very end of the unit. All of the code blocks appear in this section, so this is where all of the action takes place. You can also place declarations in this section, but they will only be available within this section. Figure 3.2 shows only one code block in Pres_u01 so far—your event handler.

The first line in the implementation section shown in Figure 3.2 is {$R *.FRM}. You might think that it's a comment because of the curly brackets. The dollar sign, however, identifies this as a compiler directive, and the R indicates Range Checking.

Exterminating Your First Bug

Before I took you on that tour of Pres_u01, you encountered your first programming bug. The error message was *unknown identifier*, and Delphi identified the SelectScreen.Show statement in your btnContinueClick procedure as the problem. While describing the sections of Pres_u01, I alluded to the solution to this problem. The problem is that Pres_u01 doesn't recognize SelectScreen because SelectScreen is part of Pres_u02. Can you figure out how to fix this?

Why doesn't Pres_u01 recognize the SelectScreen form? Was SelectScreen specified in the Type section of Pres_u01? No, but OpeningScreen was. And SelectScreen is specified in the Type section of Pres_u02, the code unit that corresponds to the SelectScreen form. So now the question becomes how do you get Pres_u01 to access something in Pres_u02? Here's a hint: The answer lies in the interface section.

While it's true that a unit's code is for *local* use, local meaning within the unit, the interface section provides the means for making outside connections. The Uses clause lists other units that need to be made available for use by the current unit. Add **Spunit02** to the end of the uses clause, as follows:

```
uses SysUtils, WinTypes, WinProcs, Messages,
Classes, Graphics, Controls, Forms, Dialogs,
StdCtrls, Pres_u02;
```

Make sure there is a comma following StdCtrls, and a semicolon at the end of the statement. Now press **F9** to run your program, and see what happens.

Your OpeningScreen should appear, and when you click on the **Continue** button, the SelectScreen form appears. The SelectScreen form is still empty, because you haven't designed its components yet. But there's something else you need to handle first. When your second screen appears, you want the first screen to disappear. Otherwise you'll end up with a very cluttered screen by the end of the presentation.

Before you can continue coding, you'll need to stop Present from running (double-click on the **OpeningScreen SystemMenu** icon in the top-left corner of the form).

Disappear is not a Delphi command. What you need is the Hide method. It works just like the Show method you used to display the SelectScreen form, only this time you'll use it with the OpeningScreen form. Place it before your Show method statement, and make sure it ends with a semicolon. All statements are delimited by a semicolon, and the only reason your Show method did not need one was because it was immediately followed by the end; Your event handler should now look like the following:

```
procedure
TOpeningScreen.btnContinueClick(Sender:
TObject);
begin
OpeningScreen.Hide;
SelectScreen.Show
end;
```

If you forget the semicolon, you'll get the `Error 85: ";" expected` error message.

Now press **F9** to run the Present application again. So far, so good. OpeningScreen appears, and when you click on the button, OpeningScreen disappears and the SelectScreen form becomes visible. Now stop the program, and then select **Save Project** from the File menu to save the good work you've done. That's all the programming you're going to do for the moment, but don't close the Present project because I'm going to show you another part of it that you haven't seen yet.

The Project Unit: More of the Big Picture

You already know that when you begin a new project, Delphi automatically generates a code unit, UNIT1.PAS, to go with FORM1. And every time you add a form, another unit is generated to contain the event handlers, procedures, and functions relevant to that form. What you probably don't know yet is that when you begin a project, Delphi also generates a project unit, initially called PROJECT1. When you save your project for the first time and give it a name, Delphi renames the unit to match. So for the sample application you're working on, Present is the name of the project unit.

The purpose of the project unit is to specify the program name, list all the code units used by the program, and run the application. This unit is not automatically visible when you open your project. In order to display the project unit in the Code Editor window, you have to bring up the **Project Manager** by selecting it from the View menu. Then click your right mouse button inside the Project Manager window and select **View Project** from the pop-up menu, as shown in Figure 3.3. PRESENT.DPR should now be displayed in the Code Editor window.

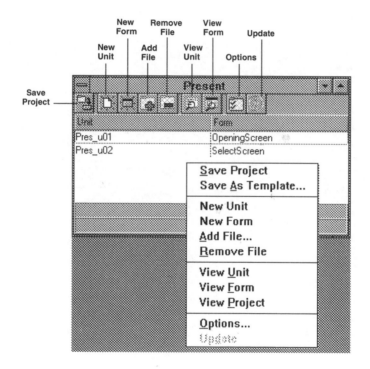

Figure 3.3 *Project Manager window with pop-up menu displayed*

Let's take a look at the following code from the Present unit:

```
unit Present;

uses
```

```
Forms,
Pres_u01 in '\Teach\Pres_u01.PAS'
            {OpeningScreen},
Pres_u02 in '\Teach\Pres_u02.PAS'
            {SelectScreen};


{$R *.RES}


begin
  Application.CreateForm(TOpeningScreen,
                         OpeningScreen);
  Application.CreateForm(TSelectScreen,
                         SelectScreen);
  Application.Run;
end.
```

The project unit consists of three sections: the **unit** header that specified the project name; the **uses** section that contains a list of all the units used in the project, the filename for each unit, and the formname with which the unit is associated; and the **begin/end** code block that contains the statements required to create each form and launch your application.

That's all there is to it, and Delphi generated all the code for you. As you continue to add other units to the project, Delphi will continue to update this unit as needed.

Before we move on, I'd like you to take another look at the Project Manager window, as shown in Figure 3.3. Some of the glyphs in this window duplicate those found on the Speedbar (Save Project, Add File to Project, and Remove File from Project), and other duplicate items on the File menu (New Unit and New Form). In addition, in the Project Manager window you have glyphs for View Form and View Unit that will display whichever form or unit you have highlighted from the list.

T I P The Project Manager is a useful tool. For example, if you wanted to make more room for Component palette pages, you could remove the Speedbar from your screen and still have access to some of the same glyphs using the Project Manager. You also wouldn't need to use the Forms... or Units... items from the View menu. With the Project Manager glyphs you can have more direct access and bypass the intermediate View Form or View Unit dialog boxes.

Statements

A statement can do a lot of things, including activate a function or procedure, assign a value, and direct the program to another statement or section of code. Delphi supports six different types of statements, and you're already acquainted with one of those types—*procedures.* As you saw earlier, a procedure begins with a heading and includes a begin/end code block containing statements that specify actions to be executed.

Some statements are *conditional,* meaning that the actions are only executed if the condition is met. *Loops* are repetitive statements where the same action is repeated a specified number of times. Another particularly useful statement type is the *assignment* statement that evaluates an expression and places the result in a variable. You'll see examples of these and other statement types as you continue to build the sample application. The *Statement Types* sidebar provides a brief description of each, and we'll point examples out to you as I go along.

Statement Types

A program is supposed to execute a series of actions, and statements describe those actions. Statements can be either simple or structured, with structured statements being the more complex.

Simple statements include:

Procedure: an individual self-contained subroutines within a unit.

> ***Assignment***: a statement that evaluates an expression and places the result in a variable.
>
> ***Goto***: a statement that allows you to direct the program to another section of code identified by a label.
>
> Structured statements include:
>
> ***Conditional***: a statement that allows you to test some condition before executing any action. Use *If* when there are one or two choices. Use *Case* when there are more than two choices.
>
> ***Compound***: a series of statements to be executed in sequence, starting with the *begin* reserved word, and concluding with *end*.
>
> ***Loops***: allow you to repeat statements. *For* repeats a specified number of times. *Repeat until* repeats until a condition is met. *While* allows you to test for a condition before repeating.
>
> ***With...do***: a statement that tells the program to use the specified components, methods, record fields, or variables, in performing the specified actions.

It's All in the Expression

Now let's talk a little about the code itself. Programming languages are a lot like human languages. In English, for example, a sentence might contain two or more phrases. In Pascal, statements may contain one or more expressions that compare things, or perform some sort of action such as an arithmetic, logical, or Boolean operation.

All expressions can be evaluated to return a result. For example, 2 + 2 is an expression that when evaluated, returns the result of 4. The plus sign used in the expression is called an *operator*. The following are called *arithmetic operators*: + (addition), - (subtraction), * (multiplication), and / (division). In Pascal, **:=** is a special symbol known as an *assignment operator*, and it is used to assign a value. You can write a simple statement to assign the value of 2 + 2 to a variable called X, as follows:

```
X := 2 + 2;
```

Notice the semicolon at the end of the statement. Pascal has its own rules of punctuation and grammar. As you saw earlier in this chapter, a period (.) indicates the end of a unit, and all statements must end with a semicolon.

The phrase *evaluate an expression* does not automatically indicate a need for operators. Sometimes a value does not need to be calculated, in which case *evaluate* simply means recognize. For example, suppose you wanted to assign a name to a variable called AuthorName. The assignment statement might look like the following:

```
AuthorName := 'Devra Hall';
```

The apostrophes before and after the value indicate that the value is a character string. In addition to assigning values to variables (a subject I'll talk more about in Chapters 4 and 5), assignment statements are also used to assign run-time properties.

Assigning Run-Time Properties

This might also be a good time to note the difference between *design-time* and *run-time* properties. In the first two chapters, you used the Object Inspector to assign values to the various components' properties. All of the design-time properties for each component are listed in the Object Inspector, so you can set their values while designing your application. Run-time properties are those whose values can be set and/or reset while your application is running.

You have the ability to set most properties at either time. This means that you can set a property's value while designing your application, and then change that value while the program is running. However, there are a few properties, such as a Form's Canvas property, that are accessible only at run-time. I'll talk more about the Canvas property in Chapter 6 when you'll use it to draw on a form.

To set a run-time property, you need to use an assignment statement where the property is identified in the following manner:

```
component.property := value
```

Now suppose, for example, that you had a form that contained a list of options with a radio button for each choice. And let's also assume that the user will have the ability to return to the list after viewing a selection. It might be useful to indicate in some way which menu selections have already been explored, and one way to do this would be to change the font color of the radio button's caption after it is selected. This color is one of the radio button's Font subproperties, and if the button was named rbFields and you wanted to change the color to green, the code would look like this:

```
rbFields.Font.Color := clGreen
```

Guess what. You're going to add this code in the next chapter. But first, you'll need to create the components for the SelectScreen form and set the design-time properties.

Summary

◆ The Show method can be used to display a form, and the Hide method can be used to make a form disappear. The method follows the name of the form, separated by a period, as follows: formname.Show and formname.Hide.

◆ If you want to view a form that is part of an open project, but not currently visible on the screen, you can use the **Speedbar** glyph, press **Ctrl-F12**, or select **Forms...** from the View menu to bring up the View Form dialog box. Alternatively, you could select the **Project Manager** item from the <u>V</u>iew menu, and use the **View Form** glyph in the Project Manager window to access the desired form.

◆ To create an event handler procedure, select the component on your form, then choose the appropriate event from the Object Inspector's event page, and double-click in the empty value area on the right. Delphi will generate the procedure heading, as well as the begin and end lines between which you must place your code.

◆ A parameter is something that allows the program to pass data to, and/or receive data from a procedure or function.

◆ Press **F9** or select <u>**Run**</u> from the <u>R</u>un menu to execute your program. To stop the program, double-click the **SystemMenu** icon in the top-left corner of the form.

◆ For every form you create, Delphi generates a corresponding unit to contain the code relevant to that form.

–Units begin with a unit heading.

–Unless specified in the interface section, all the code in a unit is available only to that unit. The uses clause lists the names of other units that are needed by the current unit.

–The type section identifies the forms, components, and procedures contained in the unit.

–The var section is used to declare variables.

–The implementation section begins with the word *implementation*, concludes with a period (.) at the end of the unit, and contains all of the procedure and function code blocks.

◆ Delphi creates one project unit for every project. It contains a list of all of the units in the project and a statement to run the application. To view the project unit code you have to select **Project Manager** from the <u>V</u>iew menu, click your right mouse button inside the Project Manager window, and select **View <u>P</u>roject** from the pop-up menu.

◆ Procedures, conditional statements, loops, and assignment statements are some of the statement types supported by Delphi.

◆ Statements may contain expressions that compare things or perform some sort of operation. Expressions are evaluated to return a result. They can use arithmetic operators such as +, -, *, and /.

◆ Design-time properties are those properties set using the Object Inspector while creating your application. Run-time properties are set using assignment statements executed when your program is running.

In the Next Chapter

In the next chapter you're going to create the components and set the properties for the SelectScreen form. You're also going to learn how to create form templates and use that technique to create the final four forms for the sample presentation program. You'll be using some familiar components and properties, and we'll introduce some new components, such as the GroupBox and BitBtn (stands for bit button). Finally, you'll finish adding the code needed to move back and forth between all of the forms.

CHAPTER 4

Adding Forms and Other Components

- ◆ Designing full-screen forms—practical considerations
- ◆ Grouping components together—the GroupBox component
- ◆ Presenting choices with RadioButton components
- ◆ Examining new properties
  - –Cursors
  - –TabStop and TabOrder
  - –WordWrap
- ◆ Aligning components
  - –Form grid
  - –Alignment palette
  - –Alignment dialog box
- ◆ Creating Form templates

- ◆ Creating a button with a glyph—the BitButton component
- ◆ Exploring statements and methods
  - –Conditional statements
  - –Assignment statements
  - –Compound statements
  - –LoadFromFile method
- ◆ Compiling an EXE file

So far you've created two forms, used the label, button, and image components, and written code to show one form and hide another. In this chapter not only are you going to add components to the SelectScreen form, but you will also add a few more forms to complete the Present application. In addition to the label and button components with which you are already familiar, you'll use the GroupBox, RadioButton, and BitButton components. You'll see the planning diagram of what the SelectScreen and SubjectScreen forms should look like, learn about the new components and their properties, and discover the Alignment palette. Throughout the chapter I'll provide you with all of the property settings for the components on each form.

If Delphi is not running with your Present project open, start it now. When you open Present, you'll see the OpeningScreen form. The SelectScreen form will not be visible. Display your SelectScreen using the View menu or Speedbar options described earlier.

Designing Full-Screen Forms

When you created the OpeningScreen, you set its WindowState to wsMaximized. I had a few reasons for designing it this way: First, because it is a presentation and I didn't want the viewer to be distracted by anything else that might otherwise be visible on the desktop; second, because presentations are often presented to groups of people, and the larger the images, the easier it is for everyone to see; and third, some of the forms need to hold a lot of information (as you're about to find out), and I didn't want the form to look too crowded.

There is one little drawback when designing full-screen forms: Either you can't see everything at once because you're working with a smaller form in order to access the Object Inspector and other tools, or you can't see the Object Inspector because you maximized the form and all the Delphi tools are hidden away underneath. Unfortunately, there is no single or simple solution. You're going to have to work it out in whichever way is most comfortable for you. I do, however, have some tips:

For full-screen forms, use the WindowState property set to maximized. That way the form will not go full-screen until you run the application, and Delphi will use the height, left, top, and width settings during design phase. Then, using your less-than-full-screen form, create your components by placing them anywhere convenient on the form. Finally, when all the components are somewhere on the form, maximize the form using the Maximize button on the top right of the form, and use the drag-and-drop method to move your components around to where you want them.

You can always maximize a window by double-clicking anywhere in its title bar. Sometimes that's easier than hitting the little button area, and quite useful when a window doesn't have a Maximize button.

NOTE

Alternatively, if you happen to know, to the exact pixel, where you want each component placed, you can use the Object Inspector to set each component's properties accordingly without having to maximize the form. Of course you won't be able to see all of your components on the form, but you can use the combo-box at the top of the Object Inspector to select a component without being able to see it. This method works best if you've made an exact diagram to see the position of each component in relationship to the others. Some would say that this method takes the visual out of visual programming—I say do whatever works best for you.

Figure 4.1 shows the drawing that was made for the SelectScreen form during the advance planning stage. It's a very simple screen that contains a list of four choices, a label to display instructions, and a button to continue. Start by placing the button and label components on the SelectScreen form. Experiment a bit with the drag-and-drop method of arranging components, if only to get the feel of it. Then you can use the following property settings for the SelectScreen form and the button and image components:

Component	Property		Value
Form	+BorderIcons		[biSystemMenu]
		biSystemMenu	True
		biMinimize	False
		biMaximize	False
	BorderStyle		bsSingle
	Caption		Teach Yourself Delphi - Sample Presentation Program
	Color		clBlack
	Name		SelectScreen
	Visible		False
	WindowState		wsMaximized
Button	Caption		Show Subject
	Cursor		crDefault
	Default		True
	Font		[Tfont]
		Color	clYellow
		Name	Roman
		Size	12
		Style	[fsBold]
		fsBold	True
	Height		40
	Left		500
	Name		btnShowSubj
	ParentFont		False
	Top		410

	Visible	True
	Width	100
Label	Alignment	taCenter
	Caption	select a category
	Cursor	crDefault
	Font	[Tfont]
	Color	clRed
	Name	Roman
	Size	24
	Style	[fsBold]
	fsBold	True
	Height	75
	Left	20
	Name	lblInstruct
	ParentFont	False
	Top	340
	Transparent	True
	Width	600

Grouping Components in a GroupBox

For the Present program, I've selected eight photos and grouped them into four subjects: field, flora, panorama, and water. You can see these four items listed inside a box in Figure 4.1. The box is known as a Group-Box component, and the word *Subject* is its caption. The four subjects are captions for the four RadioButton components inside the GroupBox. And as described in Chapter 2, these radio buttons are children of the GroupBox.

The most important rule when working with a GroupBox is that the GroupBox must be added to the form before the components you wish to place inside it. Then you must create the other components directly inside of the GroupBox. That means that you cannot create a component on the form and then drag it into the GroupBox. (Well, you can drag it in, but that won't make it a child of the GroupBox.) Now would be a good time to create your GroupBox and then the three radio button components inside it. Don't worry about the exact placement of the GroupBox or its components. When you move the GroupBox, its components move with it.

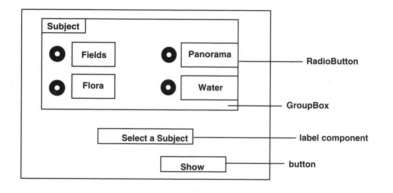

Figure 4.1 *Drawing of the SelectScreen form made during the advance planning phase*

All of the properties you need to set for the GroupBox component should be familiar to you, so we'll just do a quick recap. Following our diagram, the caption should read *Subject*. To make the GroupBox stand out even more, the color of the GroupBox area and the font for the caption are going to be different from those of the form. Don't forget, you'll also need to set the ParentColor and ParentFont properties to **False**, so that Delphi will use the GroupBox's Color and Font settings in lieu of those of the form.

The Height, Left, Top, and Width properties will define the size and placement of the GroupBox area. Of course you'll need to assign a unique name to the GroupBox component, and you'll use a prefix, gb, to begin the name as part of your naming conventions. The property settings for this component are as follows:

Component	Property	Value	Comments
GroupBox1	Caption	Subject	
	Color	clWhite	
	Font	[TFont]	
	Color	clRed	
	Name	Arial	
	Size	32	
	Style	[fsBold,fsItalic]	
	fsBold	True	
	fsItalic	True	
	Height	300	
	Left	55	
	Name	gbSubject	
	ParentColor	False	
	ParentFont	False	
	Top	25	
	Width	520	

Selecting Radio Button Components

Radio buttons are used to present the user with a group of choices, from which she or he may select only one. (For this reason, you cannot use a single radio button alone.) When a choice is selected, a small black dot appears inside the radio button. If you want one of the choices to appear preselected when the form first appears, set the Check property to **True**. In our sample application, there is no design benefit to suggesting a selection, so you'll leave the Check property set to **False**.

Just as with the label component on the first form, radio buttons have a caption, the alignment of which can be set to **taLeftJustify** or **taRightJustify** using the Alignment property. (Radio button captions don't look very good centered, so that's not an option.) The unique name given to each radio button component will begin with the prefix rb to maintain consistency and easy recognition.

As mentioned in Chapter 2, the Cursor property allows you to select a specific cursor shape. For a change of pace, you're going to use the cross-hair cursor for the radio buttons, and it will only appear in this shape when the cursor is over a radio button. The rest of the time, the cursor will resume the appropriate default shape.

Until now, you've had no reason to examine the TabOrder and TabStop properties, even though they were available to the button and image components on the OpeningScreen form. When TabStop is set to **True**, the user can use the Tab key to move to that control. When the Tab key is used, it is the TabOrder value that dictates the sequence in which the components are accessed. Delphi automatically sets the value of TabOrder in the sequence in which the components are created; however, you can change the TabOrder as needed.

NOTE

TabOrder always starts with 0, so if the TabOrder of a component is 1, it is actually the second in sequence. Also, no two components can have the same TabOrder number. If you reset the TabOrder of one component to a TabOrder number already in use, Delphi will automatically renumber all of the other components for you, bumping each component up by one.

Every component has a TabOrder setting, whether or not the TabStop property is true or false. The GroupBox, for example, has a TabOrder setting of 0 (because it was the first component you created for this form) even though TabStop is False. The TabOrder for the BitButton you're about to create will be 1, and its TabStop value will be True. You'll also notice that the child components (in this case the radio buttons) have their own TabOrder within the parent GroupBox, beginning with 0.

Instead of adding the RadioButton components and setting their properties one by one, I'm going to show you two shortcuts: the form grid and Alignment palette for easier placement, and the Paste function from the Edit menu for quickly replicating multiple components.

Replicating Components

Create one radio button component and set its properties according to the following list:

Component	Property	Value
RadioButtons	Cursor	crCross
	Font	[Tfont]
	Name	Arial
	Size	24
	Style	[fsBold,fsItalic]
	Bold	True
	Italic	True
	Height	35
	Left	40
	ParentColor	True
	ParentFont	False
	TabStop	True
	Top	90
	Width	185

Do not set the Caption, Name, TabOrder, or Top properties yet. Now make sure that the RadioButton is still selected (look for the handles around the component), and press **Ctrl-C** or select **Copy** from the Edit menu. Now press **Ctrl-V** three times. Each time you press these keys, Delphi pastes another copy of your selected radio button almost on top of the first one. Each new RadioButton has the same property settings as the first one, with the exception of the Name property that Delphi automatically increments. If you watch the Object Inspector each time you press, you'll see that the name of the selected object has changed, from RadioButton1, to RadioButton2, to RadioButton3, and so on.

There is another shortcut method. You could create each RadioButton individually and then set their properties all together. When you have more than one component with the same settings, you can select all of the relevant components together by holding down **Shift** as you select each one. The Object Inspector will change to show only those properties that the components have in common. This way you only have to set those properties once.

When you have all four RadioButtons, maximize your form and start peeling them apart (use drag-and-drop to move one at a time). Place the top one (RadioButton4) toward the bottom right of the GroupBox. The next one (RadioButton3) goes above RadioButton4. Then RadioButton2 goes below RadioButton1 and to the left of RadioButton4. Don't worry about the exact spacing yet. For now, your screen should look something like the one shown in Figure 4.2.

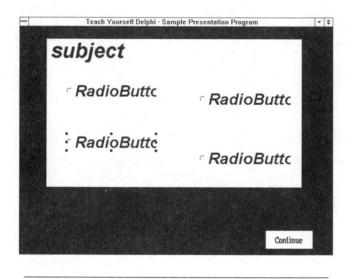

Figure 4.2 *RadioButton for a new form, before alignment*

Aligning Your Components

There are several methods for aligning your components. You can drag-and-drop your components, relying on your vision for exact placement.

Or you can drag-and-drop, relying on the form grid and its snap-to feature. Alternatively, you can select components and align them using the Alignment palette or the Alignment dialog box.

Form Grid

The form grid is responsible for those little lines of dots that you've been seeing on the background of your forms when in design mode (and before you change the background color to black). You can set their spacing to suit your needs by selecting **Environment** from the Options menu. The first Options page, called Preferences, has a section labeled Form Designer (as shown in Figure 4.3. Here you can set the X and Y grid sizes to the number of pixels. The default value for both X and Y is **8** pixels.

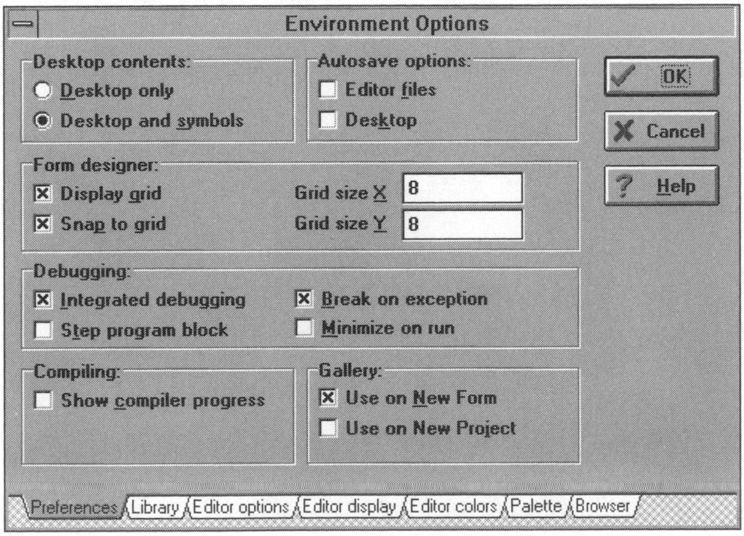

Figure 4.3 *Environment preferences*

Notice that the Snap to Grid check box is already selected. That is the default setting, allowing Delphi to snap your components to the grid as you place them. This is very helpful if you are doing a lot of manual placement, as it is easy to be off by a couple of pixels one way or the other.

You also have the option, however, of turning off the automatic snap to grid function, and selecting **Align to Grid** from the Edit menu only when you need it. Of course if you don't want to see the grid at all, you can deselect the **Display Grid** check box.

Personally, I use the grid method most often, though I generally set the grid size to a rounder number such as **10** or **20**, depending on the size of my forms and the number of components on the form. However, you might prefer the Alignment palette or the Alignment dialog box, and I encourage you to experiment with all three methods and use whatever works best for you.

Alignment Palette

You can display the Alignment palette by selecting it from the View menu. The palette (as shown in Figure 4.4) consists of ten glyphs representing your alignment options. From left to right, beginning with the top row, they are as follows:

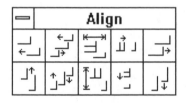

Figure 4.4 *The Alignment palette*

- ◆ **Align left edges**: align the left side of each selected component, to match that of the first selected component.

- ◆ **Align horizontal centers**: move all selected components horizontally such that the center of each is in alignment with the center of the first component selected.

- ◆ **Center in window horizontally**: places the selected component(s) in the horizontal center of the form (vertical axis ignored).

- ◆ **Space equal horizontally**: place components so that they are horizontally equidistant from one another.

- ◆ **Align right edges**: align the right side of each selected component to match that of the first selected component.

◆ **Align tops**: align the top side of each selected component to match that of the first selected component.

◆ **Align vertical centers**: move all selected components vertically such that the center of each is in alignment with the center of the first component selected.

◆ **Center in window vertically**: places the selected component(s) in the vertical center of the form (horizontal axis is ignored).

◆ **Space equal vertically**: place components so that they are vertically equidistant from one another.

◆ **Align bottoms**: align the bottom side of each selected component to match that of the first selected component.

These options correspond to the options available in the Alignment dialog box.

Alignment Dialog Box

The benefit of the Alignment dialog box, as compared to the Alignment palette, is that is allows you to select both the vertical and horizontal options at one time. To display the dialog box (as shown in Figure 4.5) select **Align...** from the Edit menu. You'll see two sets of radio buttons, one for the horizontal setting, and one for the vertical. Make your selections and click on **OK**.

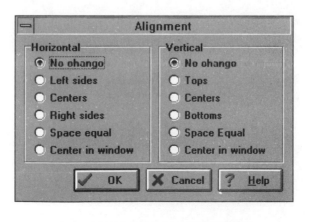

Figure 4.5 *The Alignment dialog box*

When aligning multiple components in relation to one another (as opposed to positioning one component in relationship to the form), the alignment will be based on the position of the first component selected, just as it was with the Alignment palette. If you want to align only the horizontal, or only the vertical, you can select **No Change** for the other setting.

Setting More Properties

Okay, here are the rest of the property settings for each individual RadioButton. You'll notice that I did not specify a Color setting for the radio buttons because I want you to use the same color selection as is used by the GroupBox. All you have to do is leave the ParentColor value set to **True**. You didn't do that earlier with the font settings because you needed to change the font size.

Before I move on, take a moment to be sure that you have completed the property settings for the SelectScreen and all of its components.

Component	Property	Value
RadioButton1	Caption	Fields
	Height	35
	Left	40
	Name	rbFields
	TabOrder	0
	Top	90
RadioButton2	Caption	Flora
	Height	35
	Left	40
	Name	rbFlora
	TabOrder	1
	Top	190

RadioButton3	Caption	Panorama
	Height	35
	Left	295
	Name	rbPanorama
	TabOrder	2
	Top	90
RadioButton4	Caption	Water
	Height	35
	Left	295
	Name	rbWater
	TabOrder	3
	Top	190

Making Template Forms

When the user clicks on the SelectScreen's **Continue** button, the next screen to be displayed will depend on which RadioButton was selected. You are going to create four new forms, one for each subject choice. But wait before you go off and create each form and set the properties individually. I've got another shortcut for you. Because each of the four forms is basically the same, you're going to create a Template form.

N O T E   You might wonder why you need four different forms if they are all basically the same. The truth is, this isn't the only way to design this application. One form could be used to handle all four subjects. However, it would involve programming that is slightly more complex than I want to introduce right now. As you set out to design your own applications, you will find that there are usually several different ways to achieve the same results. And each way you think of will have its own tradeoffs.

Your Template form is going to look something like the advance drawing shown in Figure 4.6.

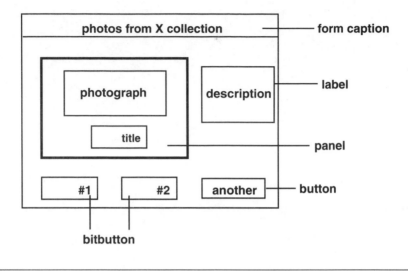

Figure 4.6 *The drawing of the Subject screen made during the advance planning stage*

Select **New Form** from the Speedbar. First add a panel component. It's very similar to the GroupBox component you used earlier, but it has a few different properties, one of which I want you to use—BevelWidth. Now add an image component and a label component, placing each inside the panel. Then add another label and place it to the right of the panel. Add two BitButtons, placing them below the panel as shown in Figure 4.5, and one regular button toward the bottom-right side of the screen.

In a moment you are going to set the component properties that are common to all four of the forms you will need. But before you do, I want to discuss a couple of the settings. First you will notice that I indicated font settings for the form. Even though you won't be placing any text directly on the form, when the ParentFont property is set to **True**, the settings will be inherited by the child and grandchild components. You will also see that I have indicated a color setting for the panel (clSilver), so it will not inherit the form's color setting (clBlack). Label1, on the other hand, will inherit the clSilver color setting of the panel, by leaving its ParentColor set to **True**. In order for Label2 to also be silver, however, you do have to set the Color property because Label2's parent is the form itself, and the form color is black.

Another property you haven't used yet is the WordWrap property. Label2 is going to contain a brief text description of the photo that is currently displayed. Because the descriptions are of varying lengths, it is better to allow Delphi to make the label grow to fit the text. You might have thought that setting AutoSize to **True** would take care of that. AutoSize will expand the length of the label to fit the text, but when there is no more room, it just stops growing and you may not be able to see some of your text. AutoSize will not expand a component vertically.

Finally, before you get to your settings, I want to talk about BitButtons. This is a component you have not used before in our sample program. A BitButton is a button that has an image or glyph inside. You've seen lots of them before, for example, the OK button that has a green check mark or the Cancel button with the red X.

To select an image for the button, use the Object Inspector, select the glyph property, and click on the ellipsis (**...**). When the Picture Editor dialog box appears, click on **Load** to bring up the Open dialog box, and select the bitmap file. The bitmap files you need were on the Teach Yourself diskette that you installed earlier. The bitmap file names for the BitButton components are **Button1.bmp** and **Button2.bmp**.

When you select **OK**, Delphi displays the image in the Picture Editor window. From there you can select **Save** to bring up a Save As dialog box so that you can save the image under a different filename, if desired. Clear will remove the image from the Picture Editor, and Cancel is self-explanatory. When you select **OK**, you will see the image displayed to the left of the caption. Why the left? Good question. Actually you have a choice of left, right, top, or bottom—left happens to be the default.

NOTE BitButtons are not the answer if you are looking for a way to place text cues on top of an image so that you can click one to get more detail. For example, if you wanted to show a picture of a piece of machinery with annotations identifying individual parts, and enable the user to click on an annotation to bring up further information, you need to use a regular image component, and place individual label components on top of it. You would set the labels' Transparent property to **True**, and use the labels' OnClick event, just as you would for a button.

Okay, it's time to set the properties for the Template form, as follows:

Component	Property	Value	Load
Form	+BorderIcons	[biSystemMenu]	
	biSystemMenu	True	
	biMaximized	False	
	biMinimized	False	
	BorderStyle	bsSingle	
	Caption	*	
	Color	clBlack	
	Font	[Tfont]	
	Name	Arial	
	Size	10	
	Style	[fsBold]	
	Bold	True	
	WindowState	wsMaximized	
Panel	BevelWidth	5	
	Caption	*	
	Color	clSilver	
	Height	240	
	Left	65	
	ParentColor	False	
	Top	40	
	Width	320	
Image	Height	160	
	Left	40	
	Width	240	
Label1	Alignment	taCenter	
	Caption	*	

	Height	20
	Left	96
	Top	200
	Width	120
Label2	Caption	*
	Color	clSilver
	Left	430
	WordWrap	True
BitButton1,	Height	40
BitButton2,	Top	370
and Button1		
BitButton1	Caption	Display
	Glyph	(TBitmap) Button1.bmp
	Left	65
	Width	145
BitButton2	Caption	Display
	Glyph	(TBitmap) Button2.bmp
	Left	240
	Width	145
Button1	Caption	Select Another
		Subject
	Left	438
	Width	155

Wherever you see an asterisk * in the above chart, set the value to blank, i.e., no value. Just delete the default caption.

The components and their settings thus far will be the same on each of the four forms you need, so before you set any of the form's specific properties, select the **Save as Template** item from the Edit menu. When the Save Form Template dialog box appears, as shown in Figure 4.7, type **PhotoScreen** in the title box and **subject screen for sample program** in the description box. Leave the default value of Unit1 in the file name box. You can select your own bitmap icon, but for now just go with the default. Now click on **OK**.

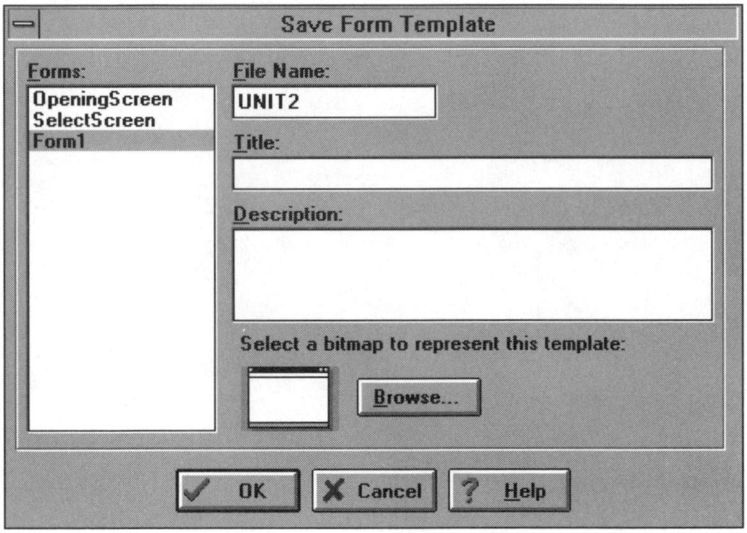

Figure 4.7 *The Save Form Template dialog box*

Now that the template has been saved, you can use it to create the other three forms. All you have to do is click on **New Form** and select **PhotoScreen** from the Gallery. Do this three times, so that you have Unit1, Unit2, Unit3, and Unit4 tabs showing at the bottom of your Code Editor window. Then, before you start coding, you should set the Name property for each component on each of the four forms, as well as the Caption property for each form. Be careful to note that Form4 should currently be visible, not Form1. Use the View Form dialog box, or Project Manager, to move between forms. The component names are as follows:

Component	Name Property	Caption
Form1	FieldsScreen	the Fields collection
Panel	pnlFields	
Image	imgFields	
Label1	lblFieldsTitle	
Label2	lblFieldsDesc	
BitButton1	bbtn1Fields	
BitButton2	bbtn2Fields	
Button1	btnFieldsGoSubj	
Form2	FloraScreen	the Flora collection
Panel	pnlFlora	
Image	imgFlora	
Label1	lblFloraTitle	
Label2	lblFloraDesc	
BitButton1	bbtn1Flora	
BitButton2	bbtn2Flora	
Button1	btnFloraGoSubj	
Form3	PanoramaScreen	the Panorama collection
Panel	pnlPanorama	
Image	imgPanorama	
Label1	lblPanoramaTitle	
Label2	lblPanoramaDesc	
BitButton1	bbtn1Panorama	
BitButton2	bbtn2Panorama	
Button1	btnPanoramaGoSubj	

```
Form4        WaterScreen     the Water collection
  Panel        pnlWater
  Image        imgWater
  Label1       lblWaterTitle
  Label2       lblWaterDesc
  BitButton1 bbtn1Water
  BitButton2 bbtn2Water
  Button1      btnWaterGoSubj
```

Select the **Name** property, type in the name value, and press **Enter**. Then when you select the next component using the Object Inspector, the Name property will already be selected. Be sure to press **Enter** after you type in each value, or else the setting won't take effect.

Now would be a good time to save your project. You'll be prompted to save the new unit files, but don't use the suggested default. The file names for the newest four units are **Pres_u03.pas**, **Pres_u04.pas**, **Pres_u05.pas**, and **Pres_u06.pas**.

Creating and Coding Events

Now it's time for some action, starting with the code needed to move from the SelectScreen form to the four new forms you just created. Your program needs to know which of the four subjects the user chooses so that it can move to the corresponding screen. There are a couple of ways to do this, but I'm only going to show you one simple approach.

There's a reason I chose to use RadioButton components for the four subject choices. When a radio button is selected, Delphi automatically places a black circle inside the RadioButton and sets its Checked property to **True**. So all you have to do is add some code that tells your program that if the Checked property for rbFields is True, to go to FieldsScreen, or if the Checked property for rbFlora is True, to go to FloraScreen, and so on.

This might sound a little familiar. In Chapter 3 I talked a bit about statements and mentioned conditional statements using the word *If*. What you'll do is create an OnClick event for the Continue button that contains code to look at each radio button's Checked property, and when it finds one that is set to **True**, show the corresponding screen. You'll also use an assignment statement to change the color of the RadioButton's caption text to indicate that the subject has been selected.

N O T E   When Delphi goes to show one of our subject forms, the SelectScreen form will remain on display, but you won't be able to see it because the Subject form will cover it over. Generally speaking, it's not usually a good idea to use up resources by keeping a lot of screens open at the same time, but two should not be a problem. (Don't try adding the code to hide the SelectScreen form. If you do, you'll be setting up a circular dependency that Delphi will not allow, and it's a subject more advanced than we want to tackle right now.)

To create the event handler, display the SelectScreen form and make sure btnShowSubj is the active component in the Object Inspector. Then select the **Events** page in the Object Inspector and double-click on the **OnClick** event. Delphi will automatically create the event handler and display it for you in the code window.

The code you will be adding involves the use of compound statements. A compound statement is like a code block that contains more than one statement but is treated as if it were a single statement. Because each statement, including the ones within a compound statement, must end with a semicolon, keywords are used to define where the compound statement starts and concludes, for example, *begin* and *end*.

When the Code window appears showing the event handler, it will already have one begin/end pair of lines. Notice that I said pair. For every begin, there must be an end, and pairs can be nested within other pairs. Enter the following code exactly as shown:

```
procedure TSelectScreen.btnShowSubjClick(Sender:
                                     TObject);

begin                                {begin
                                      event}
```

```
If rbFields.Checked = True Then      {condition}
begin rbFields.Font.Color := clBlue; {compound
                                     1}
        FieldsScreen.Show            {   "   }
end;                                 {   "   }
If rbFlora.Checked = True Then       {condition}
begin rbFlora.Font.Color := clBlue;{compound
                                    2}
        FloraScreen.Show             {   "   }
end;                                 {   "   }
If rbPanorama.Checked = True Then    {condition}
begin rbPanorama.Font.Color := clBlue; {com-
                                       pound 3}
        PanoramaScreen.Show          {   "   }
end;                                 {   "   }
If rbWater.Checked = True Then       {condition}
begin rbWater.Font.Color := clBlue {compound
                                   4}
        WaterScreen.Show             {   "   }
    end;                             {   "   }
  end;                               {end of
                                     event}
```

In order to avoid getting the same error message you got in Chapter 3, you'll also need to add the four new form names to the Uses statement in the Interface section. Now your Uses statement should look like the following:

```
uses
   SysUtils, WinTypes, WinProcs, Messages,
Classes, Graphics, Controls,
   Forms, Dialogs, StdCtrls, Pres_u03, Pres_u04,
Pres_u05, Pres_u06;
```

When you're done, save your project again. After you save it, take it for a test run (select **Run** from the Run menu, or press **F9**). The opening screen should appear, and when you click on the **Continue** button, the SelectScreen should appear. When you click on one of the radio buttons with the cross-hair cursor, a black dot should appear inside the radio button. Finally, when you click on the **Show Subject** button, the Subject form corresponding to the selected radio button should appear. To stop the program, close each window by double-clicking on the **SystemMenu** button in the upper-left corner, then when you're back in Delphi, select **Program Reset** from the Run menu.

All that remains now is to create and code OnClick events for buttons and bitButtons on each of the four subject forms. When you created the four forms, I deliberately did not ask you to load a bitmap for the image component's Picture property. I also instructed you to blank out the caption value for the label components. When one of the subject forms appears, the image and labels will be blank. However, when the user chooses to display #1 or #2 by clicking on the appropriate bitbutton, the corresponding photo, title, and description will appear. To make this happen, you will need to use the LoadFromFile method for the Picture, and assignment statements to place the text inside the caption of each label.

To create the first event handler, display the FieldsScreen form, and make sure bbtn1Field is the active component in the Object Inspector. Then select the **Events** page in the Object Inspector and double-click on the **OnClick** event. Delphi will automatically create the event handler and display it for you in the code window. The code for the bbtn1Fields OnClick event is as follows:

```
procedure TFieldsScreen.bbtn1FieldsClick(Sender:
TObject);
begin
imgFields.picture.LoadFromFile('\teach\field
1.bmp');
lblFieldsTitle.caption := 'Field of Clouds';
lblFieldsDesc.caption := 'Summer, 1993. It was
```

```
not warm. The approaching storm chilled the
air.'
end;
```

Now add an OnClick event for bbtn2Fields, using the same procedure and the following code:

```
procedure TFieldsScreen.bbtn2FieldsClick(Sender:
TObject);
begin
imgFields.picture.LoadFromFile('\teach\field
2.bmp');
lblFieldsTitle.caption := 'Stillness Field';
lblFieldsDesc.caption := 'Calm before a storm.
Cloudless. You could sense the approaching
storm.'
end;
```

Try running the program now, but first save your project. When you select **Run** from the <u>R</u>un menu or press **F9**, OpeningScreen should appear. When you click on the **Continue** button, SubjectScreen should appear. Select the **Fields** radio button and click on the **Show Subject** button. FieldsScreen should appear. Then click on **#1 Display**. The image should load and the title and description should appear as well. Now click **#2 Display**. It should be working pretty well now.

Finally, you need some code for the Select Another Subject button. It's really simple; can you guess what it is? Because you left the SelectScreen open when you displayed the subject screen, all you need to do now is use the Hide method to close the current subject screen. Create an OnClick event for btnFieldsGoSubj and add the following statement:

```
procedure
TFieldsScreen.btnFieldsGoSubjClick(Sender:
TObject);
```

```
begin
FieldsScreen.Hide
end;
```

Now save your project and try running the program again. Even though you haven't added the code for the other three forms, you should be able to select the **FieldsScreen**, view two photos, return to the **SelectScreen**, notice that the Fields radio button text is now blue, and select another subject form. Then you'll have to stop the run and finish coding the events for the FloraScreen, PanoramaScreen, and WaterScreen buttons.

The code for the three OnClick events in the FloraScreen form is as follows:

```
procedure TFloraScreen.bbtn1FloraClick(Sender:
TObject);
begin
imgFlora.picture.LoadFromFile('\teach\flora
1.bmp');
lblFloraTitle.caption := 'Tree Tops';
lblFloraDesc.caption := 'Amazing, dense, green
treetops. Growing, swaying in the breeze.'
end;


procedure TFloraScreen.bbtn2FloraClick(Sender:
TObject);
begin
imgFlora.picture.LoadFromFile('\teach\flora
2.bmp');
lblFloraTitle.caption := 'Wild Flowers''
lblFloraDesc.caption := 'A patch of wispy wild
flowers along the roadside.'
end;
```

```
procedure
TFloraScreen.btnFloraGoSubjClick(Sender:
TObject);
begin
FloraScreen.Hide
end;
```

The code for the three OnClick events in the PanoramaScreen form is as follows:

```
procedure
TPanoramaScreen.bbtn1PanoramaClick(Sender:
TObject);
begin
imgPanorama.picture.LoadFromFile(
                        '\teach\Panorama-1.bmp');
lblPanoramaTitle.caption := 'Indian Village';
lblPanoramaDesc.caption := 'Ramshackle huts, old
and abandoned. Brand new dam just behind.'
end;
```

```
procedure
TPanoramaScreen.bbtn2PanoramaClick(Sender:
TObject);
begin
imgPanorama.picture.LoadFromFile(
                        '\teach\Panorama-2.bmp');
lblPanoramaTitle.caption := Vista';
lblPanoramaDesc.caption := 'Wide open and green,
lush color all the way to the mountains.'
end;
```

```
procedure
TPanoramaScreen.btnPanoramaGoSubjClick(Sender:
TObject);
begin
PanoramaScreen.Hide
end;
```

The code for the three OnClick events in the WaterScreen form is as follows:

```
procedure TWaterScreen.bbtn1WaterClick(Sender:
TObject);
begin
imgWater.picture.LoadFromFile('\teach\Water
1.bmp');
lblWaterTitle.caption := 'Columbia River I';
lblWaterDesc.caption := 'Two great states. One
narrow body of water.'
end;

procedure TWaterScreen.bbtn2WaterClick(Sender:
TObject);
begin
imgWater.picture.LoadFromFile('\teach\Water
2.bmp');
lblWaterTitle.caption := 'Columbia River II'
lblWaterDesc.caption := 'Looking northward from
the Oregon side.'
end;

procedure
TWaterScreen.btnWaterGoSubjClick(Sender: TObject);
```

```
begin
WaterScreen.Hide
end;
```

When you're done, save your work and run your program again to test it more thoroughly. Assuming everything runs okay, the last thing to do is to create an executable file that will run your program without opening Delphi.

Building an EXE File

This is really quite simple. All you have to do is select the **Compile** item from the Compile menu, or press **Ctrl-F9**, and Delphi does the rest. If Delphi encounters any compiler errors, it will notify you by displaying an error message at the bottom of your Code Editor window and highlighting the offending line of code. If you entered all the code as shown in Chapters 3 through 4, you shouldn't have any problems. It only takes a moment. When it's done, close Delphi and run your **Present.exe** file. Then take a break—you've earned it!

Summary

◆ When you create full-screen forms, using the WindowState property set to **Maximized** allows you to resize the form during the design phase without affecting run-time.

◆ There is no immaculate conception for components. A GroupBox component must be added to a form before its child components. And the child components must be created within the GroupBox area.

◆ RadioButtons are used to present several choices from which a user must select only one. A small black dot appears inside the radio button when selected. When a RadioButton is selected, the Check property is set to **True**.

◆ TabOrder, the sequence in which the components may be accessed using the Tab key, always begins with 0. TabStop determines whether or not a user can use the Tab key to reach that component. The sequence in which you create the components determines the default value of TabOrder. Every component has a TabOrder value, even if TabStop is False.

◆ You can set properties for more than one component at a time, by holding down **Shift** as you select the components. The Object Inspector will adjust to show only those properties that the selected components have in common.

◆ The Glyph property of a BitButton contains the bitmap file name. To find and preview a bitmap file, click on the ellipsis to bring up the Picture Editor dialog box. Use the Layout property to specify the placement of the glyph in relation to the caption: left, right, top, or bottom.

◆ If you want to create or edit a bitmap, use the Tools menu to launch the Bitmap Editor.

◆ When you want to have a label caption with multiple lines, set the WordWrap property to **True**. If you want Delphi to automatically determine the size of a label's area to fit the caption, set the AutoSize property to **True**. The label will grow or shrink horizontally to fit the caption. If WordWrap is set to **True**, the label will grow or shrink vertically to fit the caption.

◆ You can copy a component by selecting it and then pressing **Ctrl-C** or choosing **Copy** from the **E**dit menu. When you paste a component copy, the new one will have identical property settings, except for Name.

◆ The settings for Form Grid spacing and Snap To Grid are found on the Preferences page of Environment Options dialog box. (Select **Options** from the **E**nvironment menu.) You can set the X and Y axis separately—the default value is 20 pixels in each direction. Snap To Grid is selected by default, as is Display Grid.

◆ The Alignment palette and the Alignment dialog box are tools to help you align your components in relationship to the form and one another. Alignment can be based on matching left, right, top, and bottom sides, as well as center points. The dialog box also contains an option for equal spacing between the selected components.

In the Next Chapter

In the next chapter you're going to take a break from creating forms and components. You will learn about data types, variables, and other things you'll need to know before you embark on the next sample application.

CHAPTER 5

Variables and Data Types

- ◆ Examining scope
- ◆ Defining variables and constants
- ◆ Using functions to assign variable values
- ◆ Using variables as parameters
- ◆ Examining data types
- ◆ Considering data type compatibility
- ◆ Employing operators and routines

Pascal program code is made up of many elements, including statements, reserved words, headings, methods, and special clauses that you've seen in the unit code already. In this chapter you will learn in more detail about variables and data types.

In Chapter 3 I talked about some of the different types of statements, and you used an assignment statement to set a run-time property. Assignment statements are the ones that use a colon and an equal sign (:=). The property name goes on the left, and the new value goes on the right. Values can also be assigned to variables, or conversely, the value in a variable can be assigned to a property. But there are some rules, first and foremost of which is that the value and the type must be compatible. But before I get into describing different data types, I want to take a look at variables, constants, and their use with parameters and functions.

Variables and Constants

In Chapter 3 I talked about evaluating expressions and assigning the result to a variable, but I did not discuss what a variable really is. What, exactly, is a variable? A variable is a place in memory where you can store numeric and character values. Also, the value stored in a variable can change. I also said that expressions are evaluated for a result, but I did not explicitly tell you that the result is placed in a variable. In the two examples I used in Chapter 3:

```
x := 2 + 2
AuthorName := 'Devra Hall'
```

and Authorname are variables, that is, places in memory where the values are stored while the program is running. You access these values by using the *identifier.*

A variable can't exist unless it is declared, and that means giving it a name and specifying its data type. Each variable has its own name, known as an identifier. In Chapter 2 I talked about how Delphi uses the Name property to identify each individual component. Delphi uses the term identifier to refer to a descriptive name you assign to a program element, whether it is a unit, procedure, variable, constant, and even a component. The rules for naming a variable are the same rules as for naming a form or component. The key is to pick meaningful names.

Once you pick a meaningful name, you have to decide where you are going to put the declaration. This brings up the concept of *scope*. The scope of a variable is within the block in which it was declared, so where you put your declaration determines the variable's availability. If you declare a variable within an event handler, for example, then that variable is only accessible from within the scope of that event handler. That variable might also be described as a *local* variable, one that is only available locally within that procedure and ceases to exist when the procedure or function is finished executing.

The opposite of local is *global*. If you declare your variable in the interface section of a unit, the variable will be accessible from anywhere within the scope of the unit. That means that global variables are available to all procedures, functions, and methods within the unit. The variable will also be available to other units that have access to the unit containing the variable declaration.

You experienced the "scope" phenomena when you wrote the first line of code for the Present application in Chapter 3. The code line was `SelectScreen.Show`, and you got an error message ("Unknown identifier") because you were trying to show a form that was not defined in the unit Pres_u01. In other words, it was not within the scope of that unit. But once you included the name of the other unit Pres_u02—the one that contained the form's declaration—by including its name in the uses section, you were able to access that form.

Variables are declared in the declaration part of a unit, procedure, or function. And as I mentioned earlier, when you declare a variable, you must state its type. Declaration of a variable starts with the reserved word var. The variable name goes on the left, followed by a colon, and then the type on the right, and ending with a semicolon. The following is the declaration for a variable named SubTotal:

```
Var
SubTotal: Integer;
```

Look familiar? It looks like some of the elements in the type declaration you saw back in Chapter 3 when I first described the sections of code in a unit. In the Type section, you saw that a form was defined as a type, and each component on the form was listed using this same format of name: type;.

When declaring variables, you may declare several of the same type in one line, by using commas (,) to separator each name, like this:

```
Var
LineTotal, SubTotal, GrandTotal: Integer;
```

The code above declares three separate variables, each of which are integers.

Constants

Constants are like variables in two ways: They represent a spot in memory, and they must be declared. The difference is that unlike the value of a variable that can change, constants may only have one value—the one specified in the declaration—and the value cannot change. Another difference is the use of the const instead of the var reserved word. The declaration syntax is also a little different. Instead of specifying the type, the type is determined by the declared value. Also, you don't assign a value using the assignment symbol (:=), but instead use a simple equal sign to state that the constant equals a specific value. For example:

```
Const
BookTitle = 'Teach Yourself Delphi';
```

Delphi can tell that the value is a text string and automatically creates a place in memory to hold a text string containing the declared value.

To confuse matters, there is also a special kind of variable called a Typed Constant. This is a real misnomer because the value of the typed constant may change, but the type may not. Delphi describes a typed constant as "a variable with an initial value."

Use with Functions and Parameters

Earlier you saw how expressions are evaluated for a result that is then placed in a variable. Functions use variables too. A function returns a value that is then assigned to a property or variable, or used to determine the flow of code. IntToStr, for example, is a function that converts an integer into a string type. It is one of Delphi's many predefined functions.

Suppose you wanted to show the result of a numeric calculation in a label component on a form. If you try to assign the result of 2 + 2 using:

```
label1.text := 2 + 2;
```

you'll get a "type mismatch" error. Delphi knows that the result of 2 + 2 is an integer, and it knows that label1.text is, well, text. The solution is to convert the integer to a string.

Try it. Open a new project, place a label component on the form, and place the following code in the form's OnClick event:

```
procedure TForm1.FormClick(Sender: TObject);
var
   counter: integer;
begin
   counter := 2+2;
   label1.text := IntToStr(counter);
end;
```

Notice that the code includes a variable named counter that is used to hold the integer result of the calculation. And it is the value inside the counter variable that is then converted from Integer To String. When you select **Run** from the Run menu, your form appears with the text Label1 showing in the label box. When you click your mouse anywhere on the form, the text in the label box changes to show the number 4.

Variables can also be used as parameters to pass values to code in a procedure. In Chapter 3 you created your first procedure—a Click event handler for the button on OpeningScreen. Delphi generated the procedure's header, begin, and end code lines, and I mentioned that the parentheses in the header line contained a list of that procedure's formal parameters. Sender:TObject was the parameter in that case, and it is one that was created automatically by Delphi to identify for the procedure, the object in which the event occurred. (The same is true for the FormClick procedure you just created.) In Chapter 6 you'll use the X and Y parameters of type TPoint that are automatically passed to all mouse events.

Because parameters are used to pass data between two elements, the parameter exists in two places. For example, the value of Sender:TObject originates automatically inside the Delphi system, but the value is passed to a specific event. The variable that initiates the value is the *actual* parameter, but on the receiving end it's called a *formal* parameter, and how you list formal parameters has an effect on how Delphi handles them.

Unless you specify otherwise, the code in the receiving routine can alter the value of the parameter without altering the original value. In these cases the formal parameter is actually a copy of the original, so changes only affect the copy. If, on the other hand, you want to change the value of both the copy and the original (the formal and the actual), making it a variable parameter, you need to list the parameter using the VAR keyword, like so:

```
procedure TForm1.Button1Click(var SubTotal:
Integer);
```

If you want to ensure that neither the actual nor the formal parameter gets changed, you can specify it as a constant, like so:

```
procedure TForm1.Button1Click(const Price:
Integer);
```

Data Types

While you can assign values contained in constants, literals, variables, or properties to other variables or properties, there is one catch: It has to be of the same type, or a compatible type. The type determines which values and operations can be applied to the programming element. I use the word element because it is inclusive of objects, components, properties, procedures, variables, and anything else you can think of. Delphi's online Help groups data types into five classes: simple, string, structured, pointers, and procedural.

Originally, I was going to describe each type in detail, but I decided that it would result in an unnecessarily long and complex chapter. That's one of the terrific things about Delphi. You can create fairly complex applications with a minimum of programming code. I'm going to selectively describe some of the types in more detail than others, and discuss a few other concepts that will be immediately useful to the Delphi novice. With these definitions and explanations, you can easily continue to create the rest of the sample applications and many of your own design.

NOTE Just because you can create applications without complex programming does not mean that Delphi is not a full-strength programming language. Delphi uses Object Pascal, a full-scale programming language. The Delphi environment is quite powerful, and programmers can create complex applications and even create their own objects and components.

Simple Types: Ordinal and Real

Simple types are either real or ordinal. Ordinal types contain a specified number of elements and are ordered or sequenced such that the values are always in the same order. Some ordinal types can be accessed using an index number. Ordinal types encompass integer, Boolean, character, enumerated, and subrange types; you will learn about each of these.

Real types are subsets of real numbers represented with floating-point notation in a fixed number of digits. I like to think of real numbers as either predictable or unpredictable, but the proper terms are rational or irrational.

A rational number is one that can be expressed as an integer or quotient of an integer. For example, when you divide 4 by 2, the result is 2, or 2.0 when represented as a floating-point decimal. Rational numbers have a repeating decimal pattern that makes them "predictable." Let's take an example where you can see the resulting pattern: 1 divided by 7, for example. The answer equals .1428571428571, and you can see (predict) the repeating pattern. The next number should be a 4, then a 2, and so on.

An irrational number cannot be expressed as an integer or quotient of an integer. You cannot express irrational numbers as fractions. Pi, for example, is an irrational number. It is expressed as a decimal, but the number goes on and on without a pattern. No matter how great the precision (how many decimal places are used), you cannot predict the next number.

Square roots are also irrational. Use a calculator to take the square root of 2. Depending on how many decimal places your calculator uses, you may get 1.41421 or 1.414213562 or 1.414213562373. My Windows desktop calculator uses 12 decimal places. The more decimal places, the greater the precision or accuracy. Take 1.414 and multiply it by itself. You get 1.999396. Try using a few more decimal positions, say 1.414213. Now you get 1.999998409369. Multiply 1.414213562 by itself and you get even closer: 1.999999998945. Finally, when I use all 12 decimal positions, I get the exact result: 1.414213562373 x 1.414213562373 = 2.

There are five different real types, and when to use which real type depends on the amount of precision required. Advanced programmers sometimes need to define variables with more precision, and so they choose their variables accordingly. The range of numbers included within each type also varies, as does the number of bytes required to store each type. Table 5.1 shows the types, the range of values, and the number of bytes for each real type:

Table 5.1 *The Range of Values and Number of Bytes Required to Store Real Types*

Type	Range	Bytes
real	$2.9 \times 10(-39)$ .. $1.7 \times 10(38)$	6
single	$1.5 \times 10(-45)$ .. $3.4 \times 10(38)$	4
double	$5.0 \times 10(-324)$ .. $1.7 \times 10(308)$	8
extended	$3.4 \times 10(-4932)$ .. $1.7 \times 10((4932)$	10
comp	$-2(63) + 1$ .. $2(63) -1$	8
[or	$-9.2 \times 10(18)$ .. $9.2 \times 10(18)$]	

Now, getting back to those ordinal types, there were five: integer, Boolean, character, enumerated, and subrange.

Integer Types

Integers are whole numbers, positive and negative, including zero. As with real number types, each integer type has a range as shown in Table 5.2.

Table 5.2 *Integer Types and Their Range of Values*

Type	Range of values
Integer	32,768 .. +32,767
Short Int	-128 .. +127
Long Int	-2,147,483,648 .. 2,147,483,647
Byte	0 .. 255
Word	0 .. 65,535

NOTE

The number of digits in a numeric value does not equal the number of bytes required to store that value. One byte can actually be used to represent any number between 0 and 255. Two bytes together, known as a word, can represent any positive number between 0 and 65,535. If you split a word in half, giving half to positive numbers and half to negative numbers, you get a range of –32,768 to +32,767—the range of the integer type.

Integer math ignores the remainder. Remember in school, before you learned fractions. The answer to 5 / 2 was 2 with 1 left over, or 2 remainder 1. To deal with fractions, you'll need to use one of the real type numbers.

Boolean Types

All four Boolean types evaluate to either **True** or **False**. In the plain Boolean type, False always equals 0, and True always equals 1. When using the other three Boolean types (ByteBool, WordBool, and LongBool), False always equals 0, but any nonzero value is treated as True. The plain Boolean type takes up the least amount of memory (as shown in Table 5.3), and unless you have a need to use one of the other Boolean types (such as compatibility requirements with some other programming language), it's the one you should stick to. I'll talk a little more about the use of Boolean types later in this chapter when I get to the section on operators.

Table 5.3 *Boolean Types and Their Storage Size Requirements*

Type	Size
Boolean	1 byte
ByteBool	1 byte
WordBool	2 bytes
LongBool	4 bytes

Character Type

Character types consist of a single character. The character must be surrounded by single apostrophes, like so: **'V'**. You may have occasion to need a single character, but most often when dealing with characters, you are more likely to be needing the string type.

Enumerated Types

Enumerated types are user-defined types that assign sequential values to elements in an identifier list, values identified numerically beginning with 0.

When you declare an enumerated type, you must first declare the type, and then declare a variable of that type, specifying all of the values that the type can have. For example:

```
Type
TCards = (Club, Diamond, Heart, Spade);
var
Cards: TCards;
```

This code shows a Type section declaration of an enumerated type by the name TCards with values limited to Club, Diamond, Heart, or Spade, and in the Var section, a declaration for the cards variable.

If you tried to assign a value not specified for that type, you would get an error message. For example, the following code would result in an "Unknown identifier" error:

```
Cards := HorseShoe;
```

Specifying each value also has the effect of declaring each as a variable so that they can be accessed by name. And this can be really helpful because you could then use the values in a case statement and really tighten up your code. In Chapter 4 you finished coding the Present sample application, and the code for the btnShowSubjClick event turned out to be rather lengthy. You used a compound statement with four separate If..Then segments to check the Checked property for each of the four radio buttons and then, based upon the result, changed the color of the text in the appropriate radio button caption, and moved to the corresponding form.

Now you're going to change that code by creating Click events for each of the four radio buttons, where your code wiil set the value of the new enumerated type. Then you will recode the btnShowSubjClick procedure to use the Case statement. But first you need to declare the type and variable.

First declare the type, call it TSubject, by adding the following line to the beginning of the Type section:

```
type
    TSubject = (Fields, Flora, Panorama, Water);
```

Then create a variable of this type, call it SelectedSubj, by adding the following line to the Var section:

```
var
    SelectedSubj: TSubject;
```

Now, in the click procedure for each radio button, you'll need a line of code to set the value of the new SelectedSubj variable. This will replace the If statements. The code for each of the four radio button click events is as follows:

```
procedure TSelectScreen.rbFieldsClick(Sender:
TObject);
begin                           {begin event}
    SelectedSubj := Fields   {assign value  to
                                enumerated type}
end;


procedure TSelectScreen.rbFloraClick(Sender:
TObject);
begin
    SelectedSubj := Flora
end;


procedure TSelectScreen.rbPanoramaClick(Sender:
TObject);
begin
```

```
      SelectedSubj := Panorama
end;


procedure TSelectScreen.rbWaterClick(Sender:
TObject);
begin
      SelectedSubj := Water
end;
```

And finally the new code for the btnShowSubjClick event, using the Case statement, looks like this:

```
procedure TSelectScreen.btnShowSubjClick(Sender:
TObject);
begin
  case SelectedSubj of
    Fields:    begin rbFields.Font.Color :=
               clBlue;
                  FieldsScreen.Show end;
    Flora:     begin rbFlora.Font.Color :=
               clBlue;
                  FloraScreen.Show end;
    Panorama: begin rbPanorama.Font.Color :=
               clBlue;
                  PanoramaScreen.Show end;
    Water:     begin rbWater.Font.Color :=
               clBlue;
                  WaterScreen.Show end;
  end;
end;
```

NOTE The use of **begin** and **end** within the above case statement has nothing to do with the way a case statement is constructed. These reserved words were required because for each case value, you used a compound statement. In other words you had two action statements for each case value: (1) changing the color and (2) showing a screen. If the Show method was the only action to be taken, then your case statement would have looked like this:

```
case SelectedSubj of
    Fields:    FieldsScreen.Show;
    Flora:     FloraScreen.Show;
    Panorama:  PanoramaScreen.Show;
    Water:     WaterScreen.Show;
end;
```

Subrange Types

Subrange is another user-defined data type. It is a subset of a larger group that ranges from one specific value to another. For example, in an alphabetic group ranging from A to Z, D through G could be defined as a subrange. In a set of all integers, 0 through 8 can be defined as a subset, or 15,000 through 74,000, and so on.

Subrange data types are really useful for automating the process of range checking. As with enumerated types, Delphi will not allow a value to be assigned to a subrange type unless that value is within the specified subrange.

Another similar type is the set type. (It really belongs in the structured type category, but because it represents a group of values, it has similarities to the subrange type.) A set type is a group of elements, all of the same ordinal type, that limit the set to a specified collection of integer, Boolean, character, enumerated, or subrange type values. Unlike subrange, a set does not need to contain sequential values. For example, you could create a set containing your favorite numbers between 1 and 20, like this:

```
FavoriteNumbers: set of 1..20 [4, 11, 12];
```

String Type

String type is a group of characters strung together and placed between single apostrophes, like so: 'Devra Hall'. If you need to use the apostrophe character as part of the string, use two together, like so: 'Devra''s computer'.

String length is equal to the number of characters. A null string is an empty string, expressed by two single apostrophes with nothing in between, like so: '' If you place even a single space between the apostrophes, the string will not be null, instead it will contain one character, a space.

NOTE

If you want to declare your own string element, in addition to giving it a name and specifying that it's a string type, you also need to specify the length of the string (i.e., the maximum number of characters). If you do not specify a length, Delphi assumes the default value of 255 characters.

Structured Types

Structured types contain more than one value, and each value may be accessed individually or you can access the structure as a whole. Structured types include arrays, records, objects, sets (mentioned a moment ago), and file types.

Arrays

An array is a structure that holds multiple values. Each value has an index number for reference. A one-dimensional array is like a list or table with only a single column, each item is the value, and each item number or row number is the index. For example, you could set up an array to hold the various possible values for a variable named EmailType. The values in the array could include:

```
CompuServe
America Online
```

```
AppleLink

Prodigy

eWorld

Internet

Delphi

Genie

Microsoft Network
```

and so on. Arrays must be declared so that your program knows the name of the array, the maximum number of values, and the type of data the values represent. If the EmailType array contained only the values listed above, the declaration would look like this:

```
EmailType : array [1..9] of Alpha;
```

If you wanted to allow for additional entries, you would have to declare the array to be bigger, perhaps something like:

```
EmailType : array [1..20] of Alpha;
```

EmailType is the name of the array, [1..9] or [1..20] specifies the first and last index number, and Alpha says that the value can be of type alpha, i.e., text. You can place a value into an array by assigning a value to the array name and index. For example:

```
EmailType[6] := "Internet";
```

This also works in reverse. Once the values are in the array, you can access a value by referring to the array name followed by square brackets containing the index number. For example, to select Internet, you would refer to EmailType[6], because it's sixth on the list.

Another way to get the values into the array is to define them as constants.

```
type
    TEType = (CompuServe, America Online,
AppleLink, Prodigy, eWorld, Internet, Delphi,
```

```
GEnie, Microsoft Network);
   TEmailType = array[EType] of string[20];
const
   ETypeStr := TEmailType = ('CompuServe',
'America Online', 'AppleLink', 'Prodigy',
'eWorld', 'Internet', 'Delphi', 'GEnie',
'Microsoft Network');
```

One of the drawbacks of using constants, however, is that you can't add new values without changing the code.

NOTE

Records

Records are specified groups of elements or fields of varying types. A record type is like a row in a database. It's a group of data fields that holds values. You can refer to a record as a whole, or to the individual fields within a record.

Suppose you wanted to create an employee record, consisting of elements such as the employee's name, address, and ID number. For this example, your Type section might include the following code:

```
Type
  Employee = record
    EmpNameFirst: string[15];
    EmpNameLast: string[25];
    EmpIDNumber: integer;
    EmpAddrLine1: string[20];
    EmpAddrLine2: string[20];
    EmpAddrCity: string[20];
    EmpAddrState: string[2];
    EmpAddrZip: string[10];
    end;
```

This looks a lot like a Form definition, doesn't it? Form definitions begin with a form name and type, followed by the components that are part of that form. Similarly, a record definition begins with the record name and type, followed by the fields that are a part of that record.

Files

A file type is a linear sequence of elements of any type, with two exceptions: A file type cannot contain other file type elements or objects. Suppose you created the employee record shown above. To save the employee records as a file on your computer, you need to define the file. It needs a name, and the file type must be identified by the type of records it contains. Continuing with this example, your Type section would now look like this:

```
Type
  Employee = record
    EmpNameFirst: string[15];
    EmpNameLast: string[25];
    EmpIDNumber: integer;
    EmpAddrLine1: string[20];
    EmpAddrLine2: string[20];
    EmpAddrCity: string[20];
    EmpAddrState: string[2];
    EmpAddrZip: string[10];
    end;
  EmployeeFile = file of Employee;
```

Objects

Each component has its own type, and you saw this early on when looking at the Object Inspector. If you wanted to see which component was currently active, or if you used the Object Inspector to select a different component and make it active, you saw the component name and object type in the drop-down box at the top of the Object Inspector window.

There you would see entries such as OpeningScreen:TForm or Button1: TButton. To the left side of the colon symbol, you have the component name. On the right side, the type (T stands for type).

Composite properties are also object types. The TFont object is what contains the font color, size, style and other subproperties. TWindowState is an enumerated type with three allowable values—wsNormal, wsMinimize, and wsMaximize. Some run-time properties also have types. In Chapter 6 you're going to use the TPen and TBrush object types to draw on TCanvas. (Canvas is the surface of a component upon which you can draw.)

Object type declarations use the Class reserved word, and can contain fields and methods. In Chapter 6 you'll use the TPoint type that consists of two integers, X and Y, representing X and Y position coordinates. One type that you've seen before (without knowing it was a type) is TColor. Yes, color is a property, but it has also been defined as a type; and clBlack, clBlue, and clYellow are some of the constants defined as values of the TColor type.

Pointer and Procedural Types

Pointer types are values that point to elements of a specified type. The value of the pointer is the element's address in memory. The ^ character precedes the data type, so a pointer declaration looks something like this:

```
pointername = ^Integer;
```

You might want to create a pointer for the employee record used in the prior example. If so, your Type section might look like the following:

```
Type
  EmployeePtr = ^Employee;
  Employee = record
    EmpNameFirst: string[15];
    EmpNameLast: string[25];
```

```
EmpIDNumber: integer;
EmpAddrLine1: string[20];
EmpAddrLine2: string[20];
EmpAddrCity: string[20];
EmpAddrState: string[2];
EmpAddrZip: string[10];
end;
```

In this example you can see why a special character is used to indicate that you are referring to a type. Without the caret character, Delphi might think that you were referring to the record itself instead of your user-defined type.

You can also compare pointers to see if one is equal to, less than, or greater than the other. If two pointers are equal, it means they are pointing to the same element.

Procedural types allow you to assign a procedure or function to a variable, and to pass that variable as a parameter. Here are some examples of some procedural type definitions that belong in the Type section:

```
ProcTypeName1 = procedure(NameOfString: String);
ProcTypeName2 = procedure(var X, Y: Integer);
```

Because functions return a value, the declaration for a procedural type using a function must also include the data type for the resulting value. For example:

```
ProcTypeName3 = function(X: Real): Real;
```

Data Type Considerations

An important aspect of type is that each type occupies a different amount of memory. This allows you to make the most of your available memory by selecting the type with the smallest range into which your variable's value will fit. For example, if the value of a variable is never going to exceed +/- 100, you can and should use the ShortInteger type. Integer and LongInteger will work, but it's a waste of space.

Compatibility is another important type consideration. Some data types are compatible with one another, and some are not. For example, you could take the value from a ShortInteger type variable and place that value inside a LongInteger variable, because the range of LongIntegers is inclusive of the ShortIntegers. Or to use a mathematical concept, short integers are a subset of long integers, so they're compatible. You could also place the value from a long integer into a short integer variable, providing the value in question is not outside the short integer range. What happens if you play mix and match with incompatible variables? You get an error message.

What else is important about type? At the beginning of this chapter I mentioned that the type determines which values can be used and which operations can be performed. For example, you can't multiply a text string because multiplication has to do with numbers. There are many operators and routines, and I'll describe some of those for you now.

Operators and Routines

In Chapter 3 you learned about the most common arithmetic operators—the ones for adding, subtracting, multiplying, and dividing. These can be used with integers or real numbers. You can also use **Div** to divide or **Mod** to return just the remainder of a division, but these two operators can only be used with integers.

The plus symbol (+) can also be used with string types. Adding one string to another string to form a third string is *concatenation*. Other operators that can be used with string types include:

```
=    (equal)
<>   (not equal)
<    (less than)
>    (greater than)
<=   (less than or equal to)
>=   (greater than or equal to)
```

These are known as *relational* operators and can be used with several other types as well. Also, those last two operators (<= and >=) have a different meaning when used with set types. Then they identify one set as a subset or superset, respectively, of another set.

Another set of operators are known as Boolean operators. Earlier in this chapter I mentioned that Boolean types return a value that us either True or False. Perhaps you've heard of using Boolean logic for database searches. That's when you search data for specific words, phrases, or character strings (i.e., search terms) along with special operators to include or exclude potential matches. For example, you might search a newspaper's archives for articles about crime, but you don't want to see articles about drugs. You could search for "crime Not drugs" and the word Not is a Boolean operator.

Boolean operators return a value of either True or False, and there are four simple Boolean operators:

> **A not B** includes all times when X is true and Y is not true.
>
> For **A And B** to be true, both X and Y must be present.
>
> **A Or B** is true when either X is true or Y is true or both are true.
>
> And for **A XOr B** to be true, one or the other must be true, but not both.

T I P

One last little piece of operator information: There is yet another set of operators called bitwise operators, and XOr is one of them. In Chapter 6 you'll come across the XOr concept as it relates to bits. The value of a bit is either 0 or 1. XOr reverses a bit's value, so 0 becomes 1 and 1 becomes 0.

Routines are like methods (only these functions and procedures are not declared inside object type declarations), and they too apply only to specific data types. Delphi's online help has lists and explanations of all of the different routine categories.

For example, you can use ordinal routines such as the **Dec** and **Inc** methods to decrement or increment a variable. **Addr** is one of the functions included in the pointer or address routines, and is used to return the address of a specified object. The **FileOpen** and **FileClose** functions are two of the file management routines. Arithmetic routines include the **Sqr** and **Sqrt** functions, used to calculate the square and square root of an argument, respectively. There are even string handling routines such as the **StrLen** function that tell you how many characters there are in a string.

Summary

◆ Variables and constants are places in memory where you can store numeric and character values. The value of a variable may change, the value of a constant may not change. Variable declarations use the **var** reserved word, and include the variable name and it's data type. Constant declarations use the **const** reserved word, and the data type is assumed from the declared value.

◆ The scope of a constant or variable is within the code block in which it is declared. Local variables and constants are only available locally within the procedure or function in which they are declared. Global variables and constants, declared in the unit's interface section, are available from anywhere within the unit.

◆ **IntToString** is a function that converts an integer value to a string value.

◆ Variables and constants can be used as parameters to pass values between procedures or functions. The original value is called the *actual parameter*, and the variable or constant on the receiving end is known as a *formal parameter*. If **var** is used in the header, then the parameter is variable and the value of both the actual and formal parameters can be changed. If **const** is used in the header, then the parameter is constant and you are not able to change the value of either the actual or formal parameter. If neither reserved word is used, the value for the formal parameter can be changed without affecting the value of the actual parameter.

◆ Simple data types include the ordinal and real data types. Real data types are numeric and can be represented with floating point notation in a fixed number of digits. Ordinal data types include integer, Boolean, character, enumerated, and subrange types.

◆ There are five real types (real, single, double, extended, and comp), and each covers a different range of values and requires a different number of bytes for storage.

◆ There are five integer types (integer, short int, long int, byte, and word), and each covers a different range of values. The number of digits in an integer has no bearing on the number of bytes required to store an integer value.

◆ All four Boolean types (Boolean, ByteBool, WordBool, and Long-Bool) evaluate to either True or False. False always equals 0. True usually equals 1 (always in the Boolean type) or any nonzero value.

◆ The character data type consists of a single character, surrounded by single apostrophes. This is not the same as a string data type that can contain as many characters as needed.

◆ Enumerated data types are user-defined data types that assign specific values that can be accessed numerically by their position in the list. Once you define the type (in the Type section), you can then define a variable of that type. This also allows you to call on each value as if it were a variable.

◆ The Case statement allows you to code the actions to be taken for each possible value of an enumerated data type without requiring individual If..Then statements.

◆ The subrange data type is another user-defined data type used to represent a sequential subset of a larger group of values. This data type is often used as an automatic means for range checking, because Delphi will not allow a value to be assigned to a subrange data type unless the value is within the declared range.

◆ The string data type is a group of characters surrounded by single apostrophes. String declarations must include the maximum number of characters. For example: `LastName: string[25];`. A null string, '', is a string without any values, not even a space.

◆ Structured data types include sets, arrays, records, files, and objects types.

◆ The set type is a structured data type that defines a collection of ordinal values. These values do not have to be sequential.

◆ An array holds multiple values for a single data element. For example, a variable named EmailType might have values such as CompuServe, Prodigy, America Online, etc. Each value can be accessed by an index number indicating the value's position in the array.

◆ A record is a specified group of elements or fields of varying types. You can refer to each individual element, or you can refer to the record as a whole.

◆ A file data type is a linear sequence of elements of almost any type. A file data type cannot contain other file data types, nor can it contain object data types.

◆ Object data types include a type for each component (such as TForm, TLabel, TButton, etc.), and for each composite property (such as TFont and TWindowState). These are predefined Delphi objects. Advanced users can also create their own object data types.

◆ Pointer data types are used to point to an element's address in memory. Pointer declarations require the use of the caret character when designating the data type of the pointer, like so: `pointername: ^Integer;`. If, when comparing two pointers, they are equal, it means that they are pointing to the address of the same element.

◆ Procedural data types allow you to assign a procedure or function to a variable, which can then be passed as a parameter to a different procedure or function.

◆ Data types are compatible with one another if the value in question is within the range of both types. For example, an integer variable with a value of +1,000 is compatible with a long integer variable because it covers all values within the range of +/- 2,147,483,647. However, that same integer variable is not compatible with a short integer variable because that data type only covers values within the range of +/- 127.

◆ Each data type supports the use of specific operators. **Div** and **Mod**, for example, may only be used with integer data types.

Some operators can be used with more than one data type. The equal operator (=) can be used with lots of different data types and always means the same thing. Other operators have different meanings when used with different data types. For example, <= sometimes means *less than or equal to*, but when used with a Set data type, you use it to identify a subset.

◆ Boolean operators always return a value of either True or False. The four Boolean operators are Not, And, Or, and XOr.

◆ Routines apply only to specific data types. **Dec** and **Inc** are two ordinal routines. **Addr** is a pointer or address routine. **FileOpen** and **FileClose** are file management routines. The **Sqr** and **Sqrt** functions are arithmetic routines, and **StrLen** is one of the string handling routines.

In the Next Chapter

In Chapter 6 you're going to experiment with different ways of drawing on a form's canvas. I'll show you how to access specific pixel positions and how to change the color of your drawing tools. You'll use different pen modes and styles and draw shapes with a single command. You'll also discover when and why to use the different mouse events, how to erase lines, and how to create a pixel array so that Windows can refresh your drawing screen as needed.

CHAPTER 6

Drawing

◆ Understanding the difference: painting versus drawing

◆ Accessing pixels by positions, and setting pixel color

◆ Examining the Canvas property and its Pen and Brush subproperties

◆ Looking at different Pen Modes and Styles

◆ Drawing lines with the MoveTo and LineTo methods

◆ Using complex statements: With...Do and Repeat...Until

◆ Drawing shapes with methods: Polyline, Polygon, Rectangle, RoundRect, and Ellipse

◆ Working with mouse events: MouseUp, MouseDown, and MouseMove

◆ Erasing lines by using the pmNotXor pen mode

◆ Saving line coordinates and storing them in arrays

◆ Refreshing a drawing window: code for the FormPaint event handler

In this chapter you will learn about drawing on forms. Two concepts are critical to this discussion: arrays and methods. I talked a bit about arrays in Chapter 5, now you'll get a chance to use one. In Chapter 2 I defined a method as a procedure, function, or command that is directly related to a specified object or component. By Chapter 3 you began using the Show and Hide methods to display and close forms. In Chapter 4 I introduced the LoadFromFile method, and you used it to load the bitmap images into the image components during run-time. In this chapter you'll work with several new methods including: MoveTo, LineTo, Polyline, Polygon, Rectangle, RoundRect, and Ellipse.

Later in this chapter you'll use an array to store information during run-time, assigning values to the array as events happen, and then use the array to replicate the data. (I'm being a little vague, but you'll see what I'm talking about by the end of the chapter.)

Painting

The terms *drawing* and *painting* have very specific meanings in Delphi. Drawing is when you tell the application to place a specific graphic in a specific location at a specific time, usually dictated by the occurrence of an event. Painting, on the other hand, is the Windows term for refreshing a window or screen. For example, if your Form1 window partially obscures the Object Inspector window, and you move it away so that you can see all of the Object Inspector, Windows has to paint in the part that was hidden. *When* the OnPaint event occurs is up to the Windows system, but *what* happens when it occurs depends on whether or not you have coded a FormPaint event handler.

Drawing

In Chapter 1 I suggested that a form was like a canvas of a big picture and that you could draw on it. Then in Chapter 3 I mentioned in passing that Canvas is a run-time only property of a form, meaning that while you won't see it in the object inspector, you can access it through code.

Pixels and Lines

A form's canvas is one big pixel grid. In fact, Pixels is a Canvas property. The following notation identifies the single pixel that is tenth from the left edge of the form, and twentieth from the top:

```
Form1.Canvas.Pixels[10,20]
```

If you wanted to change the color of this pixel you could use an assignment statement, like this one:

```
Form1.Canvas.Pixels[10,20] := clRed;
```

Did you ever learn about a style of painting called Pointillism? It's a style where they paint lots of small dots that appear to blend together when seen from a distance. When you draw on the canvas, you are manipulating the pixel colors using a pen for straight lines and the brush for filling in areas. (Pen and Brush are also properties of a canvas.)

A good example of this style as used by computers is the art of the icon. A Window's icon is a square, 32 pixels wide by 32 pixels high. Look at Figure 6.1. This is a Zoom view of a grayscale copy of the Delphi icon, where each box in the grid represents one pixel.

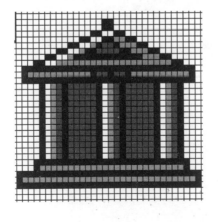

Figure 6.1 *A Zoom view of a grayscale copy of the Delphi icon*

The Pen property has its own properties—Color, Style, Width, and Mode—that control how the pixels are manipulated. By default, pen draws black (color) solid (style) lines that are 1-pixel wide (width). Mode describes the behavior of the pen. The default mode is Copy, and it over-writes whatever was already there. (Other modes allow you to combine the pen color with existing pixel values. See the "I'm in the Mode" sidebar for more information about the Mode property.)

Pen styles include psDash for a line made of dashes, psDot for a dotted line, psDashDot for a line made of alternating dashes and dots, and psDash-DotDot for a line alternating a dash and two dots. You also have the ability to make invisible lines, using psClear. And another fancy style, psInside-Frame, is one that applies lines only within the space of a closed shape.

I'm in the Mode

If you want the pen to always use black or always use white, you can use pmBlack and pmWhite, respectively. If, however, you want to control the pen color, you use pmCopy and set the color independently. The pen is automatically set to pmCopy as a default, so you may never need to change it.

Several of the modes are based on inverse colors. Inverse colors are based on the three primary colors (red, yellow, and blue), and can be plotted on a color wheel. The wheel is like a pie chart with three sections, one for each primary color. An inverse of one color is the color at the opposite position on the wheel. When you mix blue and yellow, you get green. Red and yellow mix to orange. And red and blue mix to purple. Green, orange, and purple are secondary colors and occur at the points halfway between the primary colors that made them. As you can see from the diagram in Figure 6.2, purple is opposite yellow, so they are inverse colors. Green is opposite red, and orange is opposite blue.

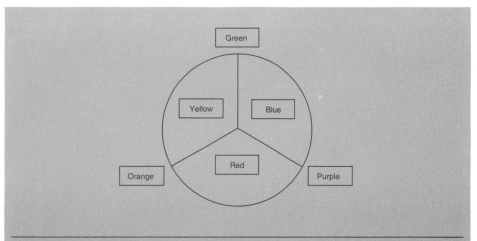

Figure 6.2 *Drawing of a color wheel showing position of primary and secondary colors*

pmMergePenNot combines the pen color and the inverse of the screen color. Why would you want to do this? To achieve better contrast. For example, if the pen is blue and the screen is yellow, then the blue pen color is combined with orange (yellow's inverse) to make a better contrast against the yellow screen.

pmMerge combines the pen and screen color to give you a blending effect, sort of like wet paints. When you draw lines with a blue pen on a yellow screen you get green lines.

If you want to disable the pen, you can set the mode to pmNop, leaving the screen unchanged. The pmXor mode creates a combination of pen or screen colors, but not both. And pmNotXor stands for *pen mode, Not Xor*, the inverse of pmXor. When using this mode, you can "erase" a line by drawing on top of it.

There are several other pen modes that are useful for paint programs and for achieving effects. You can find a list of the modes and the resulting pen behaviors by searching for Mode Property in your online Delphi Help.

Speaking of dots and lines, the actual process of drawing lines is alot like the connect the dots drawings you probably did as a kid, only now you also have to decide where to put the dots. Well, almost. What you have to do is identify the beginning and end points of the line, and then tell Delphi to draw a line between those points. You already know how to specify a point using the width and height locations, now all you need are the methods.

Seeing is believing (so they say), so launch Delphi if it's not already running, and make sure you have a blank form to play with. (Don't use your Present project, this is just for fun.) You'll need a FormPaint event handler, so use the Object Inspector's Event page for Form1, and double-click to the right of the OnPaint event. The value should be FormPaint, and your Code Editor window should appear displaying your Unit1.Pas code. Now you're ready.

PenPos (pen position) is another Canvas property, the value of which indicates the position from which the pen will begin drawing. To specify a starting position, you use the MoveTo method, as follows:

```
Canvas.MoveTo (10, 19);
```

The pen is now positioned and ready to draw a line starting with pixel 10, 19.

To draw a line, use the LineTo method to move the pen from its beginning point to a specified end point, as follows:

```
Canvas.LineTo (150, 19);
```

This line of code tells the pen to draw a line from its current pen position to the pixel that is 150th from the left of the form, and twentieth from the top of the form. The result? A straight horizontal line, 140 pixels in length, on the twentieth row of the array (don't forget arrays begin with zero). Try it and see. Enter the two lines of code in the FormPaint procedure and press **F9** to run the application. (Select **Program Reset** from the Run menu when you're ready to continue.)

Another important thing you need to know about the LineTo method is that it automatically changes PenPos to the new location. This means that if you were to issue another **LineTo** command without first using a **MoveTo** command, the new line would begin where the previous line left off. Enter the following code in your FormPaint procedure:

```
Canvas.MoveTo (10, 19);
Canvas.LineTo (150, 19);
Canvas.LineTo (150, 69);
Canvas.LineTo (10, 69);
Canvas.LineTo (10, 19);
```

Did you run the application? If so, you just drew a rectangle. You told the pen to begin at position 10, 19, and draw a horizontal line to position 150, 19. Then, because PenPos was set by the LineTo method, the next line automatically began at position 150, 19 and ran vertically down to 150, 69. Again PenPos was set by the LineTo method without our help, and the next line created was a horizontal one ending at position 10, 69; and so on.

What if you don't want to begin your next line from the end of the last one? No problem. Just use the MoveTo method each time you want to assert control over PenPos.

N O T E

Before I continue with our drawing discussion, I want to digress a moment to show you how you can code that same procedure a little more compactly using a With...Do statement. This type of statement tells Delphi to **Do** whatever code appears between the **begin** and **end** lines of the With...Do statement, using (or **With**) whatever object is specified. In this example the specified object is the canvas, and the recoded procedure looks like this:

```
procedure TForm1.FormPaint (Sender: Tobject);
begin
```

```
with Canvas do
begin
     MoveTo (10, 19);
     LineTo (150, 19);
     LineTo (150, 69);
     LineTo (10, 69);
     LineTo (10, 19);
   end;
 end;
```

N O T E

Be sure to notice that the With...Do statement has its own Begin and End lines that appear as part of the statement between the Begin and End lines of the procedure itself. In programming, this is known as *nesting*. The begin and end lines that are part of the With...Do statement are what keep the individual commands together as one statement, that is, a complex statement.

PolyLines and Pens

A rectangle is a polyline. Polylines are shapes created by connecting line segments. A square, a rhombus, even a pentogram are all polyline shapes. When you drew the rectangle in the previous section, you did it the hard way, using five separate command lines. The Polyline method allows you to draw the rectangle with one command. Using this method, your procedure looks like this:

```
procedure TForm1.FormPaint (Sender: Tobject);
begin
   with Canvas do
   Polyline ([Point (10, 19), Point (150, 19),
            Point (50, 69), Point (10, 69),
            Point (10, 19)]);
 end;
```

Try it, it works. But you probably have a couple of questions. First, what happened to the nested begin and end section? And second, what's with all the parentheses and brackets? The answer to the first question is a matter of need. The nested begin and end section was not needed here because there is only one line of code, that is, a simple statement. When there are multiple command lines, like with our first example, the begin and end lines mark the boundaries of the complex statement.

The second question brings up a discussion of parameters. I first mentioned parameters back in Chapter 3 when you examined your first event and mentioned them again in Chapter 5. Parameters are used to pass data to and/or receive data from a procedure or function. They are shown in parentheses following the method to which they apply, and when there are more than one, they are separated by commas.

Okay, that accounts for the outermost parentheses, but what about the square brackets and inner parentheses? The inner parentheses are still holding the individual pixel positions for each point in the array. The Polygon method takes an array of points as its only parameter, so by placing all of the points together (i.e., surrounded by square brackets), you are passing the whole array as one parameter.

Polygons and Brushes

What's a polygon? It's the same thing as a Polyline, only you don't have to specify the final line segment (the one connecting the last end point to the first beginning point), and the inside of the shape is automatically filled in with the brush.

Here's the code using the Polygon method to create the rectangle:

```
procedure TForm1.FormPaint (Sender: Tobject);
begin
    with Canvas do
    Polygon ([Point (10, 19), Point (150, 19),
             Point (50, 69), Point (10, 69)]);
end;
```

Now let's add some code to control the brush. The brush has three properties: Color, Style, and Bitmap. Color is self-explanatory. The Style property of the brush determines how an area is filled—it can be solid, clear, or filled with lines that are either vertical, horizontal, diagonal, or cross-hatched. The Bitmap property allows you to specify a bitmap image to use as a fill pattern instead of the lines or cross-hatching. The default values for these three properties are white, solid, and no pattern, respectively.

NOTE If you place a shape component on a form in design mode, the color and style subproperties of the shape's Brush property can be set using the Object Inspector. However, the bitmap sub-property for a brush is only available at run-time, and the bitmap needs to be 8 pixels high by 8 pixels wide.

Now add two assignment statements to set the brush color to black and to fill the polygon with back-slanting diagonal lines. The assignment statements are as follows:

```
Brush.Color := Black;
Brush.Style := bsBDiagonal;
```

and when you add these lines, your FormPaint procedure should look like this:

```
procedure TForm1.FormPaint (Sender: Tobject);
begin
    with Canvas do
    begin
        Brush.Color := Black;
        Brush.Style := bsBDiagonal;
        Polygon ([Point (10, 19), Point (150,
                19), (Point (150, 19), Point
                (10, 69)]);
    end;
end;
```

(Notice I added nested **begin** and **end** lines because the With...Do statement has become complex again, using multiple command lines.)

Sometimes properties and methods can seem confusing. You can see design-time properties in the Object Inspector, but when you're working with code how do you tell which is which? It's not hard. Whenever you work with properties in code, it's to change a property value, and that requires an assignment statement. Methods, on the other hand, are actions that are often followed by parameters, and you cannot assign a value to a method.

Prefab Shapes

If you want to draw shapes in run-time (as opposed to placing shape components in design mode) there are several methods that produce specific shapes. Remember methods are sort of like properties but instead of involving settings (using assignments), methods do things. Canvas has several shape-oriented methods including: Rectangle, RoundRect, and Ellipse. And yes, using the Rectangle method is an easier way to draw one than any way I've shown you. Like the Polygon, these shapes are automatically drawn by the pen and filled in by the brush.

Each of these three methods works in a similar way, requiring four to six parameters. The first two parameters indicate the starting pixel position (upper-left corner), the third and fourth parameters indicate lower-right corner of the shape. The fifth and sixth parameters (used with RoundRect) indicate the width and height of the ellipse corners used to round the edges. Try the following code in your FormPaint procedure (delete the whole With..Do statement that's already there):

```
procedure TForm1.FormPaint (Sender: Tobject);
begin
    Canvas.Brush.Color := bsRed;
    Canvas.Rectangle (10, 19, 200, 129);
    Canvas.RoundRect (10, 144, 200, 264, 40,
                     40);
```

```
    Canvas.Rectangle (220, 59, 410, 169);
    Canvas.Brush.Color := bsBlue;
    Canvas.Ellipse (220, 59, 410, 169);
end;
```

When you run this code, your screen should look like the one shown in Figure 6.3. Other shape-oriented Canvas methods include Arc, Chord, and Pie.

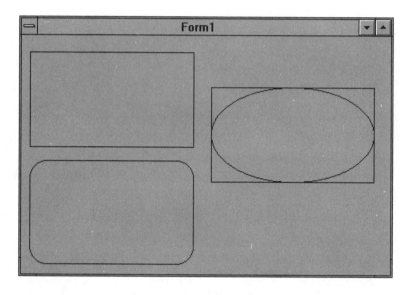

Figure 6.3 *This is what your screen should look like when running the code to draw the two red rectangles, a round rectangle, and the blue ellipse*

Interactive Drawing

Even though you're not going to create a drawing program right now, it is still important to understand what you would need to allow a user to draw lines as part of a running application. Mouse events are the key: MouseDown, MouseMove, and MouseUp.

Delphi comes with several demo programs, so let's look at one together. Launch Delphi if it's not already running, choose **Open Project** from the File menu, and select the **Scribble.Dpr** file in your Delphi\Demos\Scribble subdirectory. When the project is open, press **F9** to run it. It looks like a blank form with the caption *Scribble* in the title bar. Use your mouse to draw.

When you draw on a canvas during run-time, you press down on your mouse button as the place where you want to begin. Then holding down your mouse, you move it along the path of the line you're drawing (straight, curved, or loopy, it doesn't matter). Finally, you release your mouse, and voila, your masterpiece.

Now let's look at the code that made it work. Select **Program Reset** from the Run menu, then click on the **ScrbForm** tab to bring the Code Editor to the front displaying ScrbForm.Pas.

First is the OnMouseDown event, the code for which is in the FormMouseDown event handler or procedure. *Drawing* is a variable that keeps track of whether or not you are drawing at any given moment. As a Boolean variable, it can have one of two values, either True or False, either you are drawing, or you're not. So when you press down on your Mouse button to begin drawing, the Drawing variable is assigned a value of True. Then the Canvas.MoveTo method is used to identify the starting position. Notice that the Canvas.MoveTo method is followed by two parameters (X, Y). Delphi automatically passes these parameters with all mouse events to identify the coordinates where the mouse event occured.

The second procedure code block in the scribble demo is the FormMouseUp procedure. The only action that takes place when the OnMouseUp event occurs is the resetting of the Drawing variable to indicate that the state of Drawing is now False.

The FormMouseMove procedure is where the action takes place. It contains the LineTo method, again using the X and Y parameters. Here we encounter an If...Then statement so that the drawing action only takes place if the state of Drawing is True. If Drawing is False, then the LineTo method would not be invoked. Now you can see why it was so important to create the Drawing variable and to control its True and False settings based on the OnMouseDown and OnMouseUp events. Without it, there would be no way to tell whether or not you meant to be drawing, and the LineTo method would be invoked every time the mouse moved, whether or not you had clicked down, up, or sideways.

Before I move on, take a look at the first line of the Mouse events, specifically at the parameters inside the parentheses at the end of the header line.

Delphi automatically passes five parameters for MouseUp and MouseDown events (only four for the MouseMove event). First is the Object parameter, identifying the object or component where the event occurred. Button, the second parameter (and the one not used for MouseMove events), has three possible values—mbLeft, mbMiddle, or mbRight—to identify which mouse button was involved. The third parameter is Shift, which indicates whether the Control, Shift, and/or Alt keys were pressed when the event occurred. And finally, the fourth and fifth parameters are the X and Y coordinates where the event occurred.

Keeping Track of Points for a Straight Line

Scribble is a great little program, providing you want free-form lines. But if you need to draw straight lines, you'll either need a very steady hand or some different code. If you created a variable to remember the starting coordinates provided by the OnMouseDown event, then you could reposition the pen using the MoveTo method just before drawing the line to the end coordinates provided by the OnMouseUp event. In this case you would not need any code at all in the FormMouseMove procedure.

Try altering the Scribble program, but before you do, use **Save File As** from the File menu to save Scrbform.pas as Lines.pas and then save the project with a new name (Lines.Dpr) using **Save Project As**. (You might as well change the form's caption to Lines as well, just to avoid confusion.) This way you can make changes without affecting the actual Scribble demo.

Now, first you need a place to store the value, that is, a variable to hold the X and Y coordinates of the starting position. I named the variable Origin, and because I wanted it to hold coordinate positions, that is, points, the variable is of the type TPoint. In the Type section of the code for Lines.pas, add a new variable immediately following the Drawing variable. Beginning with the public line, your code should look like this:

```
public
    Drawing: Boolean;    {state variable}
    Origin: TPoint;      {field to store begin
                          position}
end;
```

When is the begin position determined? OnMouseDown. You'll need to assign the X and Y coordinates to the Origin variable, so add the following code after the MoveTo line in the FormMouseDown procedure, as follows:

```
Origin := Point (X, Y);
```

Now, the next change has to do with where to place the LineTo code. I decided to try drawing the line directly from origin to the line's final coordinates, so instead of drawing during MouseMove, I'll have to do the drawing in the OnMouseUp procedure—after all, that's the only time the program knows what the end coordinates are. In other words, until the user releases the mouse button, the MouseMove routine is still in control.

Add the code to move the pen to the Origin points and then the LineTo method, just before resetting the Drawing variable to False. The following should be the first code line in the FormMouseUp procedure:

```
Canvas.MoveTo (Origin.X, Origin.Y);
Canvas.LineTo (X, Y);
```

Also, comment out the code in the FormMouseMove procedure by placing curly brackets around the If...Then statement with the LineTo method. Now try running the new Lines program and see what happens.

Oops. Well, you get straight lines, but it's not very easy to draw a line when you can't see what you're doing until you're done. This won't do at all! Press **Ctrl-F2** or select **Program Reset** from the Run menu, to stop the program. Welcome to the trial-and-error process of programming. Often when you make a change to correct one thing, you affect something else. I could just tell you the final solution, but it's easier to understand when you can see what happens with each change.

Erasing the In-Between Lines

In order to see a line as it is being drawn, you have to have LineTo code in the MouseMove event handler. So take the brackets off of the LineTo statement and run the program again to see what happens. Did you try it? If so, you found that for each line you drew, you got two. Two for one is a good deal when you're shopping, but it's not what you want here. It's logical that with two LineTo statements (one in MouseMove and the other in MouseUp) you'd end up with two lines. So what can you do? You need the LineTo in MouseMove in order to see where you're drawing, and you need the LineTo in MouseUp because that's where you'll know the end-of-line coordinates.

The ideal solution would be for the line you draw during MouseMove to disappear before you draw the final straight line. You can do this by erasing the lines as they are drawn during MouseMove, and that requires a different Mode property for the pen and another variable in which to save the end-of-line coordinates. But first let's take a close look at what happens during MouseMove.

What you might think of as a single mouse-move is really many sequential mouse-moves. If you start by pressing your mouse button at position 1, for example, and move the mouse to position 4 where you release the mouse button, your system actually executes three move events. The first move is from 1 to 2, then from 2 to 3, and finally from 3 to 4. Using this same example, if you have a LineTo statement in the MouseMove event, your program will draw three lines that will appear to be one because they are joined end-to-end.

To effect the erasing solution, you'll need to save each passing end point so that you can "erase" the line between each set of beginning and ending coordinates. And that's where the new variable, combined with a different pen mode, come in. First the variable: At the end of MouseMove, you'll save the current X and Y coordinates in a variable called MovePt, and you'll need to add that variable to the Type section just as you did earlier for the Origin variable.

NOTE You can add more than one variable in a single declaration, providing they are of the same type and separated by a comma. Because MovePt and Origin are both of the TPoint type, you can declare them together. Beginning with public, your code should look like the following:

```
public
drawing: Boolean; {state variable}
Origin, MovePt: Tpoint;
end;
```

Now the pen mode: You might guess that pmNotCopy might be the way to erase a line that was drawn with pmCopy. It would make sense in a way, but that's not the way it works. pmNotCopy draws lines with the pen's inverse color, and that's not what we want here. Another logical guess might be to use pmNop, because it stands for *pen mode, No pen*. But that won't work either. With no pen you get invisible lines, and the whole point is to see where you are drawing.

The answer turns out to be a mode called pmNotXor. Remember in Chapter 5 when I talked about Boolean operators, I mentioned that XOr was a bitwise operator. The value of a bit is either 0 or 1, and XOr reverses the bit's value. That's the principle at work here. Assuming the pen color is black (that's the default), the first line you draw with pmNotXor looks kind of gray. But the magic comes the second time, when you draw another line right on top of the first one; it reverses the process, changing the pixels back to the way they were, or in effect, erasing the line.

First add an assignment statement to the MouseDown event to place the coordinates in MovePt just as you did for the Origin, like so:

```
MovePt := Point(X, Y);
```

Now for the changes in the MouseMove event. At the beginning of MouseMove you'll change the pen mode to pmNotXor, then at the end of

MouseMove you'll change it back to pmCopy. Then you'll move the pen to the original starting position (the Origin coordinates), and draw a line from there to the last known end point (the MovePt coordinates). When the mouse moves the first increment, Origin and MovePt will have the same coordinates and the program will actually be drawing a line from one position to that same position. However, from the second increment on, MovePt changes, and the line you draw then is the one that erases the previous line by drawing directly on top of it and thereby changing the pixels back to the way they were.

After the LineTo statement that erases, you'll need another MoveTo statement to get back to the original position and draw a line to the new current mouse position. This new position is the new end position and will be erased in the next go-round (unless you release the mouse button to invoke the MouseUp event), so you need to assign the new value to MovePt. And finally, change the pen mode back to **pmCopy** so that you're ready to draw the real line. Because you have several statements, you'll need an extra **begin** and **end** line to form or bracket the complex statement. Here's the code for the whole MouseMove event:

```
procedure TForm1.FormMouseMove(Sender: TObject;
Shift: TShiftState; X, Y: Integer);
begin
  if Drawing then
  begin
  Canvas.Pen.Mode := pmNotXor; {mode doesn't
      alter screen}
  Canvas.MoveTo(Origin.X, Origin.Y); {move pen
      position to origin point}
```

```
Canvas.LineTo(MovePt.X, MovePt.Y); {draw to
    see but not alter screen as mouse moves}
Canvas.MoveTo(Origin.X, Origin.Y); {back to
    start point after erasing}
Canvas.LineTo(X, Y); {draws new line, but not
    for keeps}
end;
MovePt := Point (X, Y);  {track point for next
    move}
Canvas.Pen.Mode := pmCopy; {reset pen to alter
    screen}
end;
```

After you have added the MovePt variable declaration in the Type section, the assignment statement moving coordinates to MovePt in the MouseDown event, and the code shown above to the MouseMove event, save your project and take it for a test run.

Refreshing

In the beginning of this chapter I talked about the difference between drawing and painting, and described painting as Windows's way of refreshing the screen or window. Let's try an experiment with your new Lines program. Run Lines by pressing **F9**, and draw a line across the middle of the form (see Figure 6.4). Then, while the program is still running (i.e., don't reset the program), move some other window or icon so that it sits right on top of the line you drew (see Figure 6.5). Finally move the window or icon away from the form (see Figure 6.6).

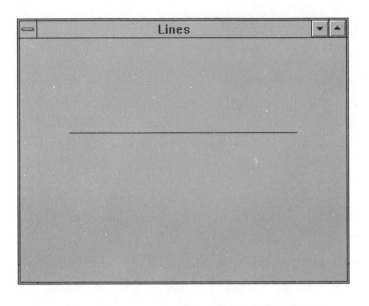

Figure 6.4 *A line drawn in the Lines program window*

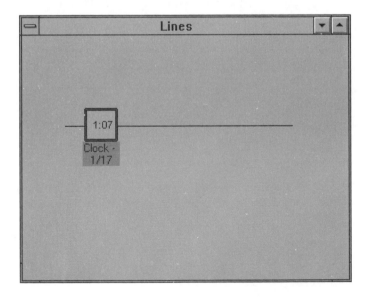

Figure 6.5 *An icon moved to cover a portion of the line in the Lines program window*

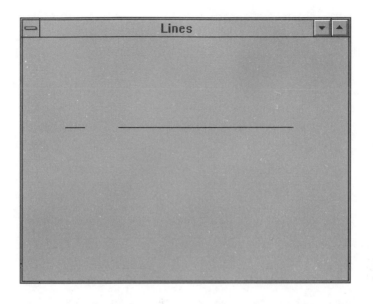

Figure 6.6 *The line, now broken, in the Lines program window after removing the icon*

The part of your line that was obscured by the other window or icon is no longer there. This could be a big problem, and it has such a simple solution. You're probably thinking about the FormPaint procedure you used earlier in this chapter. It might seem logical, but FormPaint knows nothing about the freehand drawings made by a user during run-time. Somehow, you need the Form to remember the pixel configuration of its canvas so that it can redraw it when necessary.

So far you have been saving the coordinates for each starting position, one set at a time. When you draw a line, the beginning-of-line coordinates are saved in Origin. If and when you draw a second line, the new beginning-of-line coordinates are saved in Origin, replacing the previous value. In order to save the beginning position of all lines without overwriting the previous coordinates, you'll need an array. You will also need an array in which to save the ending position of all lines.

At the beginning of this chapter I described the array declaration statement and talked about the index used to identify each element in the array. You'll need to declare each array in the Type section, providing the array name, the maximum number of elements allowed, and the type of data to be stored. You'll also need to declare a variable to be used as an index for the arrays. When you add the declarations for the keepBegin and keepEnd arrays, and the keepIndex variable, your Type section (starting with the public line) should look like the following:

```
public
drawing: Boolean; {state variable}
Origin, MovePt: TPoint;
keepBegin: array [1..1000] of Tpoint;
keepEnd: array [1..1000] of TPoint;
keepIndex: Integer;
end;
```

Now you need some code to place the coordinates in the array. The starting coordinates of each line are known in the MouseDown event, so you'll need an assignement statement there. But in addition, you'll also need to increment the index so that you don't overwrite the coordinates of the previous line. Add the following two statements to your MouseDown event between the origin and the movePt assignment statements:

```
keepIndex := keepIndex + 1;
            {increment index to next space}
keepBegin[keepIndex} := point(x, y);
            {store begin coords. in the array}
```

The ending coordinates of each line are determined in the MouseUp event, so you'll need an assignement statement there as well. This time, you do not need to increment the index, because each index number represents a line, so the index for the end position should be the same as the index for the beginning position. Add the following statement to your MouseUp event just before you set the Drawing variable to **False**:

```
keepEnd[keepIndex] := Point (x, y);
```

Finally, you're going to need some code that will use the points in these arrays to redraw your lines. The best place to put this code is in a FormPaint event, because your Windows system invokes FormPaint automatically when needed. You will need three more new variables to carry out this task. First you need two variables to hold the beginning and ending coordinates for one line at a time. Call these variables Start and Finish, and simply add them to the declaration along with the Origin and MovePt variables, as follows:

```
Origin, MovePt, Start, Finish: TPoint;
```

The third variable is an integer that will keep track of how many lines have been redrawn. The current value of the keepIndex variable tells you how many lines have been drawn, and you'll keep redrawing lines until this last new variable, call it *r* for repeat, equals the value of keepIndex. Before you create the FormPaint event, declare the *r* variable in the var section, as follows:

```
var
Form1: TForm1;
r: integer;
```

Okay, now you need a FormPaint event handler. Double-click on the OnPaint event in the Object Inspector window. Then add the following code to the procedure:

```
procedure TForm1.FormPaint(Sender: TObject);
begin
r := 0;              {set the variable to start at
zero}
repeat               {keyword used to start loop}
  r := r+1;          {increment repeat counter}
  start := keepbegin[r];
```

```
          {place begin coordinates in start
          variable}
  canvas.moveto (start.x, start.Y);
          {place pen at beginning of line}
  finish := keepend[r];
          {place end cooordinates in finish
          variable}
  canvas.lineto(finish.X, finish.Y);
          {draw line to end point}
  until r = keepindex + 1
          {is it time to stop? Yes if r =
          keepIndex}
  end;
```

I added comments to the above code so that it should be fairly self-explanatory. Once the repeat..until loop starts, it will continue looping around until r is equal to the number of postion elements in the array. Save the project again, and then test it. Run the program, draw some lines, and while it's running move another window or icon on top of a line and see what happens. You can now minimize the form while it's running without losing any lines as well.

This time, your line drawings will remain intact.

Summary

◆ An array declaration must specify the arrayname, maximum number of entries, and the type of data that the array may contain. An index is used to access a specific entry in the array, like so: `arrayname[index]`.

◆ Painting is the Windows term for refreshing a window or screen. When Windows determines the need to refresh or repaint, it automatically invokes an OnPaint event. The code contained in the OnPaint event handler, if any, is up to you.

◆ Drawing is the alteration of pixels on the canvas to create lines and shapes. Drawing is carried out by the canvas's Pen and Brush properties. The appearance of a drawing is determined by the pen and brush subproperties.

◆ A Pen has four subproperties: color, style, width, and mode. The default values are black, solid, 1 pixel, and pmCopy. A Brush has three subproperties: color, style, and bitmap. The default values are white, solid, and none.

◆ To move the pen to a specific position on the canvas, use the MoveTo method, like so—`Canvas.MoveTo (X, Y);`—where X and Y represent the coordinates. To draw a line from the pen's current position to a specified location, use the LineTo method, like so—`Canvas.LineTo (X,Y);`—where X and Y represent the end coordinates.

◆ With..Do is a type of complex statement that allows you to apply multiple command lines (i.e., simple statements) to one specified object without having to identify the object repeatedly. Like all complex statements, the command lines must be bracketed by begin and end statements.

◆ Polyline and Polygon methods allow you to draw multifaceted shapes on the canvas with a single statement. All of the points (i.e., X and Y coordinates) for the whole shape are listed as parameters within parantheses following the method. Some shapes have their own methods, including: Rectangle, RoundRect, Ellipse, Chord, Pie, and Arc.

◆ Interactive drawing generally involves code in the MouseDown, MouseMove, and MouseUp event handlers. Delphi automatically passes parameters to the mouse events. *Object* identifies the object or component where the event occurred. *Button* identifies which of the mouse buttons was pressed. *Shift* indicates whether or not the Control, Shift, and/or Alt keys were presssed when the event occurred. *X* and *Y* are the coordinates where the event occurred.

◆ In order to draw straight lines interactively, you need to save the starting coordinates so that you can move the pen to that position just before using LineTo in the MouseUp event. In order to see the line as it is being drawn (i.e., during MouseMove), without making it final, you need to use the pen's pmNotXor mode so that you can "erase" each previous segment. To do this, you also need to save the coordinates of each passing position.

◆ When you place one window or icon on top of or overlapping another window, and then move it away to reveal the underlying window again, Delphi automatically responds to Windows message to refresh the window. The OnPaint event handler, if one exists, is automatically invoked.

◆ If a window needs to be refreshed, and it contains a drawing created during run-time, you need to save all of the coordinates in an array so that the lines can be automatically redrawn. Code in the OnPaint event handler would then use the coordinates to redraw the lines, one by one. Because you do not know in advance how many lines there were, you can use the Repeat..Until statement to draw the lines. Your program would then repeat the MoveTo and LineTo statements until a counter was equal to the last index value representing the last line in the array.

In the Next Chapter

Now it's time to begin building the second sample program—an inventory application. In Chapter 7, I'm going to show you how to create a database using Delphi's Desktop Database tool. Then in subsequent chapters you'll create a front-end interface for accessing information from the database.

CHAPTER 7

Accessing Data

- ◆ Considering database application design
- ◆ Examining the Data Access components: Database, Table, Data-Source, and Query
- ◆ Building Tables with the Database Desktop
- ◆ Setting working directories and database aliases
- ◆ Defining index keys: primary, secondary, add composite
- ◆ Specifying validity requirements
- ◆ Entering data with the Database Desktop

In the Present sample application you started off with interface design. That's appropriate for a strictly presentation-type application, such as you might prepare for a lecture. It was also the best way to introduce you to the Delphi program and get your feet wet right away. However, the reality is that if your application is to involve a database (and most applications these days do), you must take the database into account during your earliest Advance Planning stages.

If your database already exists, then all you need is a list of the database(s), table(s), and fields. If your database doesn't exist yet, you should start your Advance Planning there. Until you decide how you want your data stored in the database, you won't be able to finalize the property settings for the form.

For example, the next sample application is an inventory database that I created to keep track of my computer software and hardware purchases. It goes without saying that the database will contain product names, but what does product name mean? Is it just the name of the program, for example, *Word for Windows?* Maybe it should include the version number —*Word for Windows 6.0.* Or even the manufacturer—*Microsoft Word for Windows.* Until you decide whether you want to keep each piece of information separate, or together in one field, you won't know whether to place one, two, or even three components on your form.

Sometimes experimenting with the placement of controls on the form can help you to make these database decisions, but you will not be able to actually work with the database components and test your program step-by-step until you have created your database. Luckily for you, we have already made those decisions for the sample application.

N O T E

The database components in Delphi 1.0 work with Borland's Paradox databases (versions 3.5, 4, and 5.0 for Windows), as well as with the following external databases: dBASE for Windows, dBASE IV, and dBASE III+.

Creating a Database Table

You don't have Borland Paradox, or any of the other compatible database programs? No problem! You can use Delphi's Database Desktop program to create a database. Database Desktop uses the same database engine used by Paradox, so the Paradox database format is native to Delphi as well. But before you jump right into the Database Desktop program, let's define a few terms.

What is a Database?

A *database* is a collection of information (data) stored in one or more tables. Database tables, just like tables in word processing, are made up of columns and rows. In database lingo, columns are usually referred to as fields, and each row is a record. In the sample application each row/record will represent a product, and you'll have columns/fields for product name, manufacturer, price, registration number, and other information.

Of course by now you're used to the fact that in Delphi lingo all these components are also referred to as objects—so you have database objects, table objects, field objects, even index objects. An index is one or more fields that you specify to make it easier and faster to find the information in your database. When you create an index, Delphi creates what is known as an internal pointer. Instead of reading entire records to find information, the pointers reference the chosen key field(s). You can also use indexes for sorting records and checking for duplicates.

Delphi has four main Data Access components, each created for a specific type of task. First is the Database component that you would use if you want your application to have a persistant connection to the database. If your application doesn't require a persistent connection, you will not need to use this component.

A database has one or more tables, each represented in your application by a Table component. A table's DatabaseName property defines the Database component to which it is associated, while the TableName property determines the name of the Table that it controls. The third component is the DataSource component, and Query is the fourth of the main Data Access components. I'll talk more about these components and show you how to use them in Chapter 8.

The database engine maintains the table and field information internally. It knows the name of each table, what fields belong with which tables, the size and type of each field, whether the field is required, and what if any validation requirements must be met. Index information is also maintained for each table, including the name of the index, which field or fields make up the index, and whether or not the index is the primary index.

Planning Your Database

The first thing you'll need to do is decide what tables and fields you'll need in your database. The Invntory sample application needs two tables. You'll start with a simple table containing basic information for each manufacturer. Database designers usually break down fields into the smallest logical chunks of information. For example, people's names are usually separated into first, middle, and last.

Similarly, addresses are usually split into street1, street2, city, state, and zip code. But *usually* doesn't mean that you have to do it that way. Your design decisions should be based on an assessment of user needs. In designing the Manufacturer table, I considered separating address into separate fields, but decided against it because it was not as important to be able to sort the database by state, for example, as long as I was able to search for a state within the database. Creating a search routine to search the address field for a specific state is not so difficult, so I decided on one address field that would contain the complete address. That was the trade-off, and design is full of trade-off decisions.

WARNING

Think through your choices carefully. While Delphi does allow you to change the structure of a database table after it has been defined, it can have some nasty side effects, especially if there is already data in the database. For example, if you change the size of a field, you could end up truncating data. If you change the field type, Delphi will try to handle the conversion, and if it has problems, those problem records are stored in a temporary table, allowing you the opportunity to alter the data. Nevertheless, even with Delphi's accommodations, it is best to make every effort to be sure of your fields, types, and lengths before you get started.

We've prepared a complete field listing, along with the type and size settings for the Manufact table. But before you begin building tables, you need to set your Working Directory and create a new Alias.

Changing Your Working Directory

If Delphi is not running, start Delphi's Database Desktop directly from your Window's desktop by double-clicking on the **Database Desktop** icon. If Delphi is running, you can launch the Desktop Database by selecting it from the Tools menu.

When the Database Desktop application first appears, you'll see four of its menus: File, Tools, Window, and Help. To set your Working Directory to the \Teach subdirectory you created for use with this book, select **Working Directory...** from the File menu. When the Working Directory dialog box appears, enter the name of the directory, including the path, in the top box, as shown in Figure 7.1. If you don't remember where the directory is, you can use the **Browse...** button to look for it in the Directory Browser window.

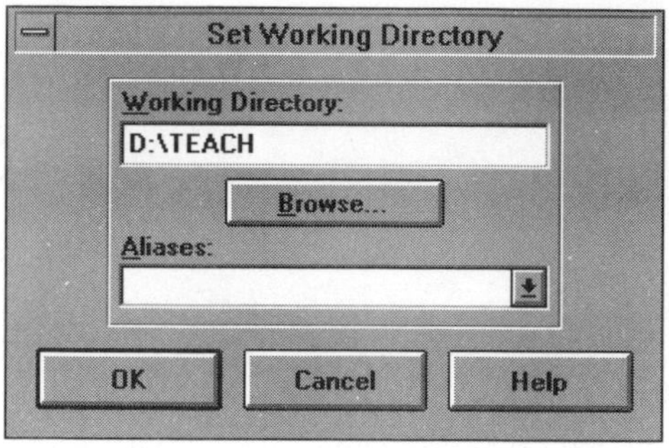

Figure 7.1 *The Working Directory dialog box*

The Database Desktop Local Configuration icon on your Windows desktop can be used to bring up the Paradox for Windows Local Settings dialog box in which you can also specify a working directory, but you need to know the path and directory name beforehand because there is no Browse button to assist you. From the Local Settings dialog box you can also change your Private Directory name and the name of your IDAPI Configuration file.

Creating a Database Alias

Now you can create an alias for the database you will be building. A database alias is used in lieu of the directory that contains the database files. In other words it is a name assigned to a directory. This saves a lot of time and hassle if your system has a lot of drives, directories, and subdirectories, resulting in long path names. Using an alias as a shortcut not only saves hassle, but it also makes your files more portable because they are not dependent or hardcoded to a specific path. This means that another user could place the application and database files in any directory, perhaps one named **\Mystuff**, and then create a database alias named to match the same alias you used (in this case the alias name will be TEACH) and assign it to their \Mystuff directory to make your application run.

Select **Aliases...** from the Database Desktop File menu to bring up the Alias Manager shown in Figure 7.2. When you click on the **New** button in the lower-right section of the window, the Database Alias box clears, allowing you to enter your own new alias name. Enter **TEACH**, and then click on the **Keep New** button to keep it as the alias in use for this session. To save it permanently in the configuration file (which you should do so that it will continue to be set for you in future sessions with this book), click **Save As...**, and when the Save Configuration File dialog box appears, click on **OK**.

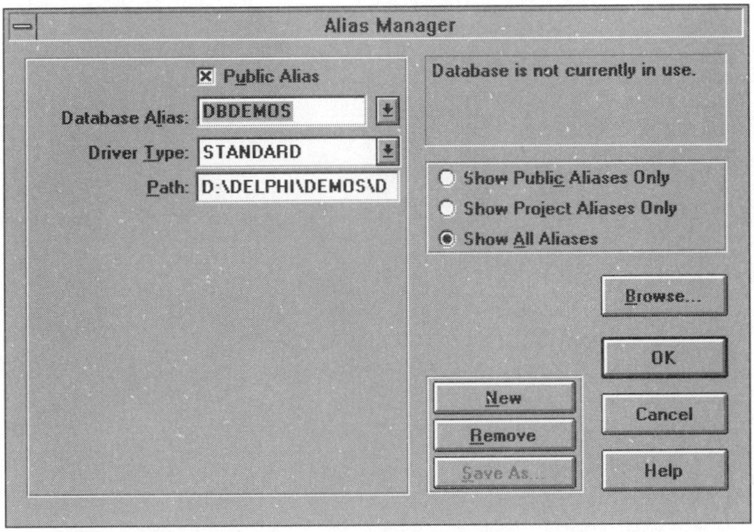

Figure 7.2 *The Alias Manager dialog box as it first appears*

There is another way you can create an alias for this (or any) directory using the IDAPI Configuration Utility program. If you wish, you can use this method instead of the one I just described. The end result is the same. (Personally, I prefer to use this utility program to set up things before I ever launch the Delphi or Database Desktop applications.) Delphi comes with an icon for your desktop that launches this program as a standalone application. When you launch the application, the IDAPI Configuration Utility window appears, containing several tabbed pages. When you click on the **Aliases** tab, your screen should look like the one shown in Figure 7.3. You'll see that DBDEMOS is the only alias defined so far.

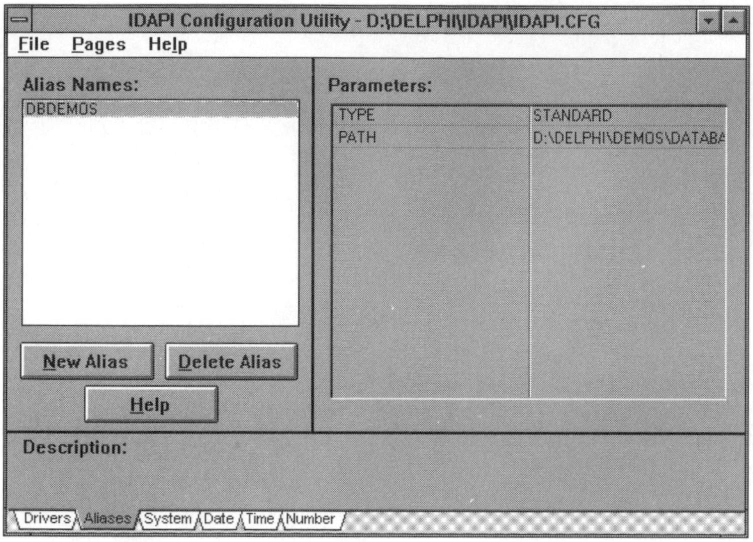

Figure 7.3 *The Aliases page of the ADAPI Configuration Utility window, before creating your new alias*

Click on the **New Alias** button and when the Add New Alias dialog box appears, type **TEACH** in the New Alias Name box. Leave STANDARD as the Alias Type, and click on **OK**. When the Utility window reappears, highlight TEACH in the Alias Names box and then enter the path and directory name in the Parameters section on the right. When you're done, the Utility window should look like Figure 7.4. Finally, select **Save** from the Utility window's **File** menu, and then **Exit**.

Building a Table

Okay, now you're ready to create your Manufacturer table using the settings shown in Table 7.1. Select **New** from the File menu, and **Table** from the submenu. When the Table Type dialog box appears, make your choice from the ComboBox. The default is Paradox 5.0 of Windows, which is just what you want. When you select **OK**, the *Create Paradox for Windows 5.0 Table: (Untitled)* window appears as shown in Figure 7.5.

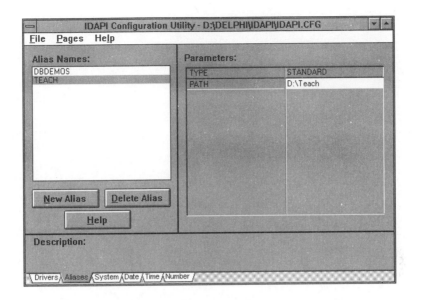

Figure 7.4 *Aliases page of the ADAPI Configuration Utility window, after creating your TEACH alias*

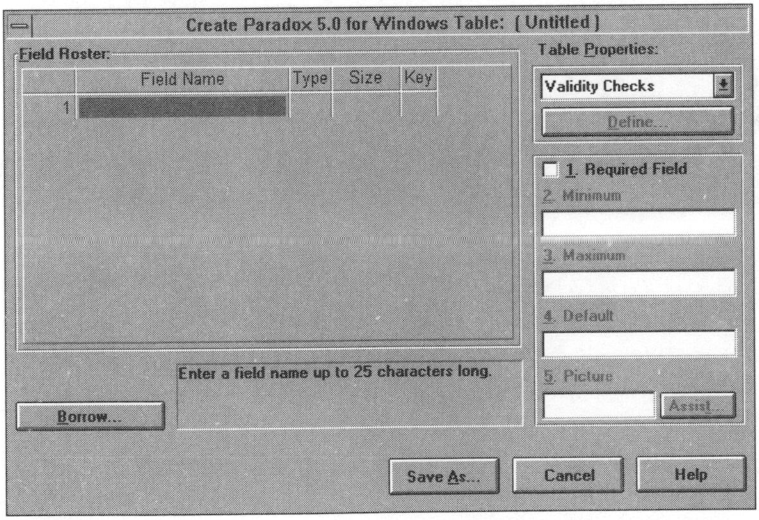

Figure 7.5 *The window used for creating Paradox for Windows tables*

The top-left portion of the window is the Field Roster section, where you will enter the **Field Name**, **Type**, **Size**, and **Key**. The right side of the window contains a section called Table Properties where you can define field requirements for validity checking, as well as Secondary Indexes, Table Lookups, and Passwords.

Just below the Field Roster section is a button, labeled Borrow..., to allow you to copy the Table Structure from another existing table. To the right of the button is an unlabeled panel that provides you with instructional prompts about what you should be doing. Right now it should still say *Enter a field name up to 25 characters long*. So what are you waiting for?

The first field name, according to Table 7.1, is Manufacturer. When you finish entering the word Manufacturer, press your **Tab** key to move to the Type column. The instructional prompt has changed and now says *Right click or press **Spacebar** to choose a field type.*.

Table 7.1 *Fields for the Manufacturer Table*

Field Name	Type	Size	Key
Manufacturer	Alpha	25	*
Location Number	Number		*
Address	Alpha	200	
Main Phone #	Alpha	12	

N O T E

For the right-click to work, you have to click where the highlight is, on the Type column in the same row as Title. Once the list is displayed, you can also use the **Up** and **Down Arrow** keys to move through the selections. Or, if you type in a letter that is the first letter of one of the available Type choices, that type will automatically be selected.

The Manufacturer field is text, so select **Alpha** from the list and **Tab** to the next column. Here you need to *Specify a field size from 1 to 255*. Table 7.1 indicates that this field will contain a maximum of 25 characters. As you move along to some of the other field types, you'll find that Size does not always apply. In fact, size only applies to eight of the data types. Table 7.2 lists database field types and their size limitations, where applicable.

Table 7.2 *Database Field Types, Symbols, and Size Limitations*

Type	Symbol	Size
Alpha	A	1 to 255
Number	N	
$ (Money)	$	
Short	S	
Long Integer	I	
# (BCD)	#	number of digits after the decimal
Date	D	
Time	T	
@ (TimeStamp)	@	
Memo	M	240 + *
Formatted Memo	F	240 + *
Graphic	G	240 + *
OLE	O	240 + *
Logical	L	
+ (Autoincrement)	±	
Binary	B	240 + *
Bytes	Y	1 to 255

*Any size, however 240 characters is the maximum that may be stored in the DB file. The rest are stored in a second file with the extension MB.

Now **Tab** to the Key column. Setting or removing a Key indicator is simple, just press any key or double-click your mouse on the highlighted area. Great, but what's a key anyway? Key is another word for index, and when using **Delphi** and **Paradox**, key refers specifically to the primary index. The primary index, or key, is used to prevent duplicate records, and is the basis for sorting all records in the table. Keys are optional, but your Manufacturer table will have one key or primary index. Why? Because you are going to need it in order to synchronize the two tables in the sample application. (You'll get to that in the next chapter.)

The instructional prompt also said *Keyed fields must be the top fields in the Field Roster.* Now you know why Manufacturer is the first field on our list. If you did not do so already, make Manufacturer a Key field, then press **Tab** to take you to the Field Name column for your next field.

The next field is Location Number. The field type is Number. I added this field so I could differentiate between records for one manufacturer with multiple locations, necessitating one record per location. Use Table 7.1 to finish entering the rest of the field names, types, and sizes. Then we'll take a second look at the fields and discuss Table Properties.

Table Properties

The Required Fields area is visible because Validity Check is the first value in the drop-down list. There are five different types of validity checking. A field can be Required, you can specify a minimum or a maximum value, you can specify a default value to be used if nothing else is entered, and you can specify a string that acts as a picture or template for how the data should look.

You can't very well have a manufacturer's record without a manufacturer name, so you should make it a Required field. That way no one can accidentally enter a record without it, or accidentally delete it when editing. To set the required marker, first select the field name, make sure that Validity Checks is showing in the drop-down properties box, then place an **X** in the Required check box by clicking on it. (If you click a second time, you can remove the X from the check box.)

Maximum, minimum, and default values don't really apply to the Manufacturer table, but you can use the Picture validity check for the Main Phone field. For example, if you want all phone numbers formatted with the area code in parentheses, you could create the following picture template where # represents a number:

(###) ###-####

Others prefer to use hyphens throughout, like this:

###-###-####

Table 7.3 shows the characters that have specific meanings when used in picture patterns. Any other character used in a picture pattern is treated as a constant. For example, if all of the phone numbers entered were to be toll-free numbers, then your pattern might look like this:

1-800-###-####

Table 7.3 *Characters with Special Meanings for Data Picture Patterns*

Character	Meaning
#	numeric digit
?	single letter
&	any letter automatically converted to uppercase
@	any character
!	any character automatically converted to uppercase
;	indicates that the next character listed is not a special pattern character
*	indicates that the following number represents the number of times the character after that will be repeated
{}	For example: {Yes, No} means either Yes or No
[]	values within square brackets are optional

Select the field name, make sure that Validity Checks is still showing in the drop-down box, then click on the **Assist...** button to help you select an appropriate picture. When the Picture Assistance window appears (as shown in Figure 7.6), you can enter your own custom picture pattern at the top, verify its syntax using the **Verify Syntax** button, and then test it by entering a value that a user might enter and clicking on the **Test Value** button.

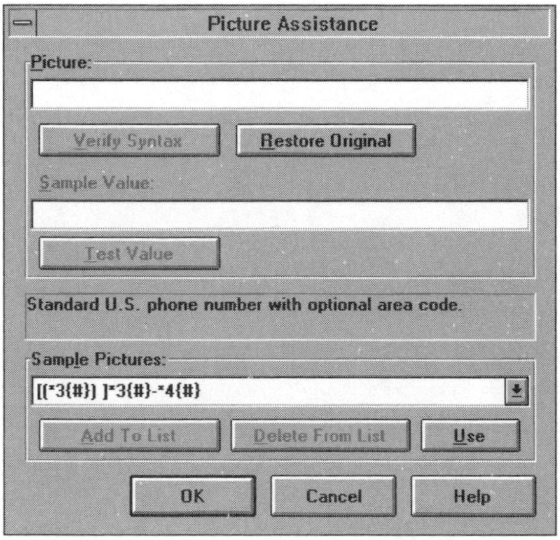

Figure 7.6 *The Picture Assistance window*

If you prefer, you can use a Sample Picture from the drop-down list at the bottom of the window. Select one and read its description shown in the panel just above. The first one shown is for standard U.S. phone numbers and is more complex than the picture patterns suggested previously because it uses the square bracket characters to indicate that the area code is optional, and uses the repeat character to specify how many numbers may be entered. You'll also find useful patterns for zip codes, lists of colors (useful for order entry forms if your products come in various colors), valid Paradox field types, time stamps, and integers.

If you find a picture pattern that you want to use, make sure it's highlighted and click the **Use** button. When the picture pattern appears in the pictures edit box at the top, you may edit it if you so choose. If you make a mistake, you can always click on the **Restore Original** button. Conversely, if you want to add your own picture pattern to the sample list, click on the **Add To List** button.

Saving a Table

When you have completed all the settings, click on **Save As...** to save your new table. Notice that the path is already set to the working directory. Enter **Manufact** as the table name (as shown in Figure 7.7) and select **OK**. When you click on **OK**, the Create window disappears and you're left looking at the empty Database Desktop window. But don't worry, your table was saved, as you'll see shortly. But before you take a look at it, you need to create the second table.

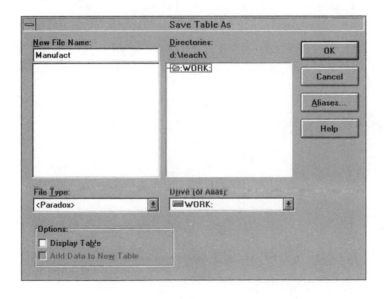

Figure 7.7 *The Save Table As dialog box*

Building Another Table

Now it's time to create the Inventory table—the main table needed for this sample application. The difference between the Invntory table and the Manufact table, other than the fact that Invntory has a few more fields, is that Invntory uses a few different data types and will have a composit primary key and two secondary indexes. The fields for the Invntory table are listed in Table 7.4. Select **New>Table** from the File menu, **OK** the Paradox 5.0 table type, and define those fields now.

Table 7.4 *Fields for the Inventory Table*

Field Name	Type	Size	Key
Product	Alpha	25	*
Version Number	Alpha	15	*
Date Purchased	Date		*
Manufacturer	Alpha	25	
Registration Number	Alpha	25	
Place Purchased	Alpha	20	
Purchase Price	$		
Technical Support Phone	A	12	
Technical Support Terms	M	100	

I could have designed the table differently. For example, I could have created a Record# to be used as a primary index. Then Record# might also have provided me with an ongoing count of the number of records in the table. However, there are other ways to get that information, if needed; and besides, Record# would not be a very useful field for sorting.

I would prefer that the products be sorted by product name, but that alone is not enough because over time I am likely to have more than one version of a product. I could create a composite secondary index composed of the product and version number, but if I purchase multiple copies of a product with the same version number (perhaps for use at other sites), it would be useful if the records were also sorted by date purchased. When you specify more than one key field, Paradox groups them together to form one Primary key, also known as a composite key. This is useful when no other single field in the table is guaranteed to be unique.

Creating Secondary Indexes

If you're done entering all the fields, types, sizes, and keys, you're ready to create the two separate secondary indexes for the Inventory table. When you select **Secondary Indexes** from the drop-down box at the top of the Table Properties section, the Define button just below becomes available. Click on **Define** to bring up the Define Secondary Index window with a list of fields from which you can create the index (shown in Figure 7.8). Notice that one of the fields shown in the Fields area on the left is grayed out so that you cannot select it. This field (Technical Support Terms) is a Memo field and as such cannot be used in a secondary index.

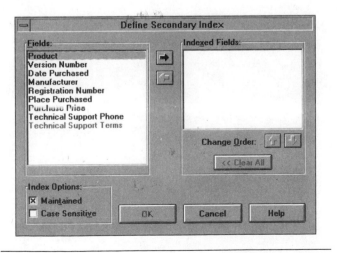

Figure 7.8 *The Define Secondary Index window used to specify the field or fields to be used in a secondary index for a table*

Memo fields are not the only field types that cannot be used in an index. Binary Large Object types (known as BLOBs) are not allowed. These include Memo, Formatted Memo, Graphic, OLE, Binary, and fields. Logical and Bytes field types are also exempted from use in an index.

N O T E

You are going to use the Product and Purchase Price fields for the first of the two secondary indexes. Select the first field, **Product**, then click on the **Right Arrow** button. Repeat this process for the Purchase Price field. Each time you move a field to the list of Inde<u>x</u>ed Fields on the right, the field name in the <u>F</u>ields list is grayed out. Now look at the **Index Options** in the lower-left corner. The two check box options are Maintained and Case Sensiti<u>v</u>e. Leave **Main<u>t</u>ained** checked. It tells Delphi to automatically update the index whenever changes occur in the table. When you're done, your screen should look like Figure 7.9.

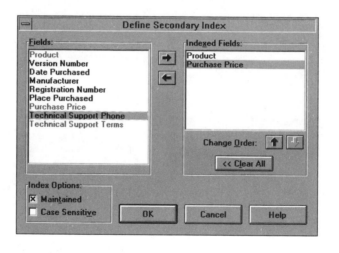

Figure 7.9 *The Define Secondary Index window after making your selections for the first of two secondary indexes*

Finally, click on **OK**. The Save Index As dialog box appears, prompting you to enter a name for the index. Because you selected more than one field, creating a composite secondary index, you'll need to use a name that is different from any of the field names. Call it ProdPrice (it's best to be as descriptive as possible), then click on **OK**. Delphi returns you to the Create window, and now you can see ProdPrice listed on the right as shown in Figure 7.10.

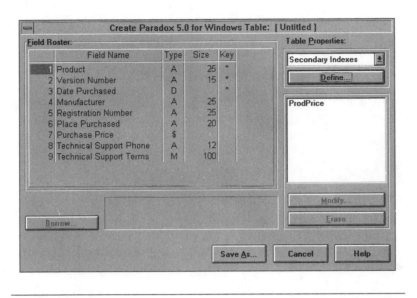

Figure 7.10 *The Create Paradox for Windows 5.0 Table: (Untitled) window after entering all of the field definitions and the ProdPrice secondary index*

Because there are occasions when you will want to sort records in a variety of sequences, you can have as many secondary indexes as needed. I thought there might be occasions when it would be useful to sort the records by **Registration Number**, so that is the second of the two secondary indexes. Again, you begin by selecting **Secondary Index** from the drop-down box (if it's not already selected) and clicking on the **Define** button. Select **Registration Number**, click on the arrow to move it to the Indexed Fields list, and click on **OK**. Even though you only selected one field for the index, Delphi wants you to select a name for the index (some other programs would automatically assign the field name). When the Save Index As dialog box appears, enter **RegNum** and click on **OK**. Now both secondary indexes should be listed.

If you have finished entering all the field definitions and created both secondary indexes, save this new table using the name Invntory.

Using the Database Desktop to Enter Data

Before you move on to creating the form, you're going to take advantage of one more Database Desktop function. You are going to use the Database Desktop to enter some data into your Manufact and Invntory tables. Select **Open** from the File menu, and **Table** from the submenu. Your new tables should be visible in the Open Table dialog box as shown in Figure 7.11. Select **Manufact** and click on **OK**.

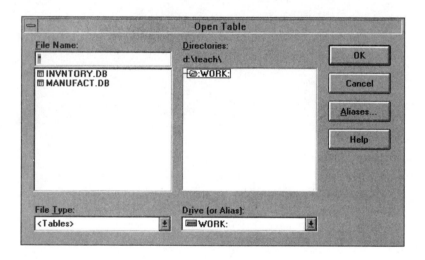

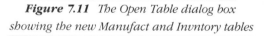

Figure 7.11 *The Open Table dialog box showing the new Manufact and Invntory tables*

When your table appears, your screen should look similar to Figure 7.12. You may think it's missing, but the Main Phone # field is still there—you just have to use the horizontal scroll bars at the bottom to see it.

Notice that several new menus have appeared as well. Let us take a look. Did you notice the toolbar? On the left side there are four glyphs.

In addition to the Cut, Copy, and Paste glyphs that correspond to options on the Edit menu, the fourth glyph is called Restructure, and it corresponds to the Table menu option of the same name. Restructure allows you to rearrange the sequence of your fields. (Don't forget though, key fields must be first.)

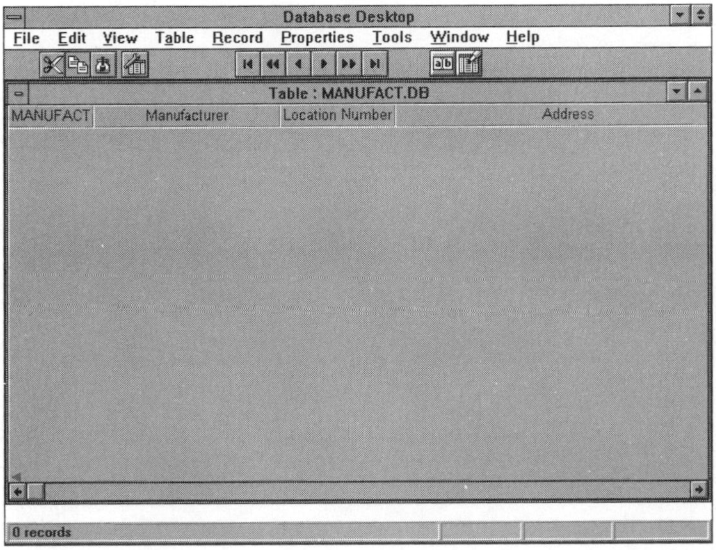

Figure 7.12 *Desktop Database window with the MANUFACT table open for editing*

The Database Desktop program has fly-by helo to remind you of which glyph is which. The only difference between the help for these glyphs and those in the Delphi main program is that when you place your mouse over a glyph here, you have to look at the status bar in the lower-left corner of the window to see the hint.

N O T E

In the middle are some arrow glyphs that allow you to move from one record to another. From left to right, they represent the First Record, Previous Record Set, Previous Record, Next Record, Next Record Set, and Last Record, respectively. Record set, in this case, refers to a screenful of records, and the Previous Record Set and Next Record Set buttons have the same effect as using the **PgUp** and **PgDn** keys on your keyboard. Other keystrokes can also help you to navigate. For example, **Cntl+PgDn** moves to the right so that you can see the Main Phone # field in the Manufact table.

On the right side of the toolbar are two more glyphs: Field View and Edit Data. These two options, which correspond to the first two options on the View menu, determine whether you are just looking at the table data, or editing the records. At the moment, your tables are empty. However, once a table is open, you can either View records, or Edit them. Editing includes adding, updating, and deleting records. When you open a table, the default setting is View Data. In order to edit, select **Edit Data** from the View menu, use the glyph, or press **F9**.

To add a record, simply begin filling in the fields, using your **Tab** or **Enter** key to move from field to field. You can add your own data, or use the values provided in Table 7.5. The data validation settings are not tested field-by-field, but rather record-by-record. For example, in our sample application you could leave the Manufacturer field blank and still move on to the Location Number field. However, when you reach the last field in the record (Main Phone #), and try to move on to the next record, Delphi will display an error message in the status bar in the lower-left corner of the window. The error message reads *Field value required* and the field name is also specified.

Table 7.5 *Sample Data for the Manufact Table*

Rec	Field Name	Value
1	Manufacturer	Borland International Inc
	Location Number	1
	Address	100 Borland Way, Scotts Valley, CA 95066
	Main Phone #	408-431-1000

```
2        Manufacturer      Compaq Computer
         Location Number   1
         Address           20555 SH 249, Houston, TX
                             77070
         Main Phone #      800-345-1518
3        Manufacturer      Microsoft Corp.
         Location Number   1
         Address           One Microsoft Way,
                           Redmond, WA 98052
         Main Phone #      206-882-8080
```

NOTE Delphi requires that you enter data for a key field, whether or not you specified the field as Required using the data validation settings.

When entering data for the Main Phone # field, were the dashes inserted automatically for you? If you used the ###-###-#### picture pattern when defining this field in the table, all you need enter are the numbers. In fact, if you used this picture pattern and tried to enter the dashes yourself, you'd get an *Illegal character for picture validation* error message.

When you finish entering the data for the final record, select **Close** from the Database Desktop File menu. Your data is saved for your automatically. Now open the Invntory table and enter the data listed in Table 7.6.

Table 7.6 *Data for New Invntory Sample Records*

Rec	Field Name	Value
Record 1	Product	Word for Windows
	Version Number	6.0

	Date Purchased	01-01-95
	Manufacturer	Microsoft Corp.
	Registration Number	12345-123-1234567
	Place Purchased	The PC Zone
	Purchase Price	298.98
	Technical Support Phone	206-462-9673
Record 2	Product	Paradox for Windows
	Version Number	5.0
	Date Purchased	01-15-95
	Manufacturer	Borland Intl Inc
	Registration Number	999999999
	Place Purchased	Egghead Software
	Purchase Price	339.98
	Technical Support Phone	
Record 3	Product	Delphi
	Version Number	1.0
	Date Purchased	3-1-95
	Manufacturer	Borland International Inc
	Registration Number	666666
	Place Purchased	Fry's
	Purchase Price	
	Technical Support Phone	

When you are finished entering the data, select **Close** from the File menu. Again your table will be saved automatically.

Summary

◆ Delphi's Database Desktop works with Borland's Paradox databases (versions 3.5, 4, and 5.0 for Windows), dBASE for Windows, dBASE IV, and dBASE III+.

◆ A database is a collection of data stored in one or more tables. Each table consists of defined fields and indexes. When you create an index, Delphi creates an internal pointer for faster access. Indexes are also used for sorting records and checking for duplicates.

◆ Delphi has four main Data Access components: Database, Table, DataSource, and Query.

◆ You can start the Database Desktop program by clicking on the **Database Desktop** icon from your Window's desktop, or selecting the option from the Tools menu inside the main Delphi program. To create a new table, select **New** from the File menu, and select **Table** from the submenu.

◆ Define your Field Names, Types, Sizes, and Key designations in the Field Roster section of the Create window. (The key column refers specifically to a primary key.) Alternatively, you can borrow the table structure from another existing table.

◆ The Table Properties section of the Create window allows you to define criteria for validity checking, table lookups, secondary indexes, passwords, and more. Validity checking includes: requiring that a field contain data; specifying minimum, maximum, and default values; and defining picture patterns, using the Picture Assistant.

◆ Delphi supports the use of an alias to designate the directory in which a database resides. You can access the Alias Manager from the Database Desktop File menu or from within the Save Table As dialog box.

◆ A field that is not unique cannot be used, by itself, as a primary key. If you want to have a primary key and no single field is unique, group two or more fields together such that when combined, the values will be unique. This is called a composit key. You may also create one or more secondary keys that can be used for sorting and other procedures when specifically called upon.

◆ Some data types may not be used as an index field. Memo, Formatted Memo, Graphic, OLE, Binary, Logical, and Byte fields may not be used.

◆ To edit an existing table, select **Open** from the Database Desktop File menu. Then select **Edit Data** from the View menu (or press **F9**). If you only wish to view data in an existing table, open the table and select **View Data** from the View menu.

◆ Arrow buttons at the top of the table window allow you to move from record to record. You can jump to the first or last record in the table, move to the previous or next screenful of records (sometimes called a record set), or move to the prior or next single record. Additionally you can use keystrokes, such as **PgUp** and **PgDn**, to navigate through records in a table.

In the Next Chapter

In the next chapter you will learn how to create a data-aware form, and you'll begin designing the interface for our TechSupport sample application.

CHAPTER 8

Creating Data-Aware Forms

- ◆ Examining data access components
- ◆ Using the Active property to design with live data
- ◆ Using the ReadOnly property to prevent or allow users to edit table data
- ◆ Synchronizing tables using the MasterSource and MasterFields properties
- ◆ Defining MasterFields with the Field Link Designer
- ◆ Controlling sort sequences with the IndexName property
- ◆ Using the DBEdit, DBLabel, and DBGrid components
- ◆ Navigating with DBNavigator (no code required)
- ◆ Examining Table Lookups and Referential Integrity
- ◆ Limiting field selection with the Dataset Designer
- ◆ Calculating run-time fields with the Dataset Designer

If you're not already running Delphi, double-click on the **Delphi** icon on your desktop to start the program. If you are already running Delphi, be sure that you have closed the Database Desktop program and that all existing projects are closed. It's time to start a new sample project using the database tables that you created in the last chapter.

Examining Data Access Components

To create a form with data-aware components, you'll be using different components than the ones you've used so far. For example, instead of using an edit or label component, you'll need the DBEdit or DBLabel components found on the Data Controls component page. But before you can use them you'll need to use some Data Access components through which you can connect the Data Controls to the database. Click on the **Component Palette** tab that says Data Access and I'll describe each one briefly, from left to right.

You might think that the first and most crucial component is the database component, but that is only true if you need to maintain a persistent connection to a database (usually a remote database) and/or require the user to log-on and provide a password. So the truth is that you probably won't have to use this component unless you're using the Client/Server edition of Delphi that supports remote database access.

The most important data access component for our purposes here is the Table component. This is the component that identifies the table you wish to access. If your project uses more than one table, you will need a separate component for each one. Alternatively, you may wish to use the query component to create a set of data from a specified table using an SQL statement. I'll talk more about that in Chapter 10. Both the table and query components communicate with the Borland Database Engine.

The second most important component is the DataSource component. Without this one, you will not be able to connect your table or query components to your data control components. The DataSource component identifies a set of data (either a group of records from a table, or the results of a query) and makes that data available to components such as DBEdit,

DBLabel, and others. For every table or query component used, you will need a corresponding DataSource component.

The BatchMove component allows you to perform operations with groups of records. For example, you would use this component if you wanted to append a group of records (i.e., a dataset) to another table, or delete a dataset from a table. The report component lets you print reports created in ReportSmith. We won't be using these two components in this chapter.

The last four components on the Data Access page of the Component palette provide you with lists that you can use in your application: a DatabaseList, TableList, FieldList, and IndexList. When you are designing forms that allow the user to select the database, table, field, and/or index with which to work, it helps to provide them with a list of what's available.

Setting Up Data Access Components

Placing a table component on a form is no different from any other component. Find the component on the palette, click on it, and then click on your form. Do this twice, because you will be using both the Invntory and Manufact tables and you'll need a separate table component for each. Each table component is going to need a companion DataSource component, so place two of these on your form as well. There is no need to drag out an area on the form, because the component only comes in one size. Also, when your application is running, the Data Access components will not be visible, so their placement is a matter of your convenience.

The properties of a table component are shown in Table 8.1, along with the default values and the settings for each of the tables in the new sample application. This is followed by Table 8.2, showing the DataSource properties, default values, and settings for the sample application. You will find that some settings cannot be set before others. For example, the value for a MasterSource property is the name of a specific DataSource component. So you can't set the MasterSource property for the table component before you have set the Name property for the DataSource component that you want to use.

Table 8.1 *Properties and Settings for the Table Component*

Property	Default	Table1	Table2
Active	False	True	True
AutoCalcFields	True		
DatabaseName		Teach	Teach
Exclusive	False		
IndexFieldNames			
IndexName			
MasterFields			Manufacturer
MasterSource			ISource
Name	Table1 or 2	ITable	MTable
ReadOnly	False		
TableName		Invntory	Manufact
TableType	ttDefault		
Tag	0		

Table 8.2 *Properties and Settings for the DataSource Component*

Property	Default Value	DataSource1	DataSource
AutoEdit	True	True	True
DataSet		ITable	MTable
Enabled	True	True	True
Name	DataSource1 or 2	ISource	MSource
Tag	0	0	0

Table Settings

The first thing you might notice is that I've asked you to change the setting of the **Active** property from its default of False, to **True**. Actually, this is a property that you can't set until after you set the DatabaseName and TableName properties. Even then, you won't notice anything right away, but when you start placing your data control components, this setting is what will allow you to see live data while designing your form. When the Active property remains set to **False**, then Delphi is unable to open the table to access data when still in design mode.

Other properties that have default settings include AutoCalcFields (True), Exclusive (False), ReadOnly (False), and TableType (ttDefault). If your table has any calculated fields, AutoCalcFields must be set to **True** in order for the calculation code to be automatically executed. (I'll show you how to create a calculated field at the end of this chapter.) When the Exclusive property is set to **False**, it means that other applications may access the table while you are using it. You may set this property to **True** if you wish to prevent such access, but you cannot change the setting when the Active setting is True. The setting of the ReadOnly property is what determines whether or not your users will be able to add, edit, or delete data from the table. The default setting, **False**, means that users may alter the table's data. If you want to limit the users of your application to viewing table data, set **ReadOnly** to **True**. One other property has a default setting. As long as **TableType** is set to **ttDefault**, Delphi will automatically identify the appropriate TableType when it opens the table. If you prefer, however, you may set **TableType** to **ttParadox** for the sample application.

In addition to setting the DatabaseName and TableName properties, which are self-explanatory, you will also set the **MasterFields** and **MasterSource** properties. (Don't forget to set the **DataSource** properties first.) When you are using two or more tables, Delphi allows you to synchronize their access so that when you move to a new record in one table (called the primary table), the corresponding record in the other table (secondary table) is accessed automatically. MasterFields identifies the names of the fields that the two tables have in common, and MasterSource identifies the name of the DataSource component controlling the primary table.

The Manufact table is going to be the secondary table, so that's the one for which you need to set the **MasterSource** and **MasterField** properties. But before you set them, you'll have to set the **Active property** back to **False**. Now set the **MasterSource** property to **ISource** (the name of the DataSource component controlling the primary table, i.e., your Invntory table). Then click on the ellipse (**...**) next to the MasterFields property to bring up the Field Link Designer dialog box shown in Figure 8.1.

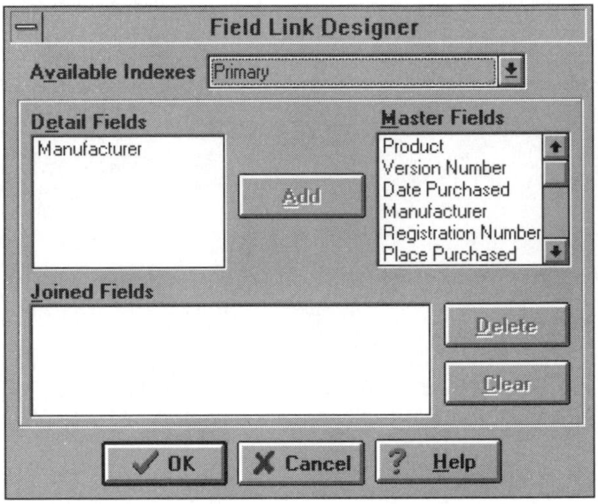

Figure 8.1 *The Field Link Designer dialog box*

In the Field Link Designer dialog box you'll see all of the fields from the Invntory table listed in the Master Fields box. The Manufact table has one field in common with the Invntory table, Manufacturer, and it is listed in the Detail Fields box. When you click on the **Manufacturer field** in both lists, the Add button becomes available. Click on **Add** to make Manufacturer a Joined field as shown in Figure 8.2. And when you do, notice that the Manufacturer field is no longer available in either of the Fields lists.

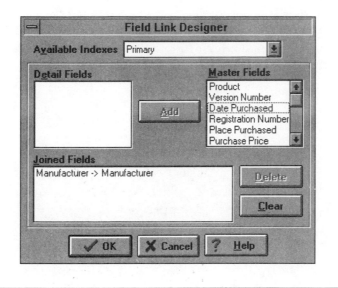

Figure 8.2 *The Field Link Designer dialog box after making Manufacturer a Joined field*

From now on, whenever the sample application is running and the value of Manufacturer from the Invntory table changes (either because of editing or moving to a new record), the program will automatically display the data from the corresponding record in the Manufact table. Of course, first you need to place some data control components on your form, and you'll get to that shortly.

IndexName identifies the name of a secondary index that you wish to use instead of the primary index. The primary index for your Invntory table is a compost based on the Product, Version Number, and Data Purchased fields. Right now, this is the most useful sort sequence for the application, so you'll leave the IndexName property blank. If, on the other hand, you wanted your table sorted by either of the two secondary indexes defined for the table, you would set property to either **ProdPrice** or **RegNum**, whichever of the two you desired.

IndexName is another one of those properties that you cannot set when the Table's Active property is set to **True** (i.e., when the table is open). You would have to set **Active** to **False**, set the **IndexName** to the name of the secondary index, and then reset **Active** to **True** again.

N O T E

DataSource Settings

The most important property setting for the DataSource component is DataSet, because that is the property that identifies which table or query DataSource will connect to the Data Control components. You can think of DataSource as a conduit through which data flows from a table to a Data Control component. Set the **DataSet property value** to the corresponding TableName—in this case **ITable** and **MTable**, respectively.

You can use AutoEdit to tell Delphi whether you want to automatically invoke edit mode (True) when a user begins typing inside one of the data control components connect to DataSource component. The Enabled property, when set to **True**, tells Delphi to automatically update all of the components whenever changes are made to the corresponding table or data set. This may sound good, but because updates are automatically invoked each time you so much as move to a new record, whether or not any editing has been done to change the data, a True setting can make your application run too slowly. Nevertheless, for the sample application at hand, leave the True setting, as that is the default value. The Tag property serves the same purpose here as it does for the table component, allowing you to store an integer value for your own use.

If you haven't done so already, go ahead and update the property settings as shown in Tables 8.1 and 8.2.

Connecting Data Control Components

Now that you have placed your table and DataSource components on the form, and set their properties, you can begin placing your Data Control components. In addition to having most, if not all, of the same properties as their non-data-aware component counterparts, the data control components also have a DataSource and DataField properties. These are the properties that make the controls data-aware by *binding* them to the DataSource component, and through it to the specific field in the table. The term binding refers to using the DataSource component to make a connection between the table component (ITable, for example) and the other components on the form. This connection, which you'll define in a moment using the Object Inspector, tells each component where to find the data. In other words, each of the other components will look to the DataSource component to provide the data. Which data it provides depends on the DataField setting of the data control component, and the TableName setting in the DataSource component.

This really isn't as complex as it might sound. When you're all done, your form should look like the one shown in Figure 8.3. Try creating a form with: a groupbox holding five DBEdit components on it for the Product, Version Number, Date Purchased, Registration Number, and Technical Support Phone fields in the Invntory table; and a panel holding one DBEdit component for the Manufacturer field in the Invntory table, and two DBLabel components for the Main Phone # and Address fields in the Manufact table. You'll also need to place three plain label components inside the group box. The plain label component tool is still on your component palette's Teach page, along with the GroupBox component you need. You'll find the panel component on the Standard page. The DBEdit and DBLabel components are on the Data Control page. Use the settings listed in Table 8.3.

Remember that labels only display information. Unlike edit components, labels do not allow you to type in new data, so you won't be able to add or update any Manufact data using this form.

N O T E

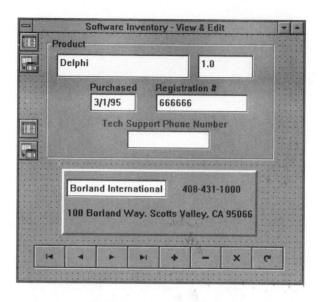

Figure 8.3 *The InventoryForm (in design mode)
after placing the Data Control components*

Table 8.3 *Properties and Settings for the InventoryForm and Its Components*

Component	Property	Value
Form	BorderStyle	bsSingle
	Caption	Software
Inventory		- View & Edit
	Height	389
	Left	166
	Name	InventoryForm
	Top	81
	Width	425

GroupBox	Caption	Product
	Height	177
	Left	40
	Name	ProdGroup
	Top	8
	Width	337
DBEdit1	DataField	Product
	DataSource	Isource
	Height	33
	Left	16
	Name	ProdEdit
	Top	24
	Width	193
DBEdit2	DataField	Version Number
	DataSource	Isource
	Height	33
	Left	224
	Name	VerEdit
	Top	24
	Width	81
DBEdit3	DataField	Date Purchased
	DataSource	Isource
	Height	25
	Left	66
	Name	DateEdit
	Top	82
	Width	65

DBEdit4	DataField	Registration Number
	DataSource	Isource
	Height	25
	Left	162
	Name	RegNumEdit
	Top	82
	Width	135
DBEdit5	DataField	Technical Phone Support
	DataSource	Isource
	Height	25
	Left	120
	Name	TechPhEdit
	Top	136
	Width	121
Label1	Caption	Purchased
	Height	16
	Left	64
	Name	DateLabel
	Top	64
	Width	73
Label2	Caption	Registration #
	Height	16
	Left	160
	Name	RegNumLabel
	Top	64
	Width	95

Label3	Caption	Tech Support Phone Number
	+Font	
	Color	clRed
	Height	16
	Left	82
	Name	RedLabel
	Top	117
	Width	189
Panel	BevelWidth	3
	Caption	(blank)
	Height	97
	Left	64
	Name	ManuPanel
	Top	200
	Width	289
DBEdit6	DataField	Manufacturer
	DataSource	Isource
	Height	24
	Left	8
	Name	ManuEdit
	Top	16
	Width	169
DBLabel1	DataField	Main Phone #
	DataSource	MSource
	Height	16
	Left	192

	Name	MainPhLabel
	Top	20
	Width	88
DBLabel2	DataField	Address
	DataSource	MSource
	Height	16
	Left	8
	Name	AddrLabel
	Top	56
	Width	268

Because you set the Active property to **True** for both the table components, you should see data appear in your DBEdit and DBLabel components as soon as you set their properties—even though you're still in design mode. When you set the properties for the DBEdit components, the data that appears from the Invntory table is the Delphi record. It's true that in the last chapter the first record you entered into the table was Word for Windows, but you'll remember that the primary index (Product + Version Number + Date Purchased) automatically sorts the table for you; that means that Delphi comes first.

When you get to the DBLabel components displaying data from the Manufact table, you'll see the data for Borland—the first record in the Manufact table. Why? Not because it's the first record, but because that's the record where the value in the Manufacturer field matches the value in the Invntory table's Manufacturer field. That's what you accomplished by setting the **MasterSource** and **MasterFields** properties.

When you're all done with the settings, save your new project, using the **Sa̲ve Project** option from the F̲ile menu. When the Save Unit As dialog box appears, don't forget to change to the \Teach subdirectory. Then save the unit as **Invn_u01.pas**. When the Save Project1 As dialog box appears, you'll have to change again to the \Teach subdirectory. Save the project as **Invntory.Prj**. Now try running it (just press **F9**). It should look pretty good, but there's definitely something missing. There's no way to see the next record, no way to navigate.

Select the **Reset Program** option from the Run menu to stop the program. Now I'll show you how to set up automatic database navigation, without writing any code!

Navigating with the DBNavigator Component

What you need is a DBNavigator component. The DBNavigator component can only be associated with one table. That would imply that you should have a DBNavigator for every table you are using. In the Invntory sample application, however, you used the MasterSource and MasterFields properties to synchronize the two tables. When you move from one record to another in the Invntory table, the matching record from the Manufact table will display automatically. So for now, you only need one DBNavigator component. Go ahead and place a DBNavigator component along the bottom of your form.

As you can see in Figure 8.4, the DBNavigator component contains Navigational Arrow buttons similar to the ones you saw in the Desktop Database, and a few you haven't seen before. There are ten buttons in all, and you have the option of using only those that you want and rendering the others invisible by setting the corresponding **VisibleButtons'** sub-properties to False.

Figure 8.4 *The DBNavigator component with all ten buttons*

The first four buttons on the left should be familiar. When you first start your application running, the first button will appear grayed out. That's because it is used to move you to the first record, and when you start the application you are already looking at the first record. At that moment there can be no prior record either, so the second button is also grayed out. The third and forth buttons take you to the next record in sequence, and the last record in the table, respectively. Of course, once you're viewing the last record, the next and last buttons become grayed out.

Use the fifth button, Insert, if you want to clear the fields and input data for a new record. The sixth button, Delete, allows you to delete the current record, i.e. the record currently displayed. If you want to edit the current record, use the Edit button (it's the seventh one, or fourth from the right). The Post button (the check mark button) saves the current record. If you don't want to save the edit, use the **Cancel** button (the **X**). As long as you are not editing, the Post and Cancel buttons remain grayed out. Once you begin to edit a field, whether by clicking on the **Edit** button or by simply beginning to type inside an edit component, the Post and Cancel buttons become available again. The last button is called Refresh, and it may be used to update a table.

Don't worry about remembering which button is which. The DBNavigator component has built-in fly-by help. If you hold your mouse over one of the buttons (without clicking) when the application is running, the name of the button appears.

N O T E

It is important to note here that whenever you use the DBNavigator to move from one record to another, Delphi automatically invokes certain routines depending on various property settings. For example, if you edit a data field and the Enabled property of the DataSource to which it is connected is set to **True**, then Delphi automatically saves the current record before moving on. This is true whether or not you use the **Post** button after editing or inserting a record. This also means that if you edit a record and you want to cancel the edits you made, you must use the **Cancel** button before you navigate to another record. If you forget, the edits will automatically be saved. This all happens only if the Enabled property is set to **True**.

Table 8.4 shows the DBNavigator properties (several of which will be familiar to you by now), along with the default values and settings needed for the sample application. Most important is the DataSource property used to associate your DBNavigator component to the table by setting its value to the name of the DataSource component controlling the table you wish to navigate—in this case, the Invntory table represented by ITable and controlled by ISource.

Table 8.4 *Properties and Settings for the DBNavigator Component*

Property	Default Value	New Setting
Align	AlNone	
Ctl3D	True	
Cursor	crDefault	
DataSource		Isource
DragCursor	crDrag	
DragMode	dmManual	
Enabled	True	
Height		33
HelpContext	0	
Hint		
HintColor	$0080FFFF	
HintPause	800	
Left		23
Name	dbNavigator1	InvnNav
ParentCtl3D	True	
PopupMenu		
ShowHints	True	
TabOrder		
TabStop	False	
Tag		
Top		312
Visible	True	
+VisibleButtons	[nbFirst,nbPrior, nbNext,nbLast...]	
nbFirst	True	

nbPrior	True	
nbNext	True	
nbLast	True	
nbInsert	True	
nbDelete	True	
nbEdit	True	False
nbPost	True	False
nbCancel	True	
nbRefresh	True	
Width		372

As I mentioned, you can choose not to use all of the DBNavigator's buttons in your application. If your application were only to allow the user to view data, you would leave the nbFirst, nbPrior, nbNext, and nbLast subproperties for the DBNavigator's VisibleButtons property set to **True**, and set all the others to **False**.

For the Invntory sample application, you should set **nbPost** to **False**. You don't need the Post button, because the DataSource's Enabled property is set to **True**, so simply moving to another record will save the edited or newly inserted record. For a very similar reason, you can also set **nbEdit** to **False**. If you followed the DataSource property settings in Table 8.2, then the AutoEdit property is set to **True**. If it was **False**, you would need the Edit button to allow you to type inside the DBEdit components. The True setting, on the other hand, allows the user to edit without the use of the Edit button. I'm leaving the Refresh property set to **True** so that you have a way to update the table without having to move to another record.

N O T E

Some programmers allow the DBNavigator control to remain visible, and take advantage of its simple built-in functionality. Other programmers prefer to make the entire DBNavigator control invisible (setting its **Visible** property to **False**), using instead their own command buttons and menus. This approach gives the programmer far greater flexibility, not just with the visual interface, but in terms of writing code that does more than the component's built-in functions would do alone.

Select **Save Proj** from the File menu to save the work you've done so far. Then try running the application. When it first starts up, it should look like the screen shown in Figure 8.5. Experiment with the navigator bar. Add, edit, insert, and delete inventory records if you'd like. Depending on your experimentations, you may hit an error message or two. For example, if you insert a new record and try to use dashes in the Date Purchased field (something like 3-1-95) you'll get an error because a Date type expects slashes (3/1/95). If this happens, just stop the application using the **Program Reset** option on the Run menu. Don't forget, this is still a work in progress, and you'll learn about error handling in Chapter 11.

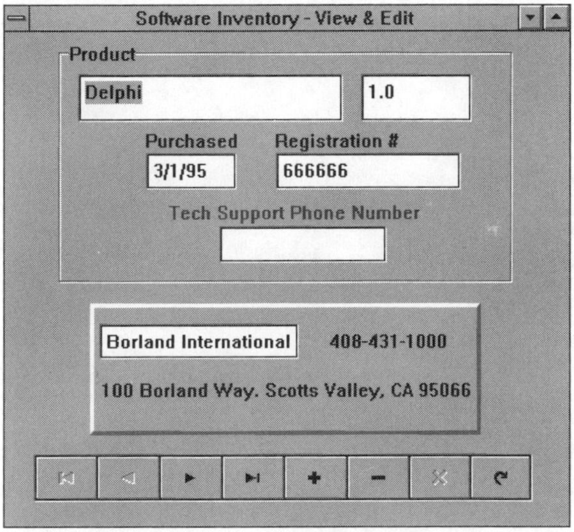

Figure 8.5 *The InventoryForm in action*

Maintaining Synchronicity

Have you thought about the fact that unless the manufacturer name is entered in the Invntory record exactly the same as it appears in the Manufact record, the synchronization achieved by using the MasterSource and MasterFields properties won't work. In other words, if your Invntory record simply lists Borland, the corresponding Manufact record will not appear because in that table Borland is listed as Borland International Inc, and Delphi won't find a match. Application designers have addressed this type of problem in many different ways. And Delphi provides the means for implementing a number of different solutions.

Table Lookups and Referential Integrity

One solution is the Table Lookup. This is a great tool for data entry because it will automatically enter the correct data found in the lookup table. The most important rule for a Delphi table lookup is that in order for a field to be "looked up," that field must be the first field in the lookup table. It doesn't have to be the same field name, but it must be the first field and it must be of the same data type.

Creating a Table Lookup

Even though I didn't want to use Table Lookup in the sample Invntory application, I thought it would be a good idea to show you how to set up one anyway. I'll use our sample application for illustration. If you want to follow along, you'll need to open the Invntory table using the Database Desktop. Once it's opened, select **Restructure Table** from the Table menu. Now your window should look like the one you used when creating the table.

Select **Table Lookup** from the Table Properties drop-down list, and click on the **Define...** button to bring up the Table Lookup dialog box as shown in Figure 8.6. First click on the **Manufact** table name in the Lookup Table list on the right side of the dialog box. When you click on the **Left Arrow** at the top of that section, the name of the first field in that table (Manufacturer) appears in the box labeled Lookup Field at the top of the window.

Then click on the **Manufacturer field name** in the Fields list on the left side of the dialog box. (This is the list of all the fields in the Invntory table.) Click on the **Right Arrow** at the top of the Fields section to display the selected field in the field name box at the top.

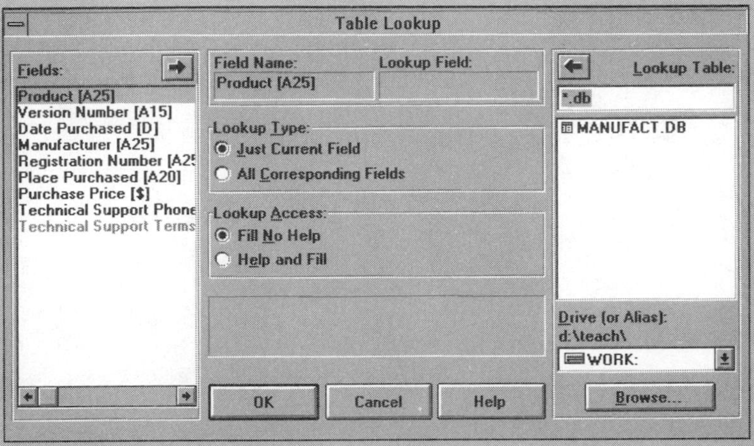

Figure 8.6 *Table Lookup dialog box when it first appears*

If the table you want is not listed, you may have to change the Drive or Alias using the drop-down box at the bottom right of the window. You can also use the **Browse...** button if you need to look for the directory holding the table you want.

Finally, you can also set some lookup options. You can choose between two Lookup Types: Just Current Field or All Corresponding Fields. In this case, you only want to look up the value for the Manufacturer field, so leave the default setting of Just Current Field. In order to use **All Corresponding Fields**, the corresponding field names would have to be identical on each of the two tables. You also have a choice between two types of Lookup Access. Fill No Help, the default, will fill in a matching value as you type in the entry, but it will not display a list of valid entries from which the user can select. I usually like to provide users with the ability to view the values in the Lookup Table, so I select the **Help** and **Fill** options.

When you're all done, your screen should look like the one shown in Figure 8.7. When you click on **OK** to return to the Restructuring window, you'll see the **Manufact.db** filename listed on the right.

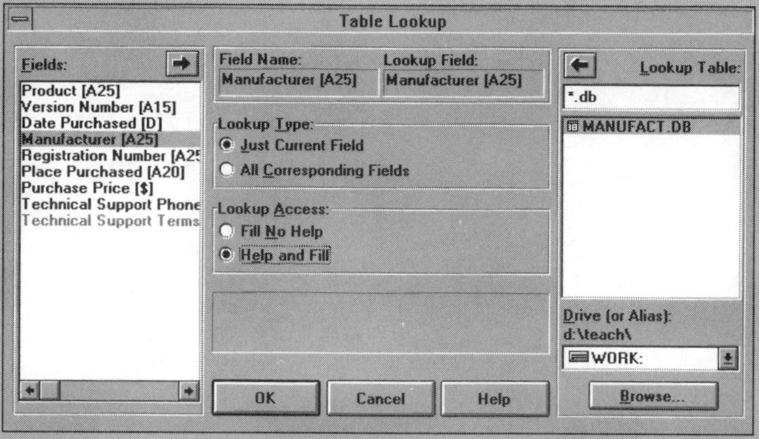

Figure 8.7 *Table Lookup dialog box with all of the settings completed*

Finally, you can also set some lookup options. You can choose between two Lookup Types: Just Current Field or All Corresponding Fields. In this case, you only want to look up the value for the Manufacturer field, so leave the default setting of Just Current Field. In order to use All Corresponding Fields, the corresponding field names would have to be identical on each of the two tables. You also have a choice between two types of Lookup Access. Fill No Help, the default, will fill in a matching value as you type in the entry, but it will not display a list of valid entries from which the user can select. I usually like to provide users with the ability to view the values in the Lookup Table, so I select the Help and Fill options.

Sounds great, but I'm not going to use it for our sample application. Table Lookup would take care of ensuring that the Manufacturer name you enter in the Invntory matches on in the Manufact table. But what if the manufacturer name changes? It could be a simple change, such as changing your records from Borland International Inc to just plain Borland. If you changed the record in the Manufact table, the existing corresponding entries in your Invntory table would no longer match, and the synchronization would no longer be effective. It would be great if when you changed the name in the Manufact table, all of the corresponding entries in the Invntory table would change automatically. Referential Integrity does just that, providing you use the **Cascade Update Rule**.

Referential Integrity, like Table Lookup, is something that must be defined when structuring a table—something I did not ask you to do when setting up the Invntory table. You could go back to the Database Desktop, Open the **Table** from the File menu, and then select **Restructure** from the Table menu to make changes. I am not suggesting, however, that you do this, because it will not really solve your problem. I will however, take a moment to tell you a little more about Referential Integrity, just in case you want to try it on one of your own applications.

Referential Integrity uses the whole primary key of the parent table. In our sample application, the parent table would be the Manufact table, and our primary key is the Manufacturer field. So you could, in fact, use this in our application, but it won't solve your problem.

 If you try to set up Referential Integrity with fields and keys that are not compatible, the OK button in the Referential Integrity dialog box will be grayed out, making it impossible to save the settings.

N O T E

Even if you did set up a referential integrity rule, it would not help you fill in the manufacturer name when entering a new inventory record. All it would do is give you an error message if you filled in a manufacturer name that did not have a corresponding record in the Manufact table. Then what would you do? If this were an advanced programming book, I might suggest that we use Referential Integrity and then program a routine to display valid names whenever such an error occurs, but there is a much simpler solution.

Sorry to have digressed, but these are considerations that go into designing an application. The solution I'm going to use right now is probably the least sophisticated of the available choices, but it will give me an opportunity to show you the DBGrid component and the Database Designer tool.

DBGrid Component

If the user of our sample application could see a list of manufacturer names currently in the Manufact table, the problem would be solved. So what you're going to do is add a button to the current form (InventoryForm), that when pressed, brings up a second form displaying the desired data. This means that you'll need to make a few changes to the InventoryForm, as well as add the second form containing three components: a table, DataSource, and DBGrid component.

If your Invntory project is not already open, open it. Then add a new form using either the Speedbar glyph or the New Form option on the File menu. Place a table component, a DataSource component, and a DBGrid component on the new form. Before you enter the final property settings, I'm going to give you some temporary settings so that you can experiment for a moment with the DBGrid component.

Set the **DatabaseName** property for the table component to **TEACH**, and set the **TableName** property to **Manufact**. Then set the **DataSet** property for the DataSource component to **Table1**. Select the **DBGrid** component and set its **DataSource** property to **DataSource1**, and finally go back to the Table component and set its **Active** property to **True**.

Now take a look at the DBGrid component. You should be seeing some data from the Manufact table. Make the component larger so that you can see more of the table's fields. See how all of the fields are there, even if you have to scroll to them. The DBGrid component automatically places horizontal and vertical scroll bars so you can scroll across to other fields, or up and down to other records.

If you take a look at the DBGrid properties in the Object Inspector, you'll see many familiar ones, and a few that will be new to you. One of the new properties is TitleFont. This is just like the font property that you are already familiar with, except that it controls the font used for the grid's column headings.

Options is another new property, and it too is one of those composite properties that has several subproperties. The dgEditing subproperty, when set to **True** (the default), allows you to edit data displayed in the grid. The dgTitles subproperty controls whether or not you display the field names at the top of each column—True, you see them, False, you don't. You can even resize the width of the columns when the application is running, as long as **dgColumnResize** remains set to **True**. The little arrow tip you saw pointing to the current record is called an *indicator*. You can get rid of it if you set **dgIndicator** to **False**. The same goes for the lines between the fields, and those separating each record—set **dgColLines** and **dgRowLines** to **False** and they all disappear. And if you want to be able to move from column to column, you need to leave the **dgTabs** subproperty set to **True**.

At this point in the design process of our sample application, all we need to see in the grid is the Manufacturer field. It happens to be the first field, so you could just size the width of the grid to match the field display, but that would still leave the horizontal scroll bars. And what if it wasn't the first field? It would be better if you could specify which field or fields you wanted to see displayed. And guess what? You can do that by using the Dataset Designer.

Dataset Designer

To bring up the Dataset Designer dialog box, double-click on the table component. Alternatively, if the table component is already selected, you can right-click on it to bring up a pop-up menu where Dataset designer... is the first item, as shown in Figure 8.8. The Dataset Designer dialog box (see Figure 8.9) shows the name of the form and table component in its title bar, but other than that it isn't much to behold at first—the Fields section empty, and all you can see are three buttons and a navigator bar.

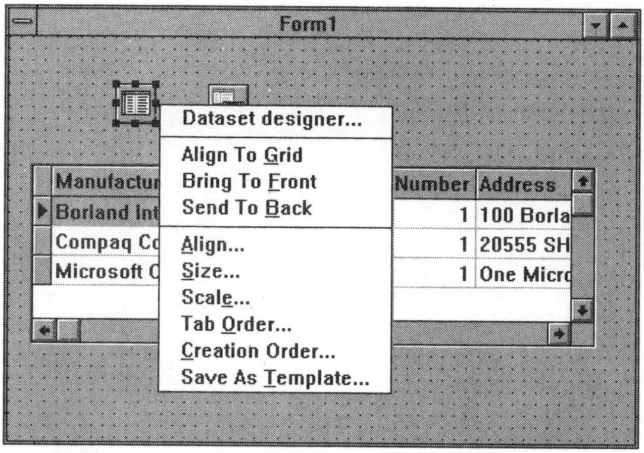

Figure 8.8 *Pop-up menu for a selected table component. Dataset designer... is the first item*

Figure 8.9 *The Dataset Designer dialog box, at first sight*

When you click on the first button, **Add...**, an Add Fields dialog box appears from which you may select one or more of the field names listed under the heading of Available Fields. (To select more than one field at a time, hold down the **Control** button while making your selections.) For our sample application, you should select the **Manufacturer** field (see Figure 8.10). When you have highlighted the field, click on **OK** to return to the original dialog box where the Fields section will now list the name of your chosen field, as shown in Figure 8.11.

Figure 8.10 *The Add Fields dialog box using the Dataset Designer with the Manufact table*

Figure 8.11 *The Dataset Designer main dialog box after selecting the Manufacturer field*

For the purposes of our sample application, that's all you really need to do. Simply close the Dataset Designer dialog box now, by double-clicking on the **System Menu** box at the top-left corner of the dialog box window. There is more to this Dataset Designer tool, and the power is behind the Define button you saw. The define feature allows you to create temporary fields to be displayed while your application is running. This is especially useful for calculated fields, such as dollar amounts. I'm going to show you how to create a calculated field, but I've put that discussion off for just a bit because I don't want it to be a part of this sample application. I'll discuss it in the next and final section in this chapter.

Now let's get back to our Invntory sample application and the new form. Table 8.5 lists all the settings that you'll need—both changes to existing components and the settings for the new ones. You've already placed the components on the forms, all except for the button component you'll need on the InventoryForm. So go ahead and place that button, and then finish up the property settings.

Table 8.5 *Changes to the InventoryForm, Settings for Its New Button, and Property Settings for the ManuListForm (Currently Known as Form1) and Its Components*

Component	Property	Value
InventoryForm	Height	428
	WindowState	wsMaximized
Button1	Caption	Show Manufacturer List
	Height	41
	Left	120
	Name	ShowManuList
	Top	352
	Width	185

Form1	BorderStyle	bsNone
	FormStyle	fsStayOnTop
	Left	400
	Height	148
	Name	ManuListForm
	Top	100
	Width	224
Table1	Active	True
	DatabaseName	TEACH
	Name	MTable
	TableName	Manufact
DataSource1	DataSet	MTable
	Name	MSource
DBGrid1	DataSource	MSource
	Name	ManuListGrid
	+Options	dgEditing
False		
	dgIndicator	False
	dgColumnResize	False
	dgColLines	False
	dgRowLines	False
	dgTabs	False
	+TitleFont	
	Color	clNavy

Go ahead and save your project before continuing. Because you've added a new form, you'll be prompted for a unit name. Call it Invn_u02, and don't forget to make sure it gets saved in the \Teach subdirectory. Now, you're going to need one single line for program code before you can test the application. Can you guess for what? You guessed it! You need to create an OnClick event for the new button on InventoryForm, and the code for the procedure is simply `ManuListForm.Show`. You will also need to add **Invn_u02** to the end of the uses clause. Your code window should look like the following:

```
unit Invn_u01;
interface
uses
  SysUtils, WinTypes, WinProcs, Messages,
Classes, Graphics, Controls,
  Forms, Dialogs, DBCtrls, StdCtrls, Mask, DB,
DBTables, Invn_u02;
type
  TInventoryForm = class(TForm)
    ITable: TTable;
    MTable: TTable;
    ISource: TDataSource;
    MSource: TDataSource;
    ProdGroup: TGroupBox;
    ProdEdit: TDBEdit;
    VerEdit: TDBEdit;
    DateEdit: TDBEdit;
    RegNumEdit: TDBEdit;
    TechPhEdit: TDBEdit;
    DateLabel: TLabel;
    RegNumLabel: TLabel;
    RedLabel: TLabel;
    ManuPanel: TPanel;
```

```
      ManuEdit: TDBEdit;
      MainPhLabel: TDBLabel;
      AddrLabel: TDBLabel;
      InvnNav: TDBNavigator;
      Button1: TButton;
      procedure Button1Click(Sender: TObject);
    private
      { Private declarations }
    public
      { Public declarations }
    end;
var
    InventoryForm: TInventoryForm;
implementation
{$R *.DFM}
procedure TInventoryForm.Button1Click(Sender:
TObject);
begin
ManuListForm.Show
end;
end.
```

Isn't it amazing that all of that code, except for one line, was generated automatically by Delphi. And you have a database application that not only affords you a synchronized view of selected fields from two different tables, but also allows you to edit most of those fields. Save your project and take it for a spin. When it's up and running, click on the **Show Manufacturers List** button—it should look something like the screen shown in Figure 8.12.

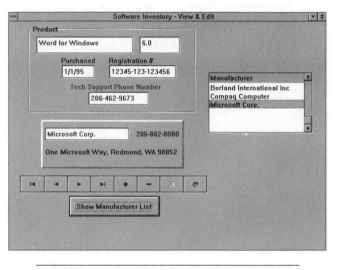

Figure 8.12 *The Inventory sample application, up and running with the Manufacturers list displayed*

Defining Calculated Fields

If the Invntory project is still open, close it. If Delphi is not running, launch it. In order to show you how to create a calculated field using the Dataset Designer, I'd like you to start with a clean slate.

Place a table component, a DataSource component and a DBGrid component on a new blank form. Set the table's **DatabaseName** and **TableName** properties to **DBDEMOS** and **ITEMS.DB**, respectively. Set the **DataSet** property of the DataSource component to **Table1**, and then set the **DataSource** property of the DBGrid component to **DataSource1**. Finally, set the table's **Active** property to **True**. (This should be old hat to you by now.) When you're done, your form should look something like Figure 8.13.

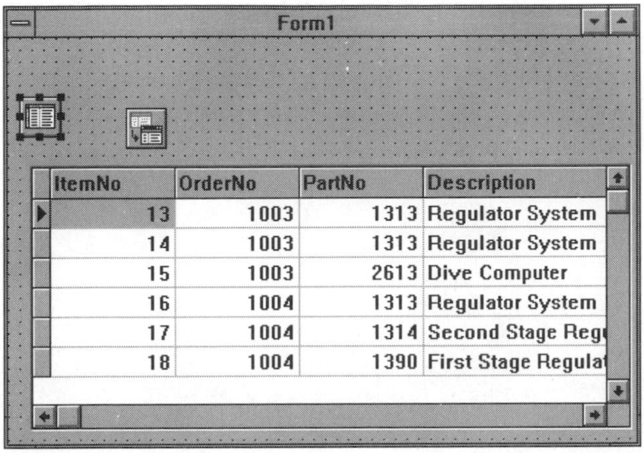

Figure 8.13 *A display of the first few fields in the Items table from the DBDEMOS database using a DBGrid component on Form1*

Now activate the Dataset Designer by double-clicking on the **table** component, or if it is still selected, right-click on it and select **Dataset designer...** from the pop-up menu. Let's start off by limiting the fields displayed to PartNo, Qty, and SellPrice. Use the **Add** button to bring up the Add Fields dialog box, select only the **PartNo**, **Qyt**, and **SellPrice** fields, and click on **OK**. You'll notice that the DBGrid component reacts immediately.

Okay, now add a special field that will exist only when the application is running. And make it a calculated field—nothing too complex, just a field to calculate how much money was paid on each order. Click on the **Define** button to bring up the Define Field dialog box. Call the new field Amount Paid. When you enter the name in the Field name box, Delphi automatically uses it to create a corresponding Component name. Then select **CurrencyField** from the Field type list so that your dialog box looks like Figure 8.14. Make sure that the **Calculated** check box is selected (i.e., has an **X** in it).

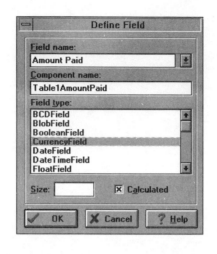

Figure 8.14 *The Define Field dialog box with all of the settings to create a calculated field named AmountPaid*

When you click **OK**, you'll find yourself back at the Dataset Designer dialog box and the new field will be visible on the DBGrid. Also notice that the Object Inspector now shows the component that Delphi created to represent your new field. Your next step takes place in the Object Inspector, so you can close the Dataset Designer now (just double-click on the upper-left corner).

Make sure that Table1AmountPaid is the current component in the Object Inspector. (If it is not, select it from the drop-down list.) Because of the selections you made in the Dataset Designer, some of the new component's properties have been preset for you. **Alignment** is set to **taRightJustify** as is appropriate for monetary values. **Calculated** and **Currency** are both set to **True**, and the DisplayLabel property shows the field name you entered in the Define Field dialog box. The component's name property has been filled in as well.

Not all defined field components have the same properties available to them. For example, a string component would not have any use for the currency property.

N O T E

Now you need to define the calculations itself, and all it will require is a single line of programming code. While your new component does have some associated events, the event you need to use, **OnCalcFields**, is associated with the table component. So select the **Table1** component (either by clicking on it or by choosing it from the drop-down list at the top of the Object Inspector), click on the **tab** for the Events page, and find the OnCalcFields event. Then double-click in the value column next to **OnCalcFields** to generate the event handler and display your Unit1 code window.

The calculation is simple. The value that belongs in the AmountPaid field is equal to the value in the SellPrice field multiplied by the value in the Qty field. I used the phrase *value in the field* quite deliberately. Value is a property of field components. It may seem obvious when stated, but you cannot multiple a field, you can only multiple the value inside the field. Likewise, when you assign a value to a field component, you must assign it to that field component's value property. With this in mind, your CalcFields procedure should look like the following:

```
procedure TForm1.Table1CalcFields(DataSet:
TDataSet);
begin
Table1AmountPaid.Value := Table1SellPrice.Value
* Table1Qty.value
end;
```

Try it out. It works.

Summary

◆ When you want to access information from database tables, you need to use Data Access and Data Control components. These components can be found on their own respective component palette pages.

◆ Table and DataSource are the two Data Access components that were used in this chapter. The table component communicates with the Borland Database Engine and connects to the table. The DataSource is the conduit between the table component and any Data Control components displaying data from that table. Data Access components are only visible while designing your forms.

◆ The database and query components are two more of the Data Access components. The database component is used whenever you need to create a persistent connection to a database. The query component is just like the table component, only it identifies a subset of the table data based on the results of a query statement.

◆ The rest of the Data Access components include: the batch component, used to perform operations on groups of records; the report component, used to print reports from ReportSmith; and four list components (DatabaseList, TableList, FieldList and IndexList), available if you need to display their data during run time.

◆ The Data Control components work just like the regular counterparts, except that they are data aware (meaning you can connect them to a DataSource) and may have a few additional features. In this chapter you used the DBEdit, DBLabel, and DBGrid components.

◆ If you want to see live data in the Data Control components while you work on your design, you can open the table by setting the table component's **Active** property to **True**. Depending on what other property settings you are working with, there may be times when you have to set and reset the Active property because some settings cannot take effect while the table is open.

◆ Table properties such as Exclusive and ReadOnly allow you some control over your data. Exclusive prevents others from accessing the table while you're using it. ReadOnly allows others to view the table data, but not to edit data, or add and delete records.

◆ Use the MasterSource and MasterFields properties, along with the Field Link Designer tool, to synchronize the display of data from multiple tables that have one or more common fields. MasterSource identifies the DataSource component of the controlling table. Use the

Field Link Designer to identify the common field(s) that will comprise the value of the MasterFields property.

◆ IndexName is the Table property that allows you to override the table's primary index by selecting one of the secondary indexes for use instead.

◆ A DataSource component has only a few properties. DataSet identifies the table to which it is connected. When **AutoEdit** is set to **True**, a user can edit the data without selecting an Edit option from a menu or clicking a button. Similarly, if you do not want the user to have to actively choose a Post or Update button or menu item, set the **Enabled** property to **True** and any changes will be automatically accepted.

◆ Data Control components look to the DataSource component to provide the data. A Data Control component, such as DBEdit, is connected to the DataSource component via DBEdit's DataSource property. After you set the property to the name of the DataSource component, you can set the DBEdit's DataField property to specify which field the DBEdit component is to display.

◆ The DBNavigator is a Data Control component that allows you to navigate through a table without writing any programming code. The Navigator bar has ten buttons, and you can control which buttons appear by setting the components **VisibleButtons'** sub-properties to **True** (visible) or **False** (invisible). In addition to buttons that allow you to move between existing records, there are buttons that allow you to insert new records, edit and delete existing records, post updated records, and cancel changes before they are saved.

◆ Table Lookups are a great tool for data entry because they can automatically enter the correct data as found in the lookup table. Table Lookups must be defined as part of a table's structure, and you can do this using the Database Desktop application. The field you wish to look up must be the first field in the lookup table, and the field must be compatible with the field in which you wish to place the found value.

◆ If you have two tables with a common field, and you want the changes made to that field in one table to automatically update the other field, or conversely, if you want to prevent changes from being made to one table to protect the corresponding entries in the other table, you need to use Referential Integrity. These settings must be defined as part of a table's structure, and you can do this using the Database Desktop application.

◆ You can show multiple fields and records using a single DBGrid component. The DBGrid's Options property affords you some control over the look of the grid. Whether or not to display field Titles, ColLines, RowLines, or the Indicator arrowtip is a function of these subproperty settings. Other Options subproperty settings enable you to allow or disallow user actions such as the ability to edit in the grid, resize the columns, or use the Tab key to move from field to field. You can also select which fields you wish to display by using the Dataset Designer's Add button and selecting the fields from the Add Fields dialog box.

◆ The Dataset Designer also has a Define button that is used to create temporary fields for display during run time. This is especially useful for calculated fields, such as totals. If you define a calculated field, you'll need to create an OnCalcFields event for the table component, and place the calculation code in the automatically generated CalcFields procedure.

◆ When you want to access the value in a table field, or assign a value to a field, you need to use that field's Value property. You cannot assign a value to Table1FieldName, but you can assign the value to Table1FieldName.Value.

In the Next Chapter

In the next chapter you will learn how to use the Menu Designer to create menus for your applications, and then I'll show you how to replace the Navigator bar with your own programming code.

CHAPTER 9

Menus and Database Methods

◆ Establishing a menu bar with a MainMenu component

◆ Designing menus in the Menu Designer window

◆ Defining menu accelerator keys and shortcuts

◆ Grouping menu items between separator lines

◆ Using the SpeedMenu

◆ Working with menu templates

◆ Creating pop-up menus

◆ Replacing the DBNavigator with table component methods

◆ Searching a table

In the first part of this chapter I am going to introduce two new components: the MainMenu and PopupMenu components, and you will use the first component to create the menus needed for the Invntory sample application. Then in the second part you will connect the menu items to programming code that will allow you to navigate through a database table without the use of the Navigator. But first I want you to take care of a small piece of business.

By now you are familiar with many different components found on various palette pages. Before you get started with menu creation, now would be a good time to get rid of the Teach page that you created at the beginning of this book. If Delphi is not already running, launch it now. You created the Teach page using the Palette page from the Environment dialog box. Bring up that dialog box by selecting **Environment...** from the Options menu, and clicking on the **Palette** page tab.

N O T E   If for some reason you prefer to leave the Teach palette page alone, you can skip to the next section. Also, if on your own you want to rearrange the components to your own liking, you may, of course, do so. From here on I will assume that the components have been restored to their original positions, or that you know where to find them.

The procedure couldn't be simpler. At the bottom-left corner of the dialog box is the Reset Defaults button. When you click on it you will be asked to confirm your intentions, because once the defaults are restored you cannot undo the restoration to return to your previous configuration. If you change your mind then, you would simple have to re-create the changes you made initially.

Now that all the components are either back where Delphi put them, or on palette pages of your own choosing, you can start designing a menu. Click on the **OK** button in the Environment Options dialog box, and then launch your Invntory project if it is not already open.

Creating MainMenus

In order to create a menu, you need a menu component. Delphi provides two—the MainMenu and the PopupMenu components—and they are on the Standard page of the Delphi Component palette. The MainMenu component is used to create a menu that attaches itself to the top of your form. Pop-up menus are not visible until you click on the form while the application is running. Let's start with a MainMenu.

Place the MainMenu component somewhere on your InventoryForm (not on the ManuListForm). This is one of those components that is invisible during run time, so it doesn't much matter where you put it. Once you place it, take a look at the Object Inspector. The MainMenu component has only four properties: AutoMerge, used to indicate whether the menu is to merge with menus on other forms; Items, the value for which contains the actual menu and item titles; Name, the name you assign to the component; and Tag, the property that allows you to store a value inside the component for later use.

You can leave the AutoMerge property set to its default value (**False**) because our sample application will not have any other menus with which to merge. Set the **Name** property to **InvnMainMenu**. To set up the value for Items, you need to use the Menu Designer, and there are a few different ways to access it. You can use the Object Inspector and double-click on the **Items property [Menu]** value, or click on the **ellipsis** next to the Items property value column. Yet another alternative is to simply double-click on the **MainMenu** component.

Introducing the Menu Designer

The Menu Designer window is like a dummy form that allows you to see how your menus look while you are building them. When the Designer window first appears you will see an empty menu bar and a placeholder for the first menu item title. To input a title, all you need to do is start typing. Actually what is happening is that Delphi is creating a new component, much the way it did when you defined new display fields using the Dataset Designer. As you type, you are entering a value for the new component's Caption property. Delphi will then use that caption to create a value for the component's Name property.

Type in **Inventory** for the first title, and then press **Enter**. Your cursor will move down allowing you to enter some items. At the same time, the next placeholder position also becomes visible, so you can click on it to enter a title for the next menu, once again creating another new menu item component. Figure 9.1 shows what your menu Designer windows should look like after typing **Inventory** and pressing **Enter**.

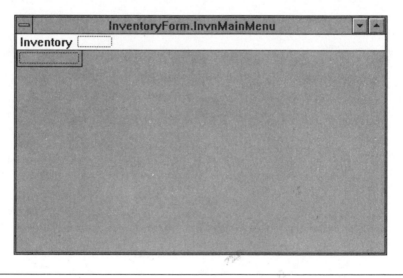

Figure 9.1 *The Menu Designer window after entering the first menu title (File)*

Our Invntory project will need three menus: Inventory, Navigate, and Find. You already created the Inventory menu title. And when you pressed **Enter**, your cursor was placed in position to enter an item for that menu. However, I want you to click on the **placeholder** for the next menu over, type in **Navigate**, and press **Enter**. Again your cursor is positioned to enter a menu item. Once again, click on the **placeholder** for the next menu over, type in **Find**, and press **Enter**. When you're done with these steps, Delphi will have created three components that are now available through the Object Inspector (one for each of the menu titles), and your Menu Designer window should look like the one shown in Figure 9.2.

```
InventoryForm.InvnMainMenu
Inventory  Navigate  Find
```

Figure 9.2 *The Menu Designer window after creating all three menu titles*

Your cursor is, once again, in position to add items to a menu—in this case the Find menu. But I want to go back to the Inventory menu to begin entering the items. All you have to do is click on **Inventory**, and the placeholder beneath it becomes visible. Click on the empty **placeholder** and you're ready to enter the first item for your Inventory menu.

 If you like to use the keyboard more than your mouse, you can return to the menubar by pressing the **Esc** key. When you do, your Navigate menu item will be highlighted (indicating that you are indeed on the menu bar), and you can then use your Arrow keys to move across.

N O T E

With your cursor in the placeholder beneath Inventory, type **Ad&d Record** and press **Enter**. Did you think that the ampersand before the d was a typo? Take a look at the result. The d in your Ad<u>d</u> Record item is underlined, and just like any other windows program, that underline indicates that it is an accelerator key. An accelerator key is one that when pressed in conjunction with the Alt key, has the same effect as selecting the item from the menu.

While you are close by, you might as well go back to the inventory menu title and make the I into an accelerator key. You can either click on **Inventory**, or use the **Esc** key to get back to the menu bar. And by the way, don't worry about the empty placeholders below Add Record and to the right of Find. They won't show up in your application, but you can't delete them from the Menu Designer window.

In addition to, or instead of, accelerator keys, you can also define keyboard shortcuts. For example, when using Delphi, you can press **F9** instead of selecting the **Run** item from the Run menu. Each menu item component has a ShortCut property, and you can select a Shortcut key or combination from a list by clicking on the **Down Arrow** key to the right of the ShortCut property's value entry—the Default for which is (None).

Separator lines are a visual element that you might want to use in your menus. When there are a lot of items on a menu, separator lines are especially useful for grouping similar items together. Personally, I like to use them even if there are only a handful of items. These lines act like landmarks. When users get used to seeing the exact location of a menu item, they are able to find what they want more quickly. All you have to do to create a separator bar is define an item with a hyphen as its caption.

Now that you know your way around the Menu Designer, go ahead and create the rest of the menu items according to the settings in Table 9.1. You'll find two new menu items plus items to match each of the eight Navigator buttons you used in the last chapter, and I've included two separator bars and some ShortCut property settings as well. When you're all done, close the Menu Designer window to return to your form. Figure 9.3 shows InventoryForm with the Navigate menu pulled down.

Table 9.1 *Menu Items for the Invntory Project Main Menu*

Menu Items	Accelerator Keys	ShortCuts
Inventory	Alt+I	
Add Record	Alt+D	F5
Delete Record		
-		
Cancel Change		
Refresh		
Navigate	Alt+N	
Next		F4
Previous		F3
-		
First		
Last		
Find	Alt+F	
Product		F6
Registration		

N O T E

Only items that are likely to be used frequently, really benefit from accelerator keys or shortcuts. It's mostly a matter of common sense and personal preference, but common is the key word, because unless you are going to be the user, your personal preferences don't really count.

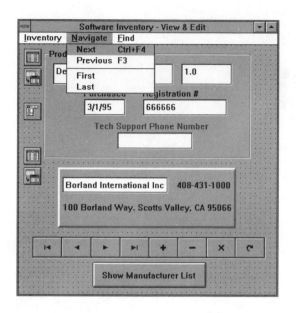

Figure 9.3 *An InventoryForm, still in design mode, with Navigate menu opened*

The Menu Designer SpeedMenu

Open up the Menu Designer window again (just double-click on the **menu component** on the form) so that I can show you the SpeedMenu. The SpeedMenu is a pop-up menu that contains some useful items when working with menus. To bring up the SpeedMenu, right-click somewhere inside the Menu Designer window. Your screen should look something like Figure 9.4.

The first two items, Insert and Delete, allow you to insert and delete menu items. For example, click on the **separator bar** in the Navigate menu, bring up the SpeedMenu again (right-click), and select **Delete**. Oops. The separator bar is gone. Of course you want to put it back, but to do so you'll need to use the **Insert** item. When you select **Insert**, an empty placeholder will appear just above whichever item was selected at the time.

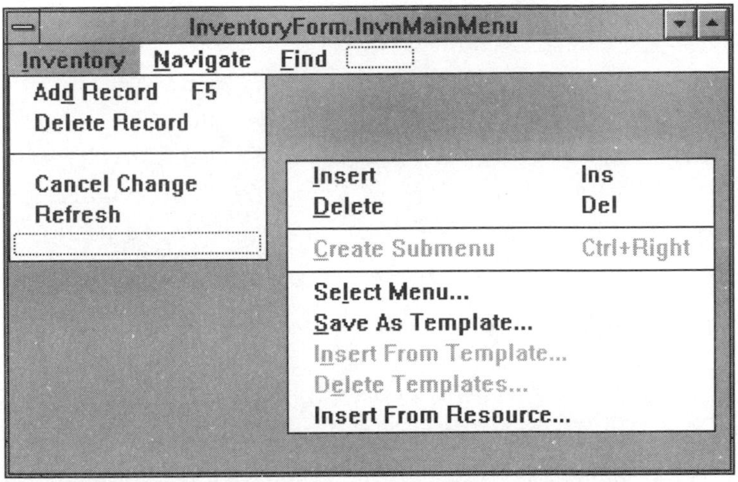

Figure 9.4 *The SpeedMenu inside the Menu Designer window,*
just after creating the menus for the Invntory sample application

The Create Submenu item on the SpeedMenu allows you to define nested menus (also known as submenus) by creating an empty place-holder to the side of whichever menu item was selected at the time. If the Create Submenu item is grayed out, then you do not have a menu item currently selected.

The Select Menu... item is useful when working with applications that have more than one menu component. Choosing this item brings up a Select Menu dialog box from which you can choose a different menu that you want to work on in the Menu Designer window.

The next three items relate to templates, so I'm going to skip those for just a moment. The last SpeedMenu item is Insert From Resource..., which allows you to import menus from other projects (all Delphi menu files have the file extension MNU). It even allows you to import individual menus created by other programs, providing the menu was saved in the standard Windows Resource format with an RC filename extension.

Before selecting this option, you would highlight the placeholder on the menu bar where you want the inserted menu to appear. When you select the **Insert From Resource...** option from the SpeedMenu, the Insert Menu From Resource dialog box appears. (It looks a lot like most Open File dialog boxes, except that the File Type is preset to list ***.MNU Files** or ***.RC files**.) Then you would select the file you want, click on **OK**, and Delphi would place the menu in the designated location on the menu bar.

Working with Menu Templates

In Chapter 4 you saved some design time by creating a form template. Once created, you were able to add several new forms, each of which already contained components with the property settings you needed. Menu templates provide a similar functionality. Delphi ships with several menu templates containing common commands, or you can create your own menus and save them as templates.

Try saving the menus you created for InventoryForm. If it is not already open, double-click on the **MainMenu** icon to bring up the Menu Designer window. Right-click in the **Designer** window to bring up the SpeedMenu, and select **Save As Template....** When the Save Template dialog box appears, give it a name (use InvnMenus) and then click on **OK**. That's all there is to creating a menu template. All of the menus titles and items that exist in the Menu Designer window at the time you make the template will be saved in that template. Sometimes, however, it is more useful to create individual templates for individual menus rather than one template for all the menus on a menu bar.

Now that you've created a menu template, let's take a look at the Insert From Template item on the SpeedMenu. Before you pop up the SpeedMenu again, click on the Navigate menu so that it is highlighted. When you pop-up the SpeedMenu and select **Insert From Template**, the Insert Template dialog box appears. Select the template you saved (**InvnMenus**) and click on **OK**.

Oooh boy! Double menus. Your screen should look like Figure 9.5. Of course you don't need two of everything, but I wanted you to see how the Insert template places the menu (or menus as the case may be) immediately preceding the position that was highlighted when **Insert From Template** was invoked. If you select the **Delete Template SpeedMenu** option, a Delete Template dialog box appears. Highlight a template name and click on **OK** to erase the template from your system. However, what you need right now is not Delete Template, but just plain delete. Highlight the extra menus you just inserted (you can highlight more than one at a time by holding down the **Control** key as you select each one) and pressing the **Delete** key.

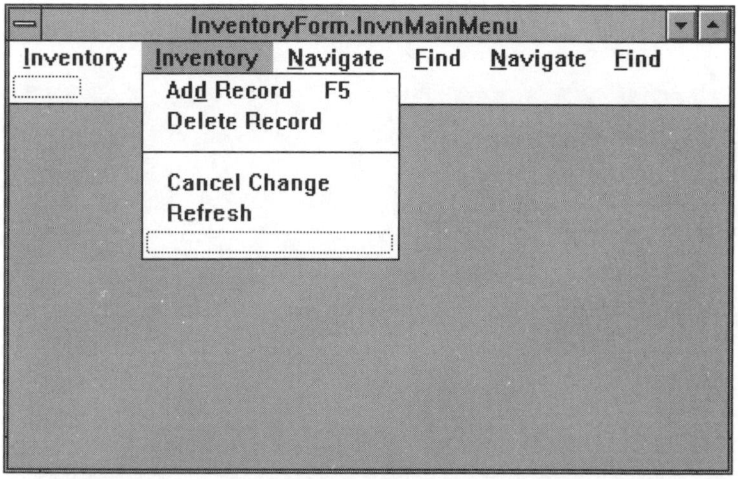

Figure 9.5 *The Menu Designer window showing double menus after using the Insert From Template SpeedMenu option*

Just one more neat feat before you close the Menu Designer window. While it's open, you can rearrange the sequence of the menus simply by dragging-and-dropping them along the menu bar. You can also move menu items from one menu to another by dragging the item up to the menu bar, along the bar to the menu in which you want to place it, and down to the position.

Now that you have menus and menu items, you'll need to make something happen when an item is selected, and that calls for some programming code. But before we get into that, I want to show you how to create a pop-up menu.

Creating Pop-up Menus

Just for the sake of experimentation, place a PopupMenu component on InventoryForm, then double-click on it to bring up the Menu Designer window. Just like before, start typing. Type **Next**, and press **Enter**. Then type **Previous**, and press **Enter**. Then type a single hyphen character, and press **Enter**. Then type **First**, and press **Enter**. And finally type **Last**, and press **Enter**. You have just re-created the items from your Navigate menu, but this time the Menu Designer window looks a little different, as shown in Figure 9.6.

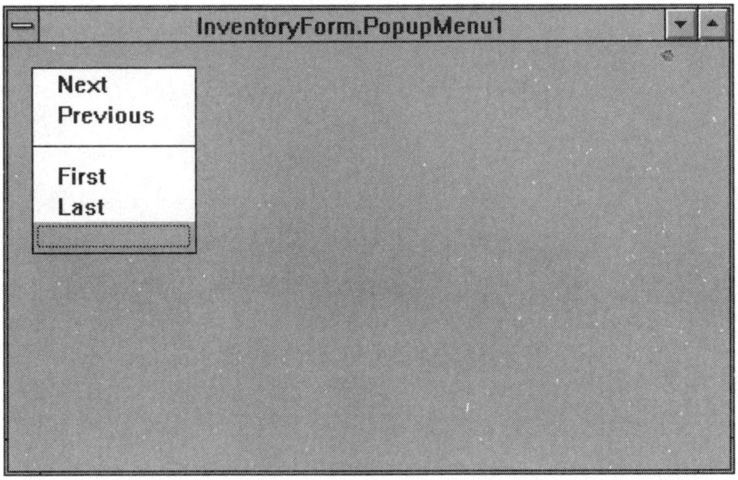

Figure 9.6 *The Navigate menu as a pop-up*

Unlike the menus that attach to menu bars, pop-up menus usually contain a single list of options. Occasionally, one or more options might lead to a submenu, and you can create submenus by using the SpeedMenu, which also works when designing pop-up menus.

That's all there is to creating a pop-up menu. Now let's get back to coding some events. Close the Menu Designer window, select the **PopupMenu** component on InventoryForm, and press the **Delete** key to remove it from the form.

Coding Events for Menu Items

Until now you have used the DBNavigator to work with the Inventory table. It provided the means for moving from record to record, as well as editing or deleting existing records and adding new ones. Now that you've created the menu items, you can write some simple code that will let you do all those same things without the Navigator. In fact, when your done, you can change the DBNavigator's Visible property to **False** if you want to use the menus exclusively.

In previous chapters I talked about methods, those action words that you add on to the end of a component name, separated only by a period. They look just like properties, only instead of property values they represent actions, so they are methods. You used the **Show** and **Hide** methods already. Now I'm going to introduce you to a some methods you can use with the table component, namely: Insert, Delete, Cancel, Refresh, Next, Prior, First, and Last. Sound familiar?

The first thing you need to do is create an OnClick event for each menu item. Click once on the **Inventory menu title** so that you can see the menu's items. Then, when you click once on the **Add Record** menu item, Delphi will create an AddRecord1Click procedure for you and will bring up the code window so that you can enter the necessary program code. All you need is a single line, as follows:

```
procedure TInventoryForm.AddRecord1Click(Sender:
TObject);
begin
ITable.Insert
end;
```

Now return to the form window and create the next event by selecting the **Delete Record** item from the Inventory menu. When the code window appears, insert a line of code containing the table name and the method needed. (The only method that does not match its corresponding menu item exactly is the Prior method that you will use for the Previous menu item.)

Repeat this process until you have coded all eight procedures for the Inventory and Navigate menus. The code for each of the remaining seven procedures is as follows:

```
procedure
TInventoryForm.DeleteRecord1Click(Sender:
TObject);
begin
ITable.Delete
end;

procedure
TInventoryForm.CancelChange1Click(Sender:
TObject);
begin
ITable.Cancel
end;

procedure TInventoryForm.Refresh1Click(Sender:
TObject);
begin
ITable.Refresh
end;

procedure TInventoryForm.Next1Click(Sender:
TObject);
begin
ITable.Next
end;

procedure TInventoryForm.Previous1Click(Sender:
TObject);
```

```
begin
ITable.Prior
end;

procedure TInventoryForm.First1Click(Sender:
TObject);
begin
ITable.First
end;

procedure TInventoryForm.Last1Click(Sender:
TObject);
begin
ITable.Last
end;
```

Finding What You're Looking for

When your table only has a couple of records in it, finding the record you need isn't very hard, you can just move from one record to the next, and in less than a moment you'll have found the one you wanted—or you'll know that the record doesn't exist. Of course, when you have lots of records in a table, it's much easier, and quicker, to let the program do the searching for you.

You'll use the **SetKey**, **GoToKey**, and **GoToNearest** methods. Before you get to the coding, you'll need to add a plain edit component and a plain label component to InventoryForm (use the settings in Table 9.2), and then create OnClick events for the Find Product and Find Registration items on the Search menu.

Table 9.2 *Property Settings for InventoryForm's New Edit Component*

	Property	Value
Edit1	Height	25
	Left	440
	Name	FindMeEdit
	Text	(blank)
	Top	320
	Width	185
Label	Alignment	taCenter
	Caption	Search For
	+Font	
	Color	clNavy
	Height	16
	Left	480
	Name	FindMeLabel
	Top	296
	Width	89

Click on the **Product** item from the Find menu to bring up the code window showing the Product1Click event. This procedure is going to need three lines of code. The first line uses the **SetKey** method to tell Delphi that you want to conduct a search. The second line of code assigns the search string to the Table's Fields property. And the third line of code tells Delphi to look at the primary key of each record and move to the first record it finds where the search string matches even a partial key.

The primary key for the Invntory table is a composite of Product + Version Number + Date Purchased. But it is unlikely that you would have all that information at hand when you want to find a record. That's why you're going to use the **GoToNearest** method for this procedure.

GoToNearest allows you to search for matches to a partial key. When the application is running, the user types the search string into the edit box under the Search For label, and then selects the Find Product item from the Search menu. The procedure code is as follows:

```
procedure TInventoryForm.Product1Click(Sender:
TObject);
begin
ITable.SetKey;
ITable.Fields[0].AsString := FindMeEdit.Text;
ITable.GoToNearest
end;
```

Did you notice the [0] following the Fields property in the second line of code? When you number the fields in a table, you always start with 0, so that 0 refers to the first field in the table.

N O T E

The code for the Find Registration menu item is going to be just a little different. In the last chapter you created a RegNum secondary index, and now it's time to use it. The table component has an IndexName property that you haven't used yet. When the IndexName property remains blank, the table automatically uses the primary index. But in order to use a secondary index, you need to assign the secondary index name to that property.

There's just one catch. You can't assign a value to a Table's IndexName property while the table is open. That means you'll have to close the table, assign the value, and then reopen the table again. It's not difficult. Close and Open are Table methods, and you already know how to assign a value to a property in runtime. And that will take care of the first three lines of code. The last three lines of code are almost identical to the code from the Find Product procedure. The only difference is that the field number is now 4 instead of 0 (Registration Number is the fifth field in the Invntory table), and you can use the **GoToKey** method this time, because the search text should be a match with the whole secondary index. The code for the TInventoryForm.Registration1Click procedure is as follows:

```
procedure
TInventoryForm.Registration1Click(Sender:
TObject);
begin
ITable.Close;
ITable.IndexName := 'RegNum';
ITable.Open;
ITable.SetKey;
ITable.Fields[4].AsString := FindMeEdit.Text;
ITable.GoToKey
end;
```

When you're done, your InventoryForm should look like Figure 9.7. Save your project and test it out.

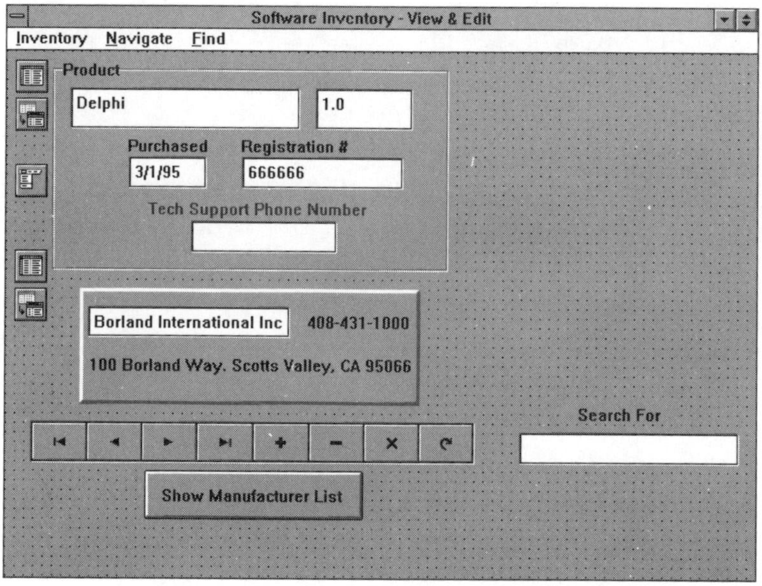

Figure 9.7 *InventoryForm with menus and Search For edit box*

Summary

◆ Delphi supports two types of menus: those that drop down from menu bars, and menus that pop up on a mouse click. You use the MainMenu component to create the menu bar type of menus, and the PopupMenu component to create pop-up menus.

◆ Once placed on a form, double-clicking on one of the menu components brings up the Menu Designer window used to define each menu title and menu item. You can create accelerator keys by placing an ampersand in front of the letter to be used with the Alt key. This letter will automatically appear underlined on the menu list.

◆ For each menu title or menu item you define, Delphi automatically creates a component that is then accessible through the Object Inspector. F-keys and other key combinations may also be defined for a menu item. These are called shortcuts, and ShortCut is one of the properties for a menu item. Use the Object Inspector to set the ShortCut value.

◆ You can use the SpeedMenu when working in the Menu Designer window. SpeedMenu options include Insert and Delete, each of which relate directly to individual menu items. The Create Submenu option is used to define nested menus. Other SpeedMenu options allow you to use preexisting menus and to insert menu templates, as well as create and delete menu templates.

◆ While in the Menu Designer window, you can rearrange the sequence of menus and menu items simply by dragging-and-dropping.

◆ Insert, Delete, Cancel, Refresh, Next, Prior, First, and Last are the Table methods that correspond not only to two of the Invntory application's menus, but also to the DBNavigator used in the last chapter.

◆ Code for menu items is placed inside the item's Click event handler. When you click on the menu item during the design phase, Delphi creates the event handler, leaving you to fill in the code between the procedure's `begin` and `end` lines.

◆ SetKey, GoToKey, and GoToNearest are three Table methods used for searching. The SetKey notifies Delphi that you wish to conduct a search. **GoToKey** is used when your search string is expected to match an index, either primary or secondary. GoToNearest, on the other hand, allows you to find matches to a partial key or index.

◆ In order to conduct a search, the search string must be assigned to the Table's Fields property. This should be done after the SetKey statement so that Delphi does not think you are trying to assign a value to a field in the table.

◆ In order to search on a secondary index instead of the primary key, you have to change the value of the Table's IndexName property. This can be done with a simple assignment statement, but it cannot be done while the table in question is open. Use the Close method to close the table, then set the **IndexName** property, and finally use the Open method to reopen the table. After that, you can conduct the search using the secondary index.

In the Next Chapter

In the next chapter you'll learn how to use ReportSmith and you'll create a report using data from the Invntory table, and some address labels using the data from the Manufact table. Then you'll use the DBReport component on a form to display a report. And finally, you get to examine a DBQuery component.

CHAPTER 10

Queries and Reports

- ◆ Examining report types and styles in ReportSmith
- ◆ Identifying tables for use in a report
- ◆ Specifying report sort sequences
- ◆ Watching ReportSmith build your SQL statements automatically
- ◆ Defining report variables for user input
- ◆ Editing reports in ReportSmith
- ◆ Creating custom report styles in ReportSmith
- ◆ Running a ReportSmith report from a Delphi application
- ◆ Using the Query component
- ◆ Building SQL statements using Delphi's String List Editor

In this chapter you'll learn the basics of using ReportSmith, and you'll create a report using data from the Manufact table. Then you'll use the DBReport component in Delphi to run a report created in ReportSmith. And finally, you get to examine Delphi's DBQuery component.

Creating Reports with ReportSmith

Working with live data is what visual programming is all about. You've been working with live data from the sample tables while designing application interfaces, and ReportSmith provides the same advantages.

When you open ReportSmith, whether by launching it from the Windows desktop or selecting it from Delphi's Tools menu, an Open Report dialog box appears. You're going to be creating a new report, so click on **Cancel** to make it go away. Your screen should now look Figure 10.1. It looks a bit like a word processor with several menus and a double-row Speedbar. Rather than give you an item-by-item name and description of each menu item and glyph, you're going to jump right in and create a report.

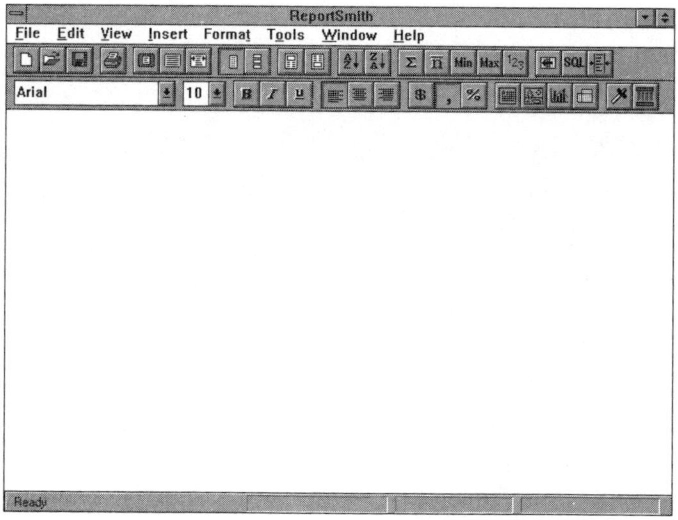

Figure 10.1 The ReportSmith main window

NOTE

ReportSmith has fly-by help, so all you have to do is hold your mouse over a glyph for a moment and look at the status bar in the lower-left corner of your screen for a hint.

You'll find that arranging the sequence of columns is a simple drag-and-drop operation, and you can change the sort sequence as easily as clicking on the title of the column by which you want to sort your data. But when it comes to style, you don't have to start from scratch each time you want to create a report. Instead you can select from a variety of predesigned report styles. Design templates can provide a sense of consistency and create an identifiable look and feel to your report communications. You can choose an existing system style or create your own design template.

Report Types and Styles

To begin, select **New...** from the File menu, and the Create A New Report dialog box appears allowing you to select one of four report types: **Columnar**, **Crosstab**, **Form**, or **Label** (see Figure 10.2). Each type has several predefined System Styles. **Columnar** is already selected, so go ahead and click on the **Style...** button on the right to bring up the New Report Style dialog box. Now you have the opportunity to select from the eight different predefined system styles (or any custom styles that may have been defined) that apply to the Columnar type.

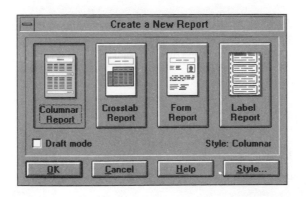

Figure 10.2 *Choose one of four report types from the Create A New Report dialog box*

When you highlight a style from the Styles list, a sample of that style is displayed on the right of the dialog box (see Figure 10.3). For example, a Columnar report type has a plain Columnar system style. But you can select the **Classic** system style to give it a more elegant look, or one of the three Colorful system styles to jazz it up, or even the Ruled system style to make it easier to read across the rows.

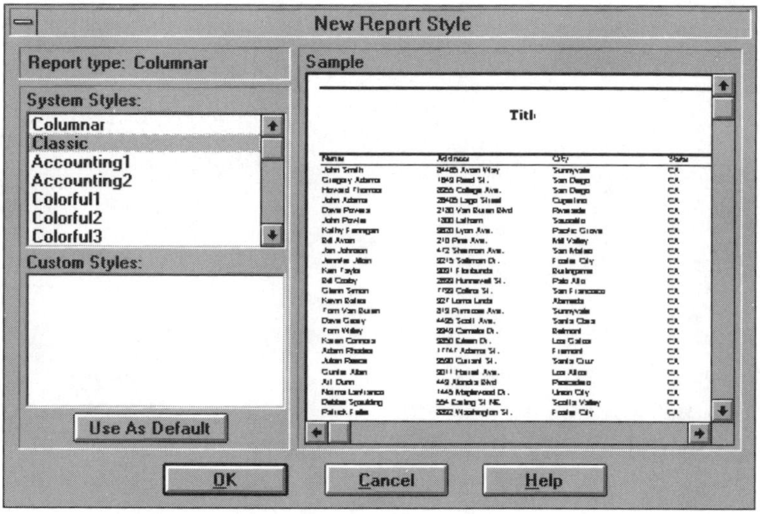

Figure 10.3 *Use the New Report Style dialog box to sample and select a style for your new report*

Take a moment to look at some of the system styles available for each of the three report types. Then select **Classic** and click on **OK**. Finally, click on **OK** once more, this time in the Create A New Report dialog box.

Selecting Tables and Other Settings

After a moment, the Report Query—Tables dialog box appears, as shown in Figure 10.4. This is where you specify the table(s) you want to use in the report. Click on **Add Table...**, and when the Select Table To Be Added dialog box appears (shown in Figure 10.5), select **MANUFACT.DB** and click on **OK**.

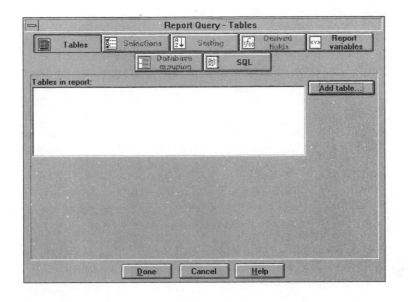

Figure 10.4 *ReportSmith's Report Query —Tables dialog box shows the table(s) selected for use in the report and provides buttons that allow you to move onto other settings such as field selection and sort sequence*

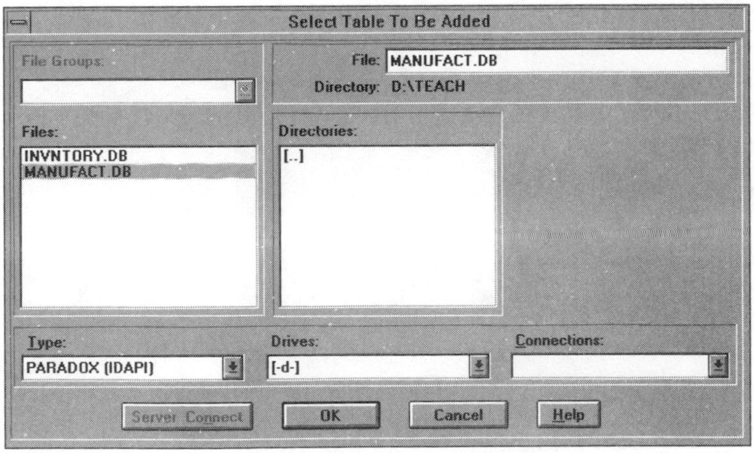

Figure 10.5 *Select a table for use in your report from the Select Table To Be Added dialog box*

If your DB files aren't showing in the Files list, make sure the Type box in the lower-left corner is set to **Paradox (IDAPI)**, and the directory is the \Teach subdirectory.

N O T E

When the Report Query—Tables dialog box reappears, its appearance will have changed. The **Manufact.db** file should be listed in the box labeled Tables in Report, and an alias is automatically assigned as shown in Figure 10.6

```
┌─────────────────────────────────────────────────────────────┐
│ ─                   Report Query - Tables                    │
├─────────────────────────────────────────────────────────────┤
│ [▦] Tables  [▤] Selections  [↓] Sorting  [∫] Derived  [<v>] Report │
│                                              fields         variables │
│              [▤] Database      [▦] SQL                      │
│                   grouping                                   │
│  Tables in report:              Alias:                      │
│  [PARADOX] D:\TEACH;MANUFACT.DB  MANUFACTxDB    [Add table...] │
│                                                [Replace table...]│
│                                                [Remove table]  │
│                                                [Table columns...]│
│       [Assign new alias →] MANUFACTxDB                      │
│  Table links:                                               │
│                                                [Edit link...] │
│                                                [Add new link...]│
│                                                [Remove link]  │
│                                                             │
│          [Done]     [Cancel]     [Help]                     │
└─────────────────────────────────────────────────────────────┘
```

Figure 10.6 *The Report Query—Tables dialog box after adding the Manufact table*

In order to specify the sort sequence, click on the **Sorting** button. The Report Table—Sorting dialog box appears listing the Report Fields on the bottom, and the fields to be used in the sort sequence at the top. To specify a sort field, highlight the field name in the Report Fields list and click on the **Insert Into Sort List** button on the right. Select the **Manufacturer** and **Location Number** fields so that your screen looks like Figure 10.7. The sequence in which you select the sort fields is the sequence in which ReportSmith will handle the sort—in this case, first by

Manufacturer name, and then within that by Location Number. If you select **Location Number** first, ReportSmith will sort the Location Numbers first, and then sort by Manufacturer within that category. If you make a mistake, or change your mind, you can always highlight a field and use the **Remove From Sort List** button.

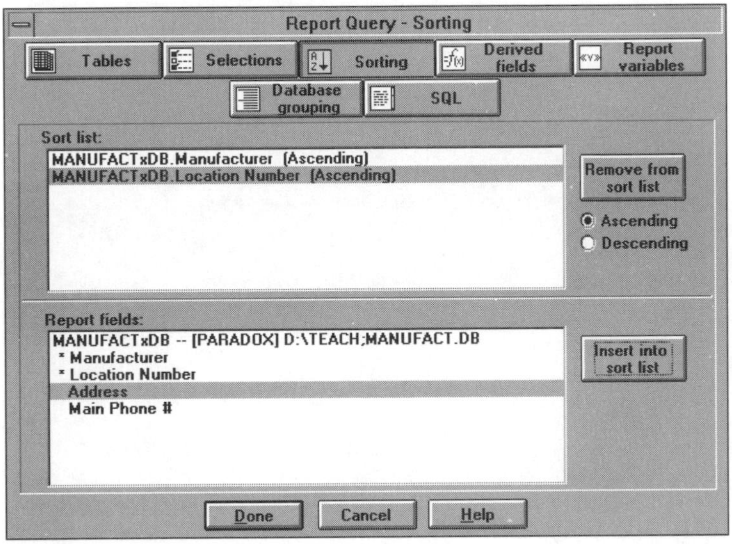

Figure 10.7 *Report Query—The Sorting dialog box after selecting the Manufacturer and Location Number fields for the sort sequence*

As you define your report, ReportSmith is automatically building an SQL statement. SQL (Structured Query Language) is the programming statement that tells ReportSmith what data you want from the table. Click on the **SQL** button at the top of the Report Query—Sorting dialog box (or another Report Query dialog box if you've been moving around on your own). Figure 10.8 shows the SQL statement built thus far.

The structure of these statements is always the same. An SQL statement begins by telling the program to select the fields named, then specifies the table in which those fields are located, and requests that the records be sorted by the designated fields. SQL statements can also be much more complex, adding criteria that determines which records from the table should be included. For example, in a table that contains names, addresses, and phone numbers, you might want to select only those records with phone numbers that begin with the 212 area code.

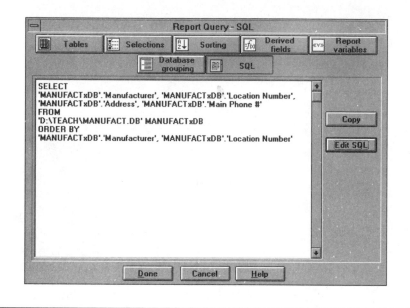

Figure 10.8 *Use the Report Query—SQL dialog box to view, copy, or edit SQL statements*

As you can see from the statement displayed in the Report Query—SQL dialog box (Figure 10.8), the keywords are SELECT, FROM, and ORDER BY. If you were specifying conditions, the statement would continue with the keyword WHERE, and an expression such as PhoneNumber ≥ 212.

The conditions for selecting records are often based on values derived from user input at the time the report is run. To obtain user input, you need to define a variable in which to store the value. To set up one or more variables, use the Report Query—Report Variables dialog box. After naming the variable and specifying its data type, you can enter the prompt you wish to display. Then you must select a type of entry—**Type-In**, **Choose From A List**, **Choose From A Table**, or **Choose Between Two Values**— and depending on your choice, you may have to define further elements such as the items to be shown on the list. Figure 10.9 shows the Report

Query—Report Variables dialog box with some sample settings. Based on the defined variables, ReportSmith will generate the appropriate dialog box and display it whenever you run the report.

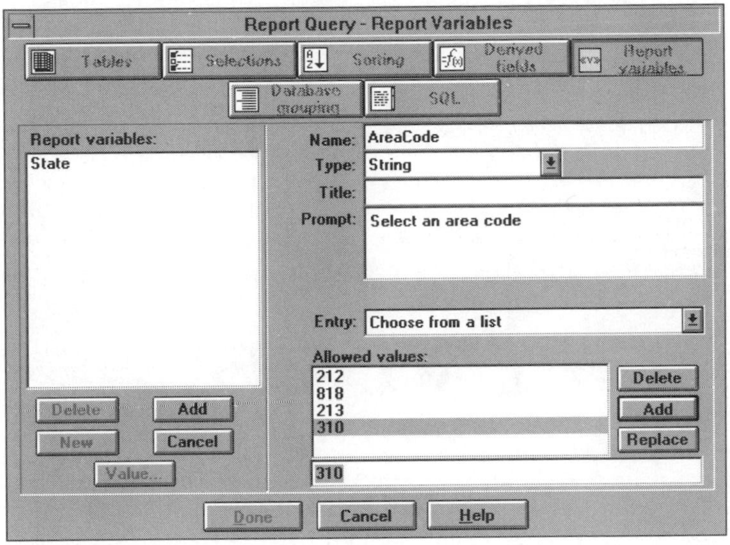

Figure 10.9 *Report Query—Report Variables dialog box with some sample settings*

There's not really much more we can do to a report using the Manufact table, so click on the **Done** button at the bottom of the Report Query dialog box and take a look at the report you created.

Formatting and Editing

Your ReportSmith window should look like Figure 10.10. First let's look at the sequence of the records. The report is in alphabetical sequence by Manufacturer name, not because that is the primary key for the table, but because that's the sequence you specified in the Report Query—Sorting dialog box a moment ago. I didn't mention it then, but when you selected the **Manufacturer** field as the sort field, you had a choice between **Ascending** and **Descending**. The default is **Ascending** and that's what you got.

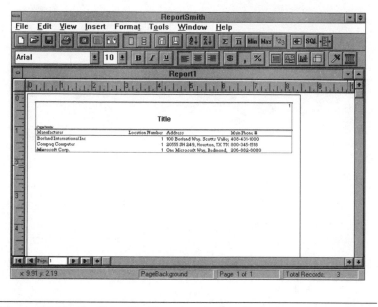

Figure 10.10 *The ReportSmith main window displaying your new report*

It is most common to sort text fields in an ascending (i.e., alphabetical) sequence, but suppose now that you're looking at the report with live data, you want to reverse the sequence. It's almost too easy; just click on the column and use the descending speedbutton (the glyph below the Windows menu showing ZA with a down arrow). Of course, you could select **Sorting...** from the Tools menu. That brings up the Sorting dialog box again, and you can alter the sequence there as well.

Now let's consider some formatting issues. Notice how Location Number column takes up a lot of space? You can change that. If you click on the **column heading**, you will see an outline around the field with two handles (little squares) at the right corners. If you place your mouse over the right edge, your cursor changes so that you may resize the column; click and drag to the desired size.

When you make the Location Number column smaller, you'll find that there isn't enough room for the column heading. If you want to leave the column small, you should edit the heading. To edit, select the heading again, and when the outline appears, double-click on it. This places an I-beam cursor inside the heading box so that you can edit the contents. Delete the word Number.

Then you might decide that all of the column headings would look better if they were centered. Select each **column heading** and use the **Text Alignment** option from the Format menu (or use the **alignment glyphs** on the Speedbar) to center the text. So far, so good, but look at the data in the Location column. It was automatically right-justified because that's how the Classic style for Columnar reports defines all number fields. In order to center the data in that column, all you have to do is click on the **column** and align the text.

When you're all done, select **Save** from the File menu. Name the report MANUS.RPT and be sure to save it in the \Teach subdirectory.

Creating Custom Styles

If you are planning to produce lots of reports and can't find a system style that you want to use without making several changes, it would be better to define your own style. That way you wouldn't have to make adjustments each and every time. Select **Report Styles...** from the Format menu to bring up the Report Styles dialog box. It looks almost exactly like the New Report Style dialog box (shown earlier in Figure 10.3), but it has different buttons at the bottom, as shown in Figure 10.11.

To create your own custom style, start by clicking on the **New...** button. When the Save As dialog box appears, give your custom style a name (perhaps Mystyle) and click **OK**. Once the name appears in the Custom Styles section, the Edit... button becomes available.

You cannot edit a system style, but you can automatically copy all of its settings into your custom style and then make your changes there.

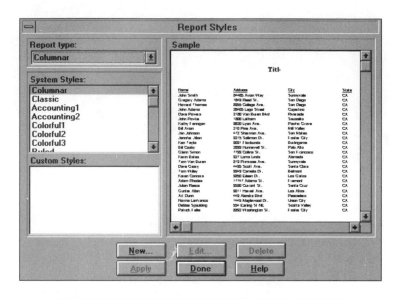

Figure 10.11 *The Report Styles dialog box is where you begin to create or edit your own custom report styles*

When you click on **Edit...**, the Edit Report Style dialog box appears as shown in Figure 10.12. The Object section contains a list of the various types of fields such as Numeric, Character, Date, and Summary. Other object types include labels, report and page headers and footers, titles, pictures, graphs, and even shapes.

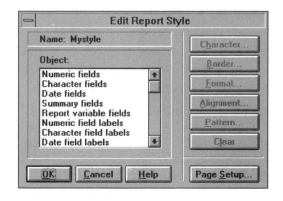

Figure 10.12 *The Edit Report Style dialog box as it first appears*

As you highlight each object, those buttons on the right that are applicable to that object type become available. The Character, Border, and Alignment buttons bring up dialog boxes that allow you to set font, border, and alignment characteristics, just as you would in a word processing program. Font name (Roman, Times, Courier, etc.), style (italic, for example), color, and size are some of the font characteristics you can set. Border settings include such things as line type, style, thickness, and shadow. Alignment options are Left, Center, or Right.

The Format button brings up the Format Field dialog box, the contents of which vary depending on what type of object you select in the Report Style dialog box. For example, when **Numeric**, **Summary**, or **Report Variable Fields** is selected, the Format dialog box provides format codes that may be applied to numeric data representing plain numbers, currency, percentage, or scientific data.

When **Date**, **Print Date**, **Print Time**, or **Print Date/Time** is selected, the Format Field dialog box changes to provide various date and time formats from which to choose. As you know from experiments in the database chapters, the value in a date field uses slashes, and you can see this in the Format Field dialog box. The lower panel always displays data as seen by Delphi. The formatted data shows how that data will look using the currently highlighted format code shown in Figure 10.13.

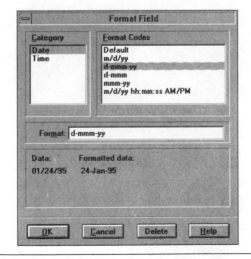

Figure 10.13 *The Format Field dialog box for a Date or Time object*

The last button, Page Setup, brings up the dialog box shown in Figure 10.14, where you can set your report margins, paper size and orientation, and label settings if applicable. From that dialog box you can bring up the Wallpaper dialog box shown in Figure 10.15 that allows you to select a bitmap file to be placed behind the report. You can treat the bitmap like wallpaper, or use it to place a corporate logo. In addition to the standard Center and Tile choices, you have the option of setting horizontal and vertical alignment, and deciding whether or not you want the bitmap to be printed along with the report.

So now that you have designed a report, what can you do with it besides run it in ReportSmith? How about using it in a Delphi application?

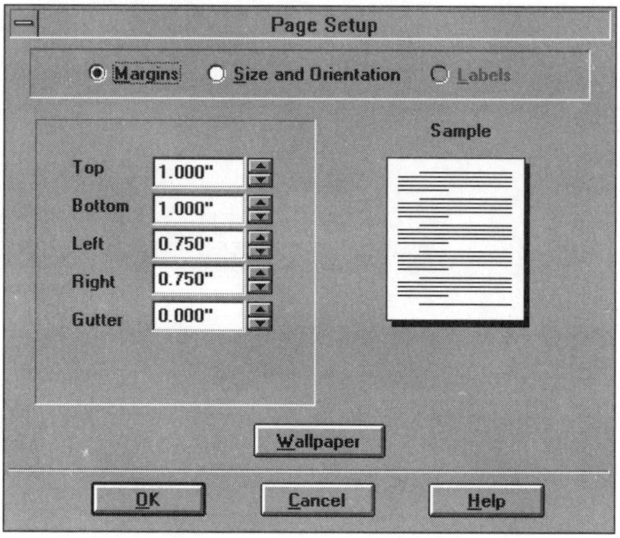

Figure 10.14 The Page Setup dialog box used when defining report styles

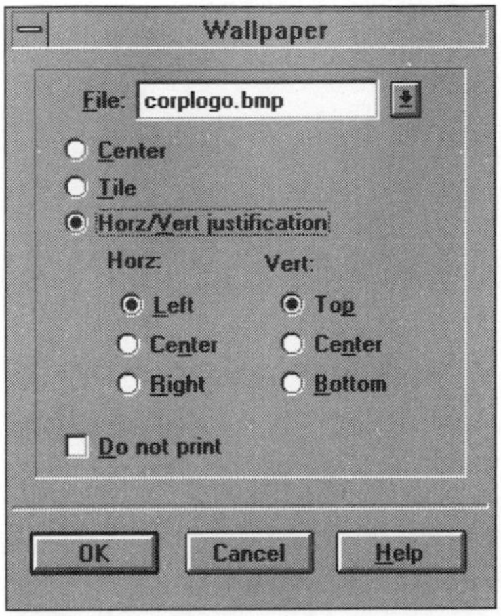

Figure 10.15 *When defining report styles, use the*
Wallpaper dialog box to place a bitmap file behind a report

Using the Delphi Report Component

Place a report component on the form, and let's take a look at its properties. The AutoUnload property relates to the ReportSmith run-time engine. In order to see a ReportSmith report inside a Delphi application, the run-time engine must be loaded into memory. When AutoUnload is set to **True**, Delphi unloads the engine from memory when the report is finished running. If AutoUnload is set to *False*, then the runtime engine continues to run in memory. Leaving it in memory does let you rerun the report more quickly, but it also means that you'll have to write code, using the CloseApplication method, to close it when you're done.

If you want to limit the number of records used in your report, use MaxRecords. This is especially useful when designing your application and a handful of records will do. StartPage, EndPage, and PrintCopies all relate to the printing of a report. The default settings specify starting on page 1 and printing one copy of the entire report (providing it's 999 or fewer pages).

When you create a report in the ReportSmith program, you have an opportunity to define variables to hold user input. Based on your specifications, ReportSmith generates the appropriate dialog box. By passing the variable values in the InitialValues property, you can prevent the dialog box from appearing when you run the report from a Delphi application.

Set the **ReportDir** property to the directory where the report is stored, and set **ReportName** to the name of the report file. Then double-click on the **component** to launch the ReportSmith application. An Open Report dialog box appears. If you have already set the **ReportName** property, just click on **Cancel**, otherwise use the dialog box to select the report you wish to use. The ReportSmith application then automatically minimizes itself, leaving you with an icon at the bottom of your screen. To show the report, click on that minimized icon.

Selecting Records with the TQuery Component

In Chapter 9 you used the DataSet Designer to select which fields you wanted to display in the DBGrid component. But that did not provide you with any way to select which records you wanted to see. If you do not wish to access all of the records in a particular database table, you can create your own dataset by querying the database table. While linguistically the word query means question, a database query is a request to see records that match certain conditions, for example all records where LastName = Jones, or all records where Salary > 40,000.

The query component is used instead of the table component, but the procedure for its use is just the same. It has most of the same properties, including the DatabaseName, and must be used in conjunction with a

DataSource component in order to connect to Data Control components. The big difference, of course, is in its SQL property, the value of which tells Delphi which fields and records to include in the dataset.

SQL stands for structured query language, and you saw how queries are constructed earlier in this chapter when I discussed SQL statements in ReportSmith. Place a query component on a blank form. Looking at the Object Inspector, you'll notice that the query component does not have a TableName property. That's because the SQL statement contains the name of the database table being queried.

You can type the SQL statement directly in the Object Inspector, or if you prefer, you can click on the **ellipsis** to the right of the value column to bring up the String List Editor dialog box. The SQL statements typed into Delphi's String List Editor are structurally the same in terms of sequence, but much simpler than the one you saw in ReportSmith. For this example you're going to use the Vendors table from the DBDEMOS database that shipped with Delphi. Set the query component's DatabaseName property to DBDEMOS, then bring up the String List Editor and type in the following text:

```
SELECT
VendorName, City, State
FROM
Vendors
ORDER BY
State
```

When you're done, your String Editor dialog box should look like Figure 10.16. If you want to save the statement as a TXT file so that you can use it again sometime, click on the **Save...** button. When you're done, click on **OK** to return to setting properties and designing your form.

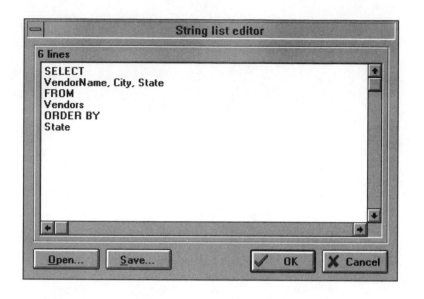

Figure 10.16 *An SQL statement as shown inside Delphi's String List Editor dialog box*

If you are working with complex queries, you might want to use the Visual Query Builder to help you connect to a database and build your statement interactively. You can access the Query Builder by double-clicking on the **query** component on your form.

Working with the query component is much the same as the table component. The DataSet Designer that you used in Chapter 9 with the table component can also be used with the query component. If you use it to select fields, you'll find that the only available fields are those fields that were specified in the SQL statement.

You need a DataSource component to act as a conduit between the query component and your Data Control components. So if you haven't done so already, add a DataSource component, and set its DataSet property to **Query1**. Then add a DBGrid component, and set its DataSource property to **DataSource1**. Finally, go back to the query component and set its Active property to **True**. Now you can see the results of the SQL statement.

The SQL statement called for a display of three fields (VendorName, City, and State) and requested that the records be sorted by state. At first glance it may look as though the vendors data is still sorted alphabetically by VendorName. But if you maximize your form window and enlarge DBGrid1 (horizontally so that you can see all three fields, and vertically to display several more records at a time), you'll find that the data is indeed sorted by state, and then subsorted by VendorName.

Summary

◆ ReportSmith may be launched from an icon on your windows desktop, or from the Tools menu inside Delphi.

◆ To create a new report, begin by selecting **New** from the File menu, choosing one of the four report types from the Create A New Report dialog box, and picking a report style from the New Report Style dialog box.

◆ Specify your report data characteristics using one or more of the seven different Report Query dialog boxes. Use **Tables** to add tables to the report as well as to define links between tables. Sequence the data in a report by selecting fields in the Sorting dialog box. The SQL dialog box allows you to view, copy, or edit the statements that ReportSmith has created based on your selections. If your report depends on user input, use the Report Variables dialog box to define variables in which to store their input.

◆ SQL statements have a basic structure. The simplest form uses only two clauses: First is the SELECT clause that lists the requested data fields, and second is the FROM clause that names the table containing those fields. If you want the records sorted, the next clause begins with the words ORDERED BY and is followed by a list of the field or fields to be sorted. Further conditions can then be added with a WHERE clause.

◆ ReportSmith allows you to make constant alterations to the report even after it is displayed in the main window. You can select elements of the report, such as a column heading, simply by clicking on them. You can edit the headings, change the alignment of the heading and/or data in the columns, alter the sort sequence, resize the column widths, rearrange the sequence of the columns—almost anything. You can also return to the various dialog boxes by selecting them from the menus.

◆ To create your own report styles in ReportSmith, select **Report Styles** from the Format menu. Once you name your new style you can bring up the Edit Report Style dialog box and define the character, border, format, alignment, and pattern styles for all types of objects including Numeric, Character, Date, Summary, and Chart fields.

◆ The Page Setup button on the Edit Report Style dialog box brings up a dialog box to set the margins, paper size, and other print-related items. You can even select a **bitmap file** (such as a corporate logo) to be placed behind a report and indicate where you want it placed and whether or not it should be printed along with the report.

◆ DBReport is the Delphi Data Access component that allows you to run an existing report from a Delphi application. Set the ReportName and ReportDir properties to the name of the report and the directory in which the report file can be found.

◆ DBReport's AutoUnload property indicates whether or not the ReportSmith engine remains in memory after the report is displayed. The MaxRecords property allows you to limit the number of records being used. StartPage, EndPage, and PrintCopies all relate to the printing of a report.

◆ If user input is required to run the report, you can use the Initial-Values property to pass the variable values to the report and thus bypass the user input dialog box that would otherwise appear.

◆ Double-click on the **DBReport** component to launch the Report-Smith engine. After displaying an Open Report dialog box, ReportSmith automatically minimizes itself. To restore, click on the **icon** at the bottom of your screen.

◆ You can use a query component in lieu of a table component if you wish to select specific records and fields from a table. The records and fields selected are a result of the SQL statement that is the value of the SQL property. You may type the SQL statement directly into the Object Inspector, or you can use Delphi's String List Editor.

◆ The query component must be used in conjunction with a DataSource component that serves as the conduit between the table data and any Data Control components such as DBGrid.

In the Next Chapter

In Chapter 11 you'll learn about types of programming errors, the process of debugging. I'll show you some of the tools that are available to assist you, and I'll close with a brief discussion of error handling.

Debugging and Error Handling

- ◆ Defining compiler and runtime errors
- ◆ Setting project options on the compiler page
- ◆ Running To Cursor
- ◆ Stepping Over and Tracing Into procedures
- ◆ Creating Breakpoints and Watch Expressions
- ◆ Setting Breakpoint Conditions and Pass Counts
- ◆ Monitoring the Watch List, Breakpoint List, and Call Stack windows

Types of Errors

A compiler error is the result of invalid code. You experienced your first compiler error in Chapter 3, when you tried to show a form that was not defined in that unit. You've probably experienced a few more since then, if you've mistyped a reserved word or forgotten a semicolon. And you'll remember, probably gratefully, that when you get a compiler error, the Code Editor appears with the cursor miraculously placed in the offending line of code. Whenever you run your application from inside the Delphi program, Delphi compiles your code first, and then runs the application, providing no compiler errors are found.

 If you want to check for compiler errors without running the application, you can use the **Syntax Check** option (it's on the Compile menu) to check for compiler errors.

N O T E

Run-time errors are not quite as considerate. You'll get an error message, but no other help—until you ask for it, that is. You can encounter two kinds of run-time errors. The first type occurs when the code is valid (i.e., no compiler errors), but executing the code causes a problem. For example, trying to open a file that cannot be found. The open statement might be correct, but the file isn't there, and the inability to successfully execute the command causes an error.

The second type of run-time error is an error in logic. The code is valid and can be executed without error, but the intended outcome or results don't happen. For example, in Chapter 6 you created two point arrays to save the beginning and ending coordinates of all of the lines drawn in the modified Scribble program so that Delphi could redraw the lines whenever Windows invoked a FormPaint event. You created a variable called r, and in the FormPaint event you set the value of **r** to **0** before starting the Repeat..Until loop. The loop was to stop when **r** was greater than the number of lines originally drawn. If you had set the value of **r** to **1**, however, the last line originally drawn would never get redrawn in the FormPaint routine.

Debugging

The key to debugging run-time errors is to pinpoint where the error occurs, and then check out what's happening. In order to figure out what's happening you'll need to know the *state of the program* at any given moment. What do I mean by state of the program? You'll want to know which function or procedure is being executed at any given time (and perhaps more specifically, exactly which line), and you'll want to know the values of the various variables and parameters. You may also need to know how many times a particular line or procedure has been executed, or if a particular condition has occurred.

Get Set

In order to use the Integrated Debugger tools, Delphi has to work with the machine code that is generated by the Delphi program compiler. Your program code (also known as source code) is written in a programming language called Object Pascal, but when Delphi compiles your program, your source code is translated into machine language. (You didn't really think that your computer was fluent in Pascal, did you?)

Now in order for the debugging tools to work, Delphi has to be able to match up the machine code with your source code. Delphi does this for you, automatically, providing the settings are right. Check the Compiler page of the Project Options dialog box (select **Options** from the Project menu) and make sure that the check boxes for the three Debugging items (Debug Information, Local Symbols, and Symbol Info) are all checked.

A programmer in the process of debugging an application will typically have several windows open at once, as shown in Figure 11.1. In addition to the window in which the application is running, and the Unit Code window, you'll want to monitor any watch expressions and breakpoints you have set up in the Watch List and Breakpoint List windows. You will also find it useful to keep an eye on the Call Stack window to track the procedures being executed. The View menu contains options to show the Breakpoints, Call Stack, and Watches windows.

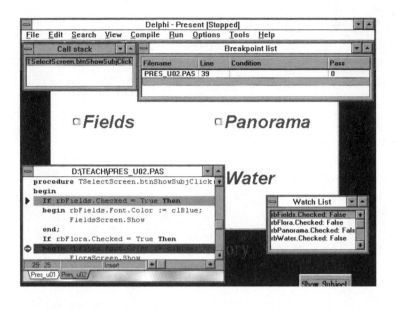

Figure 11.1 *The Present application paused during a run with the Watch List, Breakpoint List, Call Stack, and Code Editor windows displayed, and portions of the SelectScreen visible in the background*

Run to Cursor

If you execute one line of code at a time, you will ultimately arrive at the line that is causing an error. One way to begin narrowing down the possibilities is to try the **Run To Cursor** option. Place the cursor in a line of code before but near to where you think the problem is. For example, if your application uses several forms (like the Present sample application) and you think that the first two forms will work okay, but you sometimes crash while using Form3, you might place the cursor in the beginning of Form3. Delphi will run at full speed until it reaches the cursor (providing it doesn't crash earlier and prove your assumption wrong).

When Delphi reaches the cursor, it pauses, highlights a code line and marks it with an arrow in your Code Editor window as shown in Figure 11.2. The highlighted line is referred to as the execution point, and it is the next line that Delphi plans to execute—depending, that is, on what you do next. Your might step through the code using Step Over or Trace Into. You could also reposition the cursor and Run To Cursor again. Or you might just Run, in which case the program would either run successfully to the end (no bugs), run until it reaches a Breakpoint, or crashes.

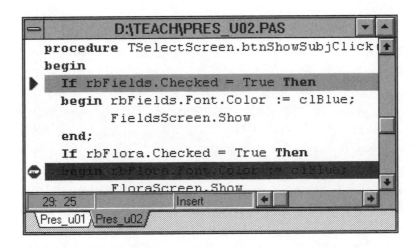

Figure 11.2 *A Code Editor window during a debugging session.*
The line with the arrow on the left is an exception point.
The line with the stop sign symbol on the left is a breakpoint.

Step through Code

If you haven't crashed yet you might want to step through the code, one line at a time. After each line, Delphi pauses and once again you can check out the state of the program by checking the value of variables in the Watch List window and so on.

If the next line to execute is a call to a specific routine, and you believe that the routine is clean, you should use the **Step Over** option. Delphi will execute the call to that routine, running whatever command lines it contains without pausing at each line, and then return to pause at the next line following the call. If on the other hand you think that the routine being called might contain the line causing an error, you should use the **Trace Into** option. Delphi will execute the call to that routine, pausing for your direction at each command line.

When you hit a line that crashes your program, you know that you've found the location of a program bug. Of course, stepping can be quite tedious, especially if you have lots of statements. One alternative is to set **breakpoints**.

Establish Breakpoints

A breakpoint is a line of code at which the program pauses. It's a little bit like running to the cursor, only you can set several breakpoints before you begin the run. Also, you have some additional options: *conditions* and *pass counts*. If you set a condition for a particular line of code, Delphi checks to see if the condition is true. If so, the breakpoint is honored and the program pauses. If the breakpoint condition is not met, the program continues executing.

Pass Count is a decremental variable. You set a number value, and each time the line is executed, Delphi decreases the value of Pass Count by 1. For example, if you set **Pass Count** equal to **10**, then the breakpoint will take effect on the tenth occurrence (when Pass Count equals **1**). But you have to be careful. If you want the breakpoint to take effect after the line has been executed ten times, then you must set the **Pass Count** to **11** and the program will pause when it reaches (not executes) that line for the 11th time.

Pass Count is useful for checking out loops. If a loop is supposed to execute 10 times, set the **Pass Count** to **10** and if the program fails during the loop, the Pass Count will tell you on which iteration of the loop the failure occurred.

A breakpoint must be an executable line of code. This means that you cannot set declaration, comment, or blank lines as breakpoints. The easiest way to set a simple breakpoint (no condition, no pass count) is from inside the code window. Just place your cursor in the code line where you want the break to occur, and press **F5**, or you can click your mouse pointer at the far-left edge of the code line. Alternatively, can use the **Toggle Breakpoint** option from the Code Editor's SpeedMenu. When you set a breakpoint, Delphi highlights the line and marks it with a little stop sign symbol. Figure 11.2 shows a Code Editor window with a visible breakpoint.

If you want to set a breakpoint condition or set the value of Pass Count, you'll need to use the Edit Breakpoint dialog box (shown in Figure 11.3). Select **Add Breakpoint** from the Run menu, or access the dialog box by using the **SpeedMenu** from inside the Breakpoint List window.

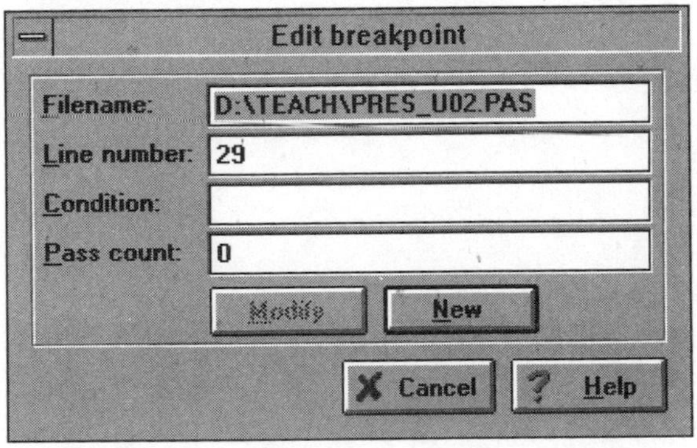

Figure 11.3 *The Edit Breakpoint dialog box*

In addition to Add and Edit, the Breakpoint List SpeedMenu also has options for enabling and disabling a breakpoint. If you want to try a program run without using a particular breakpoint, but you don't want to delete it from the List window, disable it. You can then re-enable it later. You can also choose to disable and enable all breakpoints at one time. Figure 11.4 shows a Breakpoint List window and its SpeedMenu.

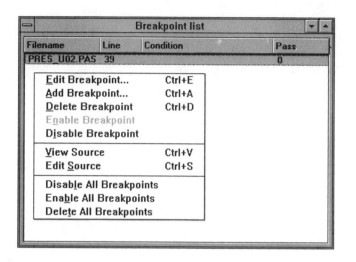

Figure 11.4 *The Breakpoint List window with SpeedMenu*

Define Watch Expressions

Okay, so what do you do when you make Delphi pause your application? You check out the state of the program. Chances are good that an error is being caused by a bad or unexpected data value. For example, one common error is dividing by zero. It's not something you would do intentionally, but it can happen if the data or variable values are unexpected. The only way to find out what is happening in these cases is to track the changing values, and you do this by setting up watch statements.

When you set a watch expression to monitor the value of a variable as it changes, the variable and its value are displayed in the Watch List window. If your Watch List window is not already visible, select **Watches** from the View menu. (Figure 11.5 shows a Watch List window with its SpeedMenu.)

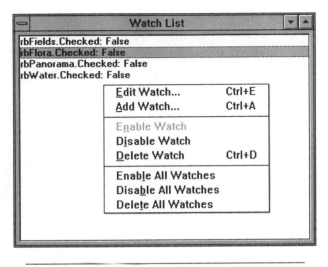

Figure 11.5 *The Watch List window with SpeedMenu*

Working with watch expressions has some procedural similarities to working with breakpoints in that you have to use a dialog box to add, edit, delete, enable, and disable your settings, and then those settings are displayed in a List window. In the case of watch expressions, you work in the Watch Properties dialog box and the expressions are displayed in the Watch List window.

To bring up the Watch Properties dialog box, select **Add Watch** from the Run menu, or press **Ctrl+F5** from the Code Editor window, or use the **SpeedMenu** from inside the Watch List window. Type the expression you want to watch in the expression box as shown in Figure 11.6. (The drop-down list contains expressions used previously in the debug session.) If your watch value is a decimal number, you can click on the **Floating Point** radio button and enter the number of digits you want to see displayed. If your watch expression is an array, you can use **Repeat Count** to indicate the number of array elements you want displayed.

Watch Properties

E**x**pression: `rbFlora.Checked`

Repeat cou**n**t: `0`   Di**g**its: `11`   ☒ **E**nabled

○ **C**haracter   ○ **H**ex integer   ○ **R**ecord
○ **S**tring   ○ **O**rdinal   ◉ **D**efault
○ **D**ecimal integer ○ **P**ointer   ☐ **M**emory dump

✓ OK   ✗ Cancel   ? **H**elp

Figure 11.6 *The Watch Properties dialog box*

In addition to watching the values as they change, you also have the option of altering a value during a pause and then continuing on with the new value. This ability to change an expression during a debug session gives you the power to test out your assumptions. For example, if you think that a logic error can be prevented by changing the expression value, this allows you to try it out without altering your program source code. The change is only used during the debug session. If it works, great, then you can modify your code. If not, you can try something else. No harm done.

To change an expression you need to bring up the Evaluate/Modify dialog box shown in Figure 11.7. Either select **Evaluate/Modify** from the Run menu, or select it from the SpeedMenu inside the Code Editor window as shown in Figure 11.8.

If you want to try out an expression, you can use the Expression Evaluator dialog box even when you are not debugging code. For example, if you enter **2 + 2** in the expression box, the value **4** shows up in the result box.

N O T E

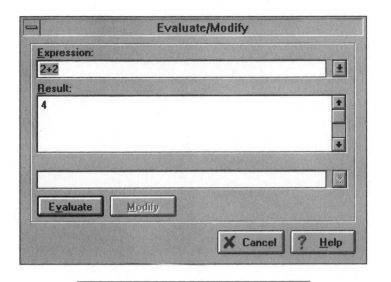

Figure 11.7 *The Evaluate/Modify dialog box*

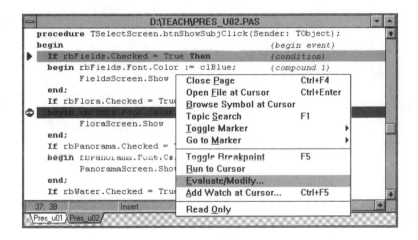

Figure 11.8 *The Code Editor window with SpeedMenu*

Monitor Call Stack

When you need to figure out which functions are being executed at any given time, you can find the information in the Call Stack window as shown in Figure 11.9. It displays the function or procedure as it occurs, and also shows the value of any parameters as identified in the procedure's header line. If the Call Stack window is not visible, select **Call Stack** from the View menu. You will find, however, that the Call Stack window will only display its information when in the midst of a debugging session.

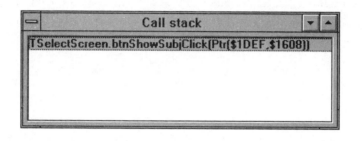

Figure 11.9 *The Call Stack window during a debugging session*

Advanced Tools

There are a few additional tools that are a bit more advanced. In addition to the tools that are part of the Integrated Debugger, external programs are available as well. Turbo Debugger, for example, lets you look at machine registers, the assembly language version of your code, dynamic link libraries, and more.

Then there's WinSpector and WinSight. WinSpector is used to examine applications that have incurred the wrath of Windows and suffered an Unrecoverable Application Error (UAE) or a General Protection Fault (GPF).

Exception Handling

It is more than likely that at some point in your Windows experience, a program froze (just stopped) on you. (That's exactly what happens if you put dashes in the Date Purchased field of your Invntory application.) It is also likely that at some time or other your entire system has crashed. Some program probably caused a dreaded General Protection Fault error, and the only way to recover was to reboot your system.

Some errors can be prevented; some can be fixed. Then there are those errors that you can neither prevent nor fix, but you can save your data before the crash. While the specifics of writing code to handle errors is beyond the scope of this book, I can give you an idea of what the process is all about.

First you have to give some thought to the things that might cause errors. For example, data type incompatibilities (like putting dashes in a Date field) and trying to open a file that does not exist are two things that will cause errors.

The second step in the process is to think about whether there is anything you can do to prevent the error from happening in the first place. For example, you might place a label component next to the edit box reminding the user that the acceptable date format is xx/xx/xx. Or if the user has the ability to open a file, you might want to use a combobox component that contains a list of the available files.

If there is nothing you can do to prevent the error, then you have to decide what you want the program to do if and when it happens. And that's the third step. Some errors can be handled, and some can't.

Using Protected Blocks to Handle Exceptions

When an error occurs, Delphi creates an *exception object*. If the error is one that can be corrected, then in the process of implementing the correction, the exception object will be destroyed and your application continues processing. If the error cannot be corrected, then at least you can stall the abrupt termination long enough to save your data. This is called *cleanup code*.

The attempt to open a file that doesn't exist is an error that can be handled. The logic used is similar to the If..Then statements you learned about earlier in this book. However, instead of using the If..Then statement, you would use the Try..Except statement. What you want to do is tell Delphi to Try to execute the code, except when a particular exception occurs, then it should do something else.

What that something else is, depends on you. It may be something as simple as displaying a message saying something like *date format not acceptable*, or *file not found*, and then giving the user another chance. Or it could be something more complex like searching the directory for existing file names and presenting them to the user so that they can select one. With errors that cannot be handled, the best you can do is save your data and then let the program crash.

Protecting Resources

System resources, such as memory, are precious and need protection. If you run out of memory, your program can freeze up or crash. Usually, running out of memory is not something that happens because you don't have enough, but because the amount you do have is not being handled efficiently. For example, one way to crash Windows is to open too many applications—and chances are that you are not using all of them at once. Closing those that are not needed at the time would be a more efficient use of your system resources.

Open files use memory. If your Delphi application uses a lot of files, you want to be careful about how many are open at any one time. If after executing a particular routine, you no longer need the file to be open, you can use the Try..Finally statement. This statement tells Delphi to try executing the code in that block, and then finally, when it's done (or if it encounters an error), it should execute whatever code is between the "Finally" keyword and the end of that block. This way you can open and close files as they are needed, and not waste resources.

NOTE Variables also use memory, but they only exist within the scope of where they are defined. Global variables need to be available at all times, but other variables may only be needed during the execution of a particular procedure. Paying attention to a variable's scope is another way to protect your memory resource.

Finally, you can create your own exception objects by defining a type derived from the exception class of objects. Suppose you want to impose a password requirement in your application, and further suppose that this password is not required to start your application, but is only needed during a specific routine—a routine that displays confidential data to which only certain persons should be privy. You could create an exception object that is evaluated as true if the entered password is not valid.

Once you create the exception object, you could use the Try..Except statement, placing the code that allows the confidential data to be displayed in the Try section. The Except section of the statement could then contain statements that display a message such as *confidential data, access denied* and cause the application to resume.

Summary

- ◆ Before running your application, Delphi compiles your source code and points to any compiler errors. A compiler error is caused by invalid code. You can use the **Syntax Check** option from the Compile menu to check for compiler errors without running the application.

- ◆ When Delphi encounters a run-time error, it displays an error message and stops running your application. Delphi does not, however, activate Reset Program for you. Run-time errors can be caused by valid code that cannot be successfully executed, or by errors in logic. Logic errors are the most difficult to spot.

- ◆ In order for the Integrated Debugger tools to work, the Debug Information, Local Symbols, and Symbol Info items on the Compiler page of the Project Options dialog box should all be selected.

- ◆ If you place your cursor in a particular line of code and select **Run To Cursor**, Delphi will run the program and upon reaching the specified line, pause the program, highlight the code line, and mark it with an arrow. This line is called an exception point.

◆ The Step Over technique of stepping through code will execute a whole routine and pause when the routine is done. The Trace Into technique, on the other hand, will pause at each line of code within the routine.

◆ Breakpoints are predefined exception points that you can use over and over. A breakpoint must be an executable line of code—no declaration, comment, or blank lines.

–If you want to set a breakpoint to pause at a specific line, the breakpoint definition must contain the unit file name and the line number. (Delphi enters these for you if you set the **breakpoint** from inside the Code Editor window by pressing **F5**.)

–If you want to set a **breakpoint** to **pause** when a specific condition is met, set the **condition** in the Edit Breakpoint dialog box so that it appears in the Breakpoint List window.

–If you want to set a **breakpoint** to **pause** when a specific line is executed a certain number of times, use the Edit Breakpoint dialog box to set the **Pass Count**. To define a breakpoint such that is pauses the program when a specific condition has been met a certain number of times, specify both the condition and the Pass Count.

◆ To monitor the value of a variable or property, define it as a Watch expression. The value is displayed in the Watch List window, and you can see the value change (or not) as you step through your program code. You can also use the Evaluate/Modify dialog box to alter the value of a watch expression before resuming processing.

◆ The Call Stack window displays the name of the current procedure or function.

◆ Delphi creates an exception object when an error occurs and automatically destroys the object if the error can be corrected or handled.

◆ The Try..Except statement directs Delphi to try to execute the code except if an error occurs, in which case it should execute the statements in the Except section. The Try..Finally statement directs Delphi to execute the code in the Try section of the block, and when it's finally done, it should execute the statements in the Finally section. If in error occurs while executing statements in the Try section of a Try..Finally statement, Delphi jumps directly to the code in the Finally section and attempts to execute it before crashing.

◆ System resources such as memory need protection from overuse. Closing unneeded files and maintaining variables only when useful can help to handle memory use more efficiently.

◆ You can create your own exception objects and use them with a Try..Except statement. The object should be derived from the Exception Class of objects.

APPENDIX A

About the Third-Party Software on the Disk

The custom controls and DLL functions provided by Sheridan Software Systems are a sample of their 3-D Widgets product. Their actual product contains far more custom controls and DLLs and you'll find an advertisement at the back of the book with more details about 3-D Widgets. Sheridan Software has also agreed to provide 3-D Widgets to readers at a special price. For more information contact:

Sheridan Software
65 Maxess Road
Melville, NY 11747
(516) 753 0985

These are the functions provided by the Sheridan Software custom-control file:

◆ **3-D Panel**. This custom control allows you to add 3-dimensional borders to your program. You can place these borders anywhere, including around other controls.

◆ **3-D Button**. A special version of the Command Button that allows you to put a picture inside a command button. The standard control only allows text inside the button.

There are two Sheridan files included on the disk in the back of the book:

SHERDN01.VBX The custom control file that you can use for both run-time and design-time. This is the file you'll use when you're building your program. *DO NOT give this file to other people—you do not have a license to distribute it!*

SHERDN01.VBR The run-time only version of SHERDN01.VBX. When you want to give your program to other people, give them a copy of this file and rename it SHERDN01.VBX. Sheridan allows you to freely distribute this file ONLY. You will not need to display a Sheridan copyright notice or pay royalties to Sheridan when using this file.

To use the 3-D Panel and 3-D Button controls, you'll need to add the SHERDN01.VBX file to your project. Follow the instructions for adding 3rd-party VBX controls to your programs that came with Delphi.

APPENDIX B

Installing the
Sample Programs

In addition to the third-party software, the disk accompanying this book holds four self-extracting zip files: Bitmaps.exe, Presfile.exe, Linefile.exe, and Invnfile.exe. You need to install the bitmap files contained in the Bitmaps.exe file in order to build the first sample application described in the book. The application is called Present, and you'll need to place the bitmap files in a directory named \Teach.

You can use the Windows File Manager to create the Teach directory. Open the File Manager and click on the root directory of your hard drive. Unless you have more than one hard drive in your system, this will the

the c:\ directory. Then select **Create Directory...** from the File menu, enter TEACH in the dialog box that appears, and click **OK**.

From the File Manager window, click once on the **TEACH** directory to make it the current directory. If you have not yet begun to create the Present sample application, there will not yet be any files in the directory. Then click on the **Run...** option from the File Manager's File menu. When the dialog box appears, enter A:BITMAPS.EXE and click on **OK**. (If you're installing from a floppy disk in drive B rather than A, enter B:BITMAPS.EXE.) The bitmap files you need will automatically self-extract into the TEACH directory. When done, your TEACH directory should show the following files:

```
BUTTON1.BMP

BUTTON2.BMP

FIELD-1.BMP

FIELD-2.BMP

FLORA-1.BMP

FLORA-2.BMP

PANOR-1.BMP

PANOR-2.BMP

WATER-1.BMP

WATER-2.BMP
```

If you don't see the files listed in the TEACH directory, refresh your Program Manager window by clicking on the drive letter at the top of the window. This will force Windows to re-read the drive and show the file.

Each of other three self-extracting zip files contain the files from the corresponding sample applications. If you follow all the instructions in the book, you will end up creating these same files for yourself. They are only included here in the event that you want to examine the finished files, or compare them to your own. Should you choose to install any of these files, create a separate directory for them so that you do not over-write your own files in the TEACH directory. For example, you could create a directory called SAMPLE, and then from that directory run one or more of the three self-extracting zip files.

The Present application is the first sample application you will create. It has six forms and six corresponding unit files. There are twenty-two files in the PRESFILE.EXE self-extracting zip file. Each graphical form is saved in a file with the extension DFM. Each unit source code file has the extension PAS, which stands for the Pascal programming language. Once compiled, Delphi translates the source code into object code and saves the object code in files with the extension DCU. Each application also has a project file with the extension DPR. Once compiled, Delphi also creates a project option file (with the extension OPT), a compiler resource file (with the extension RES), and a compiled executable file (with the extension EXE).

The following is a list of the files contained within the Presfile.exe self-extracting zip file:

```
PRES_U01.DCU
PRES_U01.DFM
PRES_U01.PAS
PRES_U02.DCU
PRES_U02.DFM
PRES_U02.PAS
PRES_U03.DCU
PRES_U03.DFM
PRES_U03.PAS
PRES_U04.DCU
PRES_U04.DFM
PRES_U04.PAS
PRES_U05.DCU
PRES_U05.DFM
```

```
PRES_U05.PAS
PRES_U06.DCU
PRES_U06.DFM
PRES_U06.PAS
PRESENT.DPR
PRESENT.EXE
PRESENT.OPT
PRESENT.RES
```

In Chapter 6, you examine the SCRBFORM.PAS file that is part of Borland's Scribble Demo application, and alter the code, saving the source code in a file named LINES.PAS and the project as LINESTRT.DPR. The Linestrt.exe self-extracting zip file contains only the following seven files:

```
LINES.DCU
LINES.DFM
LINES.PAS
LINESTRT.DPR
LINESTRT.EXE
LINESTRT.OPT
LINESTRT.RES
```

The last sample application in the book, Invntory, involves the creation of two database tables and two forms. The Invnfile.exe self-extracting zip file contains twenty-three files. In addition to the DCU (unit object code), DFM (graphical form), PAS (source code), DPR (project), EXE (compiled executable), OPT (project option), and RES (compiler resource) files, you will find two DB files (one for each Paradox table), two VAL files (one for each table's validity check), and two PX files (one for each Paradox table's primary index settings). In addition, you'll find some X, Y, XG and YG files that contain the secondary index settings for the Invntory table. The following is a list of all of the files in the Invnfile.exe self-extracting zip file:

```
INVN_U01.DCU
INVN_U01.DFM
INVN_U01.PAS
INVN_U02.DCU
INVN_U02.DFM
INVN_U02.PAS
INVNTORY.DB
INVNTORY.DPR
INVNTORY.MB
INVNTORY.OPT
INVNTORY.PX
INVNTORY.RES
INVNTORY.VAL
INVNTORY.X04
INVNTORY.XG0
INVNTORY.XG1
INVNTORY.Y04
INVNTORY.YG0
INVNTORY.YG1
```

GLOSSARY

Glossary of Terms

Accelerator key

A key specified for use in combination with the Alt key, as an alternative means for activating a menu command without using the mouse. Accelerator keys are indicated by the placement of an ampersand before the character when defining menu options.

Actual Parameter

The actual parameter is the original value before being passed to the procedure or function. (See also **Formal Parameter**.) The value of an actual parameter may not be changed, unless the formal parameter is declared with **var** in the header indicating that changes to the formal parameter will be reflected in the actual parameter as well.

Alias

A database alias is a name assigned to a directory that contains database files. The alias is then used in lieu of the directory name.

Alignment Palette

A toolbar to help you align your components in relationship to the form and one another. Alignment can be based on matching the left, right, top, and bottom sides, as well as center points of objects.

Arrays

An array is a structured data type that holds multiple values for a single data element. Each value can be accessed using the index number to indicate the value's position in the array. Arrays are declared as variables using the **array...of** keywords.

ASCI

A standard that defines how numeric values are assigned to characters inside your computer. The ASCII standard defines which numbers will be assigned to all the characters on a U.S. keyboard, and assigns the numbers 32 through 127 to these characters. Other characters, such as ü are assigned numbers in the extended ASCII set (above 127 or below 32).

Assignment operator

An assignment operator (:=) is used to assign a value to a variable, or property.

Boolean

Boolean is an ordinal data type containing an integer that is always evaluated as being either True or False. There are four Boolean types: Boolean, ByteBool, WordBool, and LongBool. False always equals 0, and True usually equals 1. In the case of ByteBool, WordBool, and LongBool, True can be any non-zero value, evaluate to either True or False.

Boolean operators

Boolean operators must always return a value of either True or False. Boolean operators include Not, And, Or, and XOr.

Boolean expressions use Boolean operators: equal to, not equal, less than, greater than, less than or equal to, greater than or equal to, not, or, XOr, equivalent, implication.

Breakpoint

A breakpoint is a line of code at which you want Delphi to pause during a debugging session so that you can examine the variables, properties and other elements. A breakpoint must be an executable line of code—no comment or blank lines, and you can set several breakpoints before you begin the run. (Also see **Stopped**).

Bug

Some type of failure in a computer program, usually caused by improper code or an error in logic. If your application does not behave in the manner intended, your program has a bug. Debugging is the process of locating the problem and solving it.

Call Stack

The Call Stack window is used in the debugging process. It lists each function or procedure as it occurs, allowing you to track the procedures and functions being executed.

Canvas

The surface of an object upon which you can draw using the pen and brush. A canvas is made up of pixels. (Also see **Drawing**.)

Case

A Case statement allows you to code the actions to be taken for each possible value of an enumerated data type without requiring individual If..Then statements.

Character

The Character data type consists of a single character, surrounded by single apostrophes. (Also see **String**.) This is not the same as a String data type that can contain as many characters as needed.

Child

A child is an object or component that is contained within another component. For example, when you place a button on a form, the button is a child of that form.

Cleanup Code

Code written to save your data in the event an exception occurs that cannot be successfully handled. (Also see **Exception Handling**.)

Code Editor

The window that contains the Object Pascal code for an application. Each unit has it's own page in the Code Editor window.

Command

Reserved words that tell your program to execute the corresponding activity. (Also see **Statement**.) Programmers sometimes use other words such as statement, instruction, and code interchangeably for the word command.

Compiler error

A compiler error is the result of invalid code, such as mistakes in syntax and unknown identifiers, detected by Delphi while attempting to compile the source code. A program cannot run without first being compiled successfully. (Also see **Source Code**.)

Components

Components, sometimes called controls or objects, are the building blocks for your applications. Text boxes, picture boxes, buttons, labels, even menus, are all examples of components.

Component Palette

The Component Palette is the right portion of the toolbar located directly under the menus that contains all of the available components. Components are categorized into eight basic groups: Standard, Additional, Data Access, Data Controls, Dialogs, System, VBX, and Samples, each group with it's own tabbed page. When you incorporate components from

	third-party vendors, they too will appear on the Component Palette.
Composite Key	A composite key is a key that is made up of more than one field. Composite keys can be primary or secondary keys. (Also see **Primary Key** and **Secondary Key**.)
Composite Property	A property that has subproperties. For example, the Font property has six subproperties: Color, Height, Name, Pitch, Size, and Style. Delphi indicates composite properties by using a plus sign (+) in the Object Inspector window.
Condition	Another word for a Boolean expression, which returns a value of True or False.
Const	A reserved word used for declaring constants.
Constant	A constant is a place in memory where you can store a numeric or character value. Once declared, the value of a constant may not change.
Database	A database is a collection of information (data) stored in one or more tables. (Also see **Table**.)
Dataset Designer	Select which fields you wish to display by using the Dataset Designer's... also has a Define button that is used to create temporary fields for display during runtime. This is especially useful for calculated fields.
Debugging session	The purpose of a debugging session is to locate and correct any runtime errors.
Design-Time	The phase during which you are constructing the interface and coding an application using the Object Inspector, Component Palette, and Code Editor, before running the program.
Design-Time Properties	Design-time properties are those properties that can be set using the Object Inspector

while creating your application. (See also **Run-Time Properties**.)

Double

One of the Real data types that can represent numbers with decimal points using what's known as floating-point calculations. Double type values fall within the range of 5.0 x 10 (-324) .. 1.7 x 10(308), allow for 15-16 significant digits, and use 8 bytes for storage.

Drawing

Drawing is when you tell the application to place a specific graphic in a specific location at a specific time, usually dictated by the occurrence of an event. Drawing is carried out by the Canvas's Pen and Brush properties, used to alter the pixels on the canvas to create lines and shapes. (Also see **Painting**.)

Element

A single item or instance in an array.

Enumerated

Enumerated data types are user-defined ordinal data types that assign specific values that can be accessed numerically by their position in the list.

Event

An event is some action relating to an object or component that is caused either by the user or the program itself. Click, MouseDown, Mouse-Up, and KeyPress are examples of events.

Event Handler

A procedure containing code to be executed whenever the corresponding event occurs. The object name and event are combined to create a method used with the form containing the object. For example: Form1.Button1Click. (Also see **Method**, **Object**, and **Procedure**.)

Event Page

One of the two tabbed pages in the Object Inspector. The event page keeps track of the events for each component on the form.

Exception

An object created by Delphi whenever an error occurs. If the error is successfully handled,

	Delphi destroys the exception object. Delphi creates an exception object when an error occurs, and automatically destroys the object if the error can be corrected or handled.
Exception handling	Code written to handle exceptions when they occur. Successful handling will cause the exception object to be destroyed. (Also see **Cleanup Code**.)
Expression	Expressions are statements that are evaluated to return a result. For example, 2 + 2 is an expression that when evaluated, returns the result of 4. Expressions use operators such as +, -, *, and /.
Expression Evaluator	This dialog box allows you to evaluate individual expressions and to change the value of expressions in an application during a debugging session.
False	When a Boolean expression is evaluated to equal zero, the condition is found to be False.
Field Link Designer	A tool used to identify the common field(s) that will comprise the value of the MasterFields property needed when synchronizing the display of data from multiple tables.
File	A File data type is a linear sequence of elements of almost any type. A File data type cannot contain other File data types, nor can it contain Object data types.
Floating-point numbers	Any number with something after the decimal point. For example 1.1 and 3.14159 are both floating-point numbers.
Focus	Focus refers to which component has the keyboard's focus of attention. The component that is current or active is said to have the focus. When an application is running and

you use the Tab key or mouse to move from one component to another, you are moving the focus.

Form

Forms are the windows inside of which you place your components. Forms are components themselves, and usually they a form is a parent. (Also see **Component** and **Parent**.)

Formal parameter

The variable or constant receiving the parameter value inside the procedure or function is known as the formal parameter. Unless declared as Const, the value of a formal parameter may be changed. (Also see **Actual Parameter** and **Const**.)

Function

A function is a special type of subroutine that computes and/or returns a value.

Global

Global refers to scope. Global variables and constants are declared in the unit's interface section, and are therefore available from anywhere within the unit.

Glyph

Small bitmaps or icons used in SpeedButtons and BitButtons.

Grid

The horizontal and vertical dotted lines on a form that are visible during design time to assist you in placing and aligning components.

Handler

(See **Event Handler**.)

Identifier

An identifier is the name given to a component, variable, constant, or other programming element.

Implementation

The implementation section of a unit begins with the word implementation, concludes with a period (.) at the end of the unit, and contains all of the procedure and function code blocks.

Index	A variable used to access an element within a structured type by its position.
Instruction	A programming command or statement. The words instruction, statement, and command, and code are sometimes used interchangeably by programmers.
Integer	Integers are whole numbers, positive and negative, including zero. There are five Integer types (Integer, Short Integer, Long Int, Byte, and Word), and each covers a different range of values. The number of digits in an integer has no bearing on the number of bytes required to store an integer value. Regular integer values range from -32,768 to 32,767 and take two bytes for storage.
Integrated Debugger	The Integrated Debugger automatically takes control whenever you run an application from inside Delphi. The options to Pause, Run to Cursor, Step Over or Trace Into, along with the ability to view the Code Editor, Watch List, Breakpoint List, and Call Stack windows, are all integrated debugging tools.
Interface section	The interface section specifies components, types, variables and procedures that are accessible by other units.
Local	Local refers to scope. Local variables and constants are only available locally within the procedure or function in which they are declared.
Logic error	(See **Run-Time Error**.)
Long or LongInt	Integers are whole numbers, positive and negative, including zero. Long Integer values range from -2,147,483,648 to 2,147,483,647 and take four bytes for storage. (Also see **Integer**.)

Loop	Loops are complex statement structures that allow you to repeat a sequence of statements for a specified number of times or until a condition is met.
Machine Code	The Delphi program compiler translates your source code into machine code. (Also see **Source Code**.)
Menu Designer	The Menu Designer window is used to define each menu title and menu item.
Method	A method is a procedure, function, or command that is directly related to a specified object or component, and represents an action that can be performed on that object. The method follows the name of the object, separated by a period—for example, formname.Show and formname.Hide.
Module	Some programs refer to code displayed in separate windows and saved in separate files as modules. Delphi call them units. (Also see **Unit**.)
Modulo	A mathematical operation that calculates the remainder of a division.
Nonvisual Component	Nonvisual components are not visible during Run-Time. The Table, Query, and DataSource components are examples of nonvisual components.
Null String	A null string, '', is a string without any values, not even a space. (Also see **String**.)
Object	Object data types include a type for each component (such as TForm, TLabel, TButton, etc.), and for each composite property (such as TFont and TWindowState). These are predefined Delphi objects. Object data types may also be user-defined.

Object Inspector   The Object Inspector is a window with two pages. The Properties page keeps track of all the properties associated with each object, and allows you to set the value for these properties. The Events page lists all of the events that may be associated with each object.

Ordinal   Ordinal types contain a specified number of elements and are ordered or sequenced such that the values are always in the same order. Integer, Boolean, Character, Enumerated, and Subrange are all Ordinal data types.

Painting   Painting is the Windows term for refreshing a window or screen. (Also see **Drawing**.)

Parameter   A parameter is a variable or constant used to pass data to, and/or receive data from, a procedure or function. It may be a variable, constant, or special keyword. Parameters are declared in the procedure or function header.

Parent   A Parent is an object or component that contains another component.

Pointer   Pointer data types are used to point to an element's address in memory.

Primary key   A database table's primary key, or index, is used to prevent duplicate records, and is the basis for sorting all records in the table. Keys are also useful for speeding up searches because Delphi creates internal pointers to key fields. A primary key is used by default, unless over-ridden by a Secondary key. (Also see **Secondary Key**.)

Private   Variables, constants, types, or other elements declared as private are exclusive to the unit in which they are declared.

Procedural

Procedural data types allow you to assign a procedure or function to a variable, that can then be passed as a parameter to a different procedure or function.

Procedure

A procedure is a subroutine, i.e. block of code nested within the main program, that can be called from anywhere in the program.

Project

A project can contain one or more forms and units in addition to the project file. A project file is a special file (with the .DPR extension) that tells Delphi which forms (.FRM files), and units (.PAS files), belong to an application.

Project Manager

The window providing access to the form and unit files that are associated with the project.

Property

A special type of Delphi variable, the value of which affects the appearance or behavior of a component or object . When you click on a component during the design phase, that components properties are shown on the Properties Page of the Object Inspector. (Also see **Properties Page** and **Object Inspector**.)

Properties Page

A tabbed page in the Object Inspector window that allows you to view and set values for a component's properties. (Run-Time Only properties cannot be accessed using the Object Inspector.)

Protected block

Blocks of code programmed to respond to or handle exceptions. Such blocks generally employ the Try..Until or Try..Finally statements.

Real

Real data types are numeric and can be represented with floating point notation in a fixed number of digits. There are five real types: Real, Single, Double, Extended, and Comp. Each type covers a different range of values and requires a different number of bytes for storage.

Record

A Record is a specified group of elements or fields of varying types. You can refer to each individual element, or you can refer to the record as a whole.

Referential Integrity

If you have two tables with a common field, and you want the changes made to that field in one table to automatically update the other field, or conversely, if you want to prevent changes from being made to one table to protect the corresponding entries in the other table, you need to use Referential Integrity. These settings must be defined as part of a table's structure.

[Running]

When working with Delphi, you are either designing, compiling and executing, or pausing the run for debugging purposes. When you select Run from the Run menu or press F9, Delphi compiles and then begins executing your application, and you see [running] appear in the Delphi title bar. (Also see **[Stopped]**.)

Run-Time Properties

Run-Time properties are set using assignment statements executed when your program is running. Most properties that can be set using the object Inspector can also be set during Run-Time. Some properties, however, are only accessible during Run-Time.

Run-Time error

You can encounter two kinds of runtime errors. The first type occurs when the code is valid (i.e. no compiler errors), but executing the code causes a problem. For example trying to open a file that doesn't exist or dividing a number by zero. The second type of runtime error is an error in logic. The code is valid, and can be executed without error, but the intended outcome or results don't happen.

Scope

The scope of a constant or variable is within the code block in which it is declared. (Also see **Local** and **Global**.)

Secondary Key

Secondary keys, comprised of one or more fields, may be used for alternative sort sequences. IndexName is the Table property that allows you to override the table's primary index by selecting one of the secondary indexes for use instead. Keys are also useful for speeding up searches because Delphi creates internal pointers to key fields.

Set

A Set is a structured data type that defines a collection of ordinal values. These values do not have to be sequential.

Shortcuts

These are key combinations assigned to menu items. Like accelerator keys, they can be used to execute menu options without using the mouse.

Simple

Simple data types include all of the Ordinal and Real data types. (Also see **Ordinal** and **Real**.)

Single

One of the Real data types that can represent numbers with decimal points using what's known as floating-point calculations. Double type values fall within the range of $1.5 \times 10^{(-45)} .. 3.4 \times 10^{(38)}$, allow for 7-8 significant digits, and use 4 bytes for storage.

Source Code

Source code is the program code you write using the Object Pascal programming language. When Delphi compiles your program, your source code is translated into machine language.

Speedbar	The Speedbar holds 14 glyphs representing shortcuts for tasks such as Open, Save, View Form, View Unit and more.
SpeedMenus	Delphi has several speed menus that pop-up with a right mouse click. Each speedmenu is associated with a different window or dialog box, and contains menu options that relate to that window or dialog box.
SQL	Standard Query Language, used to request data from database tables to select records that meet certain conditions from specified tables, presented in a defined sort sequence
Statement	Statements are command or instruction lines that end in a semi-colon. Assignment and procedure statements are referred to as simple statements. Structured statements include conditional statements, loops, and other complex statements. The words statement, instruction, command, and code are sometimes used interchangeably by programmers.
Step Over	Unlike the Trace Into technique, the Step Over technique of stepping through code in a debugging session will execute a whole procedure or subroutine, and then pause when the routine is done. (Also see **Trace Into**.)
[Stopped]	When working with Delphi, you are either designing, compiling and executing, or pausing the run for debugging purposes. When you select Pause from the Run menu, Delphi pauses the execution of your application, and you see [Stopped] appear in the Delphi title bar. Whenever the program is stopped, you can view the Call Stack, Watch List, and Breakpoint List windows to monitor your program. (Also see **[Running]**.)

Strings	The String data type consists of a multiple characters (as many as desired) surrounded by single apostrophes. If you wish to use a quotation mark as part of a string, type the quotation character twice. (Also see **Character**.)
Structured	Structured data types include Sets, Arrays, Records, Files, and Objects types. (Also see **Sets**, **Arrays**, **Records**, **Files**, and **Objects**.)
Subrange	A user-defined data type used to represent a sequential subset of a larger group of values.
Subroutine	A subroutine is a block of code that has a label (identifier), and can be run from other parts of a program. Delphi has many pre-defined subroutines such as event-handler procedures and functions.
Syntax Check	If you want to check for compiler errors without running the application, you can use the Syntax Check option (it's on the Compile menu) to check for compiler errors. (Also see **Compiler Error**.)
Table	Database tables are made up of columns and rows. In database lingo, columns are usually referred to as fields, and each row is a record.
Table Lookups	Table Lookups provide a means for automated data entry automatically enter the correct data as found in the lookup table. Table Lookups must be defined as part of a table's structure.
Template	Delphi allows you to design Forms and Menus and then save them as templates so that they may be incorporated into other projects.
Trace Into	Unlike the Step Over technique, the Trace Into technique of stepping through code in a debugging session will execute each individual line in a procedure or subroutine, pausing after

	each statement. (Also see **Step Over**.)
True	When a Boolean expression is evaluated to equal one (or a non-zero value in the case of ByteBool, WordBool, and LongBool types), the condition is found to be True.
Type section	The type section identifies the forms, components, and procedures contained in the unit.
Unit	Units are code modules that are individually compiled. The source code in a unit includes the unit heading, interface section and implementation sections, and is saved as a PAS file. Compiled units are saved as DCU files. Delphi creates a unit file for each form defined in a project, and a project unit that contains a list of all the units in the project and a statement to run the application.
User-defined type	A compound variable that you define using the Type command. Compound refers to the combination of multiple variables of different types into a single variable.
Uses clause	The uses clause lists the names of other units that are needed for use by the current unit.
Validity Checks	A validity check is a requirement defined for a field in a database table. Validity checks includes: requiring a field contain data; specifying minimum, maximum, and default values; and defining picture patterns using the Picture Assistant.
Values	The actual numbers or strings in a variable.
Var	A reserved word used for declaring variables. Units have a var section.
Variables	A variable is a place in memory where you can a store numeric or character value. The value of a variable may change

Watch expression

An expression used to monitor the value of a variable or property as it changes. Watch expressions are displayed in the Watch List window, available when debugging an application.

INDEX

SHERIDAN SOFTWARE

S heridan Software has provided two custom controls that let you add a 3-dimensional look to your program, as well as icons to the buttons in your programs.

3-D Panels

This custom control allows you to add various 3-dimensional borders to your programs:

- ◆ Add 3-D borders around other controls

- ◆ Use as a 3-D progress indicator

- ◆ Display 3-D text

3-D Command Buttons

If you need to put an icon inside a button, this is the control for you.

- ◆ Add icons to your buttons

- ◆ Change the width of the bevel

- ◆ Add a 3-D effect to the caption

ON THE DISK

SHERDN01.VBX   Design-time file

SHERDN01.VBR   Run-time file

Sheridan Software
65 Maxess Road
Melville, NY 11747
(516) 753-0985